19514

D1582636

# SHAKESPEARE'S CHARACTERY

STAGE TYPES

# SHAKESPEARE'S CHARACTERY

## A BOOK OF 'CHARACTERS' FROM SHAKESPEARE

———

Selected and Arranged by
JOHN M. LOTHIAN
With an Introductory Essay

———

OXFORD
BASIL BLACKWELL
1966

Type set by Gloucester Typesetting Company Limited
and printed in Great Britain by
Ebenezer Baylis and Son Limited
The Trinity Press, Worcester and London

# Preface

Shakespeare's apparent delight in throwing off sketches of characters real or imaginary, abstract or concrete, necessary to his play or structurally superfluous, led to the assembling of this anthology of over four hundred pieces. They are arranged so as to serve several purposes. They illustrate, firstly, by their numbers alone, the astonishing richness of the dramatist in the popular contemporary field of 'charactery', and make clear his precedence and pre-eminence in it. The grouping of identical or similar characters provides, in the second place, the means of observing, in a convenient way, the changing concepts of particular individuals or types held by the dramatist at different times. Further, it is hoped that the arrangement in categories and in roughly chronological order will make it possible to compare the artist's varying modes of presenting the same or similar concepts. The Editor trusts it will thus form a useful supplement to heavier studies in the 'mind and art' of Shakespeare, as well as a 'dippable' or bedside book for the enjoyment of the general reader. The illustrations are intended to help present the contemporary concepts of some 'characters'.

The Anthology was compiled at times and in places widely separated. The Editor found it convenient therefore to draw for his text on the easily portable one-volume 'Shakespeares' – Macmillan's 'Globe', Craig's 'Oxford Standard Authors' and Kittredge's 'Complete Works' (Ginn & Co.) : to the publishers of these editions he wishes to make acknowledgment.

The Editor wishes to thank the University of Aberdeen for the provision of typing and photographic services, and for assuming some responsibility for the cost of publication. He would wish to thank all those who have granted permission to the publishers to reproduce the illustrations used. He also owes a debt of gratitude to the editorial staff of Messrs. Basil Blackwell for their generous aid, skilled advice, and patience.

J.M.L.

# Contents

## M. ABSTRACTIONS AND ALLEGORIES 205

## N. SUPERNATURALS 214

## O. WOMEN GENERALLY 220

## List of Illustrations

# SHAKESPEARE'S CHARACTERY

# AN INTRODUCTORY

# ESSAY

# Shakespeare's Charactery

Bishop Joseph Hall, a contemporary of Shakespeare, and the first English writer to profess direct imitation of Theophrastus, the chief character-writer of antiquity, described the methods of his predecessors in this way, in 1608:

"While some [of the heathen philosophers] spent themselves in deep discourse of human felicity and the way to it in common, others thought it best to apply the general precepts of goodness or decency to particular conditions and persons. A third sort in a mean course betwixt the two other, and compounded of them both, bestowed their time in drawing out the lineaments of every virtue and vice, so lively, that who saw the models might know the face; which art they significantly termed Charactery. Their papers were so many tables, their writings so many speaking pictures, or living images, whereby the rude multitude might even by their sense learn to know virtue and discern what to detest."

Hall was in no doubt as to his purpose in drawing out his 'characters' of men 'honest', 'faithful', 'humble', 'valiant', and 'noble', and of opposing to them the 'hypocrite', the 'inconstant', the 'presumptuous', the 'vainglorious'; nor was he at a loss for models. "I am deceived", he says, anent his purpose and method, "if any course could be more likely to prevail, for herein the gross conceit is led on with pleasure, and informed, while it feels nothing but delight; and if pictures have been accounted the books of idiots, behold here the benefit without the offence. It is no shame for us to learn wit of heathens, neither is it material in whose school we take out a good lesson."

In spite of the clarity of purpose of its official initiator in English, the kind of writing known as 'character' still remains remarkably hard to define. If one chooses to define it by its content, 'characters' as varied as 'a bowling alley', a 'tavern', and 'St. Paul's Churchyard' have to be covered by terms which

3

mostly concern human beings; and yet somehow abstractions such as Nicholas Breton's 'Learning' and 'Love' and 'Time' and 'Death' have to be found shelter under the same verbal umbrella. Obviously, terms which should include *all* kinds of 'character' would define none!

Definition by technical 'form', on the other hand, is equally misleading. "The formal pattern" (of the Theophrastan character in England), says Professor Bush, "is simple. It is a paragraph which begins with a brief definition of a vice, proceeds with a series of descriptive and narrative items that show a representative of it in his everyday conduct, and ends when the author chooses to stop." Professor Bush, like Miss Gwendolen Murphy in her *Cabinet of Characters*, is aware that this description is true only of 'one of the most usual forms' of the seventeenth century character, and that there is much in the collections of Hall, Overbury and Earle to which it is quite inapplicable. Besides, a 'form' in which the end comes 'when the author chooses' is by very description somewhat formless.

It would seem best to take the 'character' as we take the novel, namely as a literary 'kind' of very great variety of form and content, of which a particular mode may be the fashion of the moment. Historically, this particular form of literary activity was very popular in the first half of the seventeenth century in England, for reasons made admirably clear by Professor Bush.[1]

It suited the satirical, analytical, self-examining spirit of the age and gave plenty of scope for the exercise of a sententious and sometimes foppish wit, while imposing few restrictions on the writer in the way of form. One of the contributors to Overbury's Characters (1614), gives in detail *What a Character Is.*

> "If I must speak the schoolmaster's language, I will confess that character comes of this infinitive mood χαρασσειν which signifies to engrave, or to make a deep impression. And for that cause a letter (as A, B) is called a character: these elements which we learn first, leaving a strong seal in our memories."

[1] Bush, D. *English Literature in the Earlier Seventeenth Century.* Clarendon Press. 1945.

"Character is also taken for an Egyptian hieroglyphic, for an impress or short emblem; in little comprehending much."

"To square out a character by our English level, it is a picture (real or personal) quaintly drawn in various colours, all of them heightened by one shadowing."

"It is a quick and soft-touch of many strings, all shutting up in one musical close; it is wit's descant on any plain song."

The writer of this description, it is clear, expects certain literary qualities in a character-sketch. It must be forceful ('a deep impression', 'a strong seal'); it must be brief and light ('a quick and soft touch'); it must be a unity ('all of them heightened to one shadowing'); and it must be vividly picturesque ('a picture, real and personal, quaintly drawn'). These specifications would not exclude a 'character' of a bowling-alley, or a tavern, and are such as would allow Shakespeare or any other of the dramatists who found 'charactery' a useful adjunct of their art and a natural outlet for their energy to claim a place among the character-writers of their time.

Shakespeare is not usually counted, as Ben Jonson is, with the Halls and Overburys and Earles of his time, as a writer of 'characters'. Few writers on the subject mention him, and no anthologies of 'characters' find a place for his work. It is the purpose of this Anthology to illustrate his work in this 'kind' and to supply the materials for its study, and of this Essay to attempt an estimate of the importance of that work for himself and for others.

For he was, from his earliest play to his latest, an inveterate 'thumb-nail' sketcher, and no one in English, in drama or elsewhere, had done comparable work before him. It is not enough to say that these 'characters' are not Theophrastan: neither, for that matter, are Breton's, or many of Overbury's, or more than a few of Hall's. But they are the fruit of a similar kind of literary activity: and to one approaching Shakespeare's work through the plays of his predecessors, his bias towards character-sketching is very noticeable. Seven such portraits in miniature appear in *The Comedy of Errors*, eight in the *Two Gentlemen of Verona*, and fifteen in *Love's Labour's Lost*. At the end of his career, *The Tempest* has six, *Cymbeline* nine, and *The Winter's Tale* fourteen. Nor is the activity confined to the Comedies. Early Histories, *Richard III* and *Richard II*, have eleven and nine respectively, and an early Tragedy, *Romeo and Juliet*, thirteen. In some plays of the middle years the sketches number at least a score; and the total for the complete canon of the plays is well over four hundred!

It is clear that even if he never drew a technically correct 'character' on the model of Theophrastus, he delighted in the same kind of character-sketching activity, in 'hitting-off' with the minimum of strokes, like a lightning-artist with crayons, the features of a wide variety of human temperaments. Many of these portraits are dramatically quite unnecessary to the plays, though often very enlivening in their effect, and the profusion with which they are distributed points to a natural bias of the poet's mind and art in this direction, and to an appreciation of this element in his work on the part of his audience.

It is customary to associate the sudden outburst of character-writing in England in the early seventeenth century, with the publication at Leyden, in 1592, of Casaubon's edition of the *Characters* of the late Greek writer and scientist, Theophrastus. Casaubon added a translation and commentary, in Latin, and the book was re-issued in 1599. Casaubon's presence in London from October 1610 until is death in 1614 may also have stimulated interest in this kind of writing. Joseph Hall's *Characterismes of Virtues and Vices*, admittedly modelled on Theophrastus, appeared in 1608, and is usually taken to be the first fruits of this influence, though Professor R. C. Jebb, in the standard modern edition of Theophrastus, thought 'the broad differences' between Hall and his model "far more striking than the indebtedness in details". Modern critics, following the lead of the late Professor G. S. Gordon, tend to give the precedence in the creation of the specifically English type of 'character' to Ben Jonson. "The English Character", asserted Gordon,[1] "is in the main a by-product of the Comedy of Humours accidentally

[1] Gordon, G. S. Theophrastus and his Imitators (in *English Literature and the Classics*).

determined, at an early moment in history, by the opportune appearance of Theophrastus's model. . . . Jonson was the first man in England to produce the set-character on scientific principles, and he deserves all the credit it may bring him, for he spoilt most of his comedies to do it." And Professor Bush (to quote a living authority), when he had summed up the conditions that made for the flourishing of the 'character', added "More than one of [them] would suggest that the genre ought to have been introduced by Ben Jonson, and it was."

It is not the purpose of this Anthology and Essay to establish Shakespeare as a rival to Jonson for precedence in the field of the 'set' character. It is plain to any reader of the collections of characters such as Morley's or Miss Murphy's or Richard Aldington's, that 'characters' were of many kinds, and that precedence in one was far from implying precedence in all. What it is hoped to show, however, firstly, is that in the ten years or so before the first of Jonson's 'characters' were drawn in the *dramatis personae* of *Every Man Out of his Humour* (1599), Shakespeare had some two hundred sketches to his credit in a closely comparable form of literary activity, and, secondly, that there is enough evidence to suggest that some, at least, of these were so well known that the more conventional character-writers drew upon them for suggestion and imitation.

To deal with the second, and less important point, first. It is difficult when one reads Overbury's description of a Chambermaid, "Her industry is upstairs and downstairs, like a drawer", *not* to remember Shakespeare's poor Francis in *I Henry IV*, pestered by the Prince and Poins, and described by the former in terms almost identical with Overbury's. "That even this fellow should have fewer words than a parrot, and yet the son of a woman! His industry is upstairs and downstairs, his eloquence the parcel of a reckoning." Something of Hotspur's contempt for the supercilious king's-messenger who condescended to tell him, sweating and bloody from the conflict, that "the sovereign'st thing on earth was parmaceti for an inward bruise", may have inspired Overbury's words about An Ordinary Fencer: "His wounds are seldom above skin-deep;

for an inward bruise lamb-stones and sweet-breads are his only
spermaceti, which he eats at night next his heart fasting."
Overbury's Noble and Retired Housekeeper is a character
very different from Puck, that supersonic traveller, who "can
put a girdle round about the earth in forty minutes", yet, in his
own way, as Overbury claimed, he "hath as it were put a gird
about the whole world, and found all her quicksands". Hall's
character of Unthrift has a smack of Falstaff, he "ranges without
the pale, and lives without compass"—which is Sir John's in-
dictment of himself—"and now I live out of all order, out of all
compass". The same worthy's mixture of sacred and profane in
"hollaing and singing of anthems" appears in the Common
Singing Men of John Earle's collection, *Microcosmographie*.
"Their skill in melody," says Earle, "makes them better companions abroad, and their anthems abler to sing catches." Both
Earle and Overbury imitate Shakespeare's Sergeant "all in
buff", "a devil in an everlasting garment", one of the earliest of
his sketches, in *The Comedy of Errors*. "His habit", says Overbury, "is a long gown, made at first to cover his knavery, but
that growing too monstrous he now goes in buff. . . . The
devil calls him his white son; he is so like him that he is the
worse for it, and he takes after his father, for the one torments
bodies as fast as the other tortures souls. . . . He goes muffled like
a thief, and carries still the marks of one; for he steals upon man
cowardly, plucks him by the throat, makes him stand, and
fleeces him." Earle's Sergeant or Catch-pole "is one of God's
judgments; and which our roarers do only conceive terrible.
He is the properest shape wherein they fancy Satan; for he is at
most but an arrester, and hell a dungeon." It is obvious that all
three authors had the leather suits of the devils of medieval
drama in mind, and that the similar suits of contemporary
sergeants, and their connection with prisons, made the mental
association a popular one. But it is when Earle comes to his
Constable that we see the clearest dependence on Shakespeare.

"No man stands more upon it that he is the king's officer . . .
and apprehends a drunkard for not standing in the king's

name. He is never so much in his majesty as in a night-watch, where he sits in his chair of state, a shop-stall, and environed with a guard of halberts, examines all passengers."

It is surely correct to surmise that Earle is here as much indebted to Dogberry and Verges as to his own observation.

There are many reminiscences, in Hall and Overbury and Earle, of Shakespeare's characters and phrasing, which are not so clear as to make indebtedness certain, but which, when taken along with those that are reasonably certain, confirm what these show, namely, that the character-writers often looked upon Shakespeare's creations as examples of the art they themselves were practising, and worthy of imitation. Earle's Blunt Man, for instance, who "will do more than he can speak, and yet speak more than he will hear", has surely something of the directness of Gadshill's companions, who "strike sooner than speak, and speak sooner than drink, and drink sooner than pray"? Earle, too, is as much aware of the danger of an "affected plain knave" as Cornwall, in *King Lear*, when he suspects the disguised Kent of being one.

> This is some fellow
> Who, having been praised for blunt-ness, doth affect
> A saucy roughness, and constrains the garb
> Quite from his nature. He cannot flatter, he!
> An honest mind and plain—he must speak truth!
> And they will take it, so; if not, he's plain.
> These kind of knaves I know which in this plain-ness
> Harbour more craft and more corrupter ends
> Than twenty silly-ducking observants
> That stretch their duty nicely.

"He is not easily bad", says Earle, summing-up his Blunt Man, "in whom this quality is nature, but the counterfeit is most dangerous, since he is disguised in a humour that professes not to disguise." The popularity of *Hamlet* accounts for many reminiscences. Overbury's courtier recalls Osric: "He puts more confidence in his words than meaning, and more in his pronunciation than his words." The same author's Amorist could pass for Hamlet disguised or distracted, and is, to use Overbury's words, "untrussed, unbuttoned, and ungartered, not out of carelessness but care. . . . He answers not, or not to the purpose". Hamlet makes his friends promise that, when he shall see fit

> to put an antic disposition on,
> That you, at such times seeing me, never shall
> With arms encumb'red thus, or this head-shake,
> Or by pronouncing of some doubtful phrase,
> As 'Well, well, we know', or 'We could, an if we would',
> Or 'If we list to speak', or 'There be, an if they might'.

Hall's 'Malcontent' behaves in this very fashion, he "shakes his head and smiles, as if his silence would say, I could and would not." Some light is thrown on the nature of the joke played on Malvolio by Overbury's comment on his old-fashioned 'Country Gentleman': "if he go to court it is in yellow stockings". Overbury, too, like Falconbridge in *King John*, finds the pick-tooth 'a main part' of the Traveller's behaviour; but for the mental qualities he pictures someone more like Armado: "His discourse sounds big, but means nothing; and his boy is bound to admire him howsoever."

Of Shakespeare's influence on the character-writers, there should now, it seems to me, be little doubt: it remains to discuss the claim made earlier for him, that he himself should be considered one of them. There need be no dispute concerning his early practice of at least *some* kinds of 'charactery', and his long continuance in them: the four hundred and twenty-six excerpts that follow in this Anthology, from every play in the canon, should surely be evidence enough. They show that Shakespeare from the first, in addition to drawing many portraits that were dramatically useful and often necessary, sketched many that were merely exercises of his quick observation and exuberant fancy. Why should he, for instance, but for very delight in his skill, have Dromio of Syracuse, in the *Comedy of Errors*, twice draw fanciful pictures of the Sergeant, in successive scenes?

ADRIANA. Where is thy master, Dromio? is he well?

DROMIO S: No, he's in Tartar limbo, worse than hell.
A devil in an everlasting garment hath him,
One whose hard heart is button'd up with steel;
A fiend, a fairy, pitiless and rough;
A wolf, nay, worse, a fellow all in buff;
A back-friend, a shoulder-clapper, one that counter-
mands
The passages of alleys, creeks and narrow lands;
A hound that runs counter and yet draws dry-foot-well;
One that, before the judgment, carries poor souls to hell.
(IV. ii. 31–40)

As if to show his fertility of fancy, his tireless virtuousity, and ability to turn about and do in prose what he had just done in verse, Shakespeare in the next scene takes up his sketch again, where Dromio is surprised to find that Antipholus of Syracuse, as Dromio thinks, has got rid of the Sergeant:

DROMIO S: What! Have you got the picture of old Adam
new-apparell'd?

ANTIPHOLUS S: What gold is this? What Adam dost thou
mean?

DROMIO S: Not that Adam that kept the Paradise, but that
Adam that keeps the prison: he that goes in the calf-skin
that was killed for the Prodigal: he that came behind
you, sir, like an evil angel, and bid you forsake your
liberty.

ANTIPHOLUS S: I understand thee not.

DROMIO S: No? why 'tis a plain case: he that went, like a base-
viol, in a case of leather; the man, sir, that when gentlemen are tired, gives them a fob, and rests them; he, sir,
that takes pity on decayed men and gives them suits of
durance; he that sets up his rest to do more exploits with
his mace than a morris-pike.

ANTIPHOLUS S: What, thou meanest an officer?

DROMIO S: Ay, sir, the sergeant of the band; he that brings
any man to answer it that breaks his band; one that

thinks a man always going to bed, and says, 'God give you good rest!'

This, obviously, owed nothing to Theophrastus; it is in the pert, fanciful, repetitive style that Overbury and his collaborators made popular: only, Shakespeare wrote it, and many others of the same vivid kind, long before Overbury's *Characters* appeared in print in 1614. The same fluent, restless fancy we can see at work in the sketch of the schoolmaster Pinch, also in *The Comedy of Errors*—a portrait that is surely a work of supererogation, since Pinch has already appeared upon the stage!

ANTIPHOLUS OF EPHESUS: One Pinch, a hungry, lean-faced villain,
A mere anatomy, a mountebank,
A threadbare juggler, and a fortune-teller,
A needy, hollow-eyes sharp-looking wretch,
A living-dead man.

The same abundance of fancy and copiousness in the vocabulary of derogation shows itself when Falstaff and the Prince have their bouts of verbal fisticuffs; and when Falstaff, the master image-maker, is absent, the insignificant Gadshill gets bestowed on him for the nonce the magnificent verbal *repertoire* of Sir John.

"Tut, there are other Troyans that thou dreamest not if, the which for sport sake are content to do the profession some grace; that would, if matters should be looked into, for their own credit sake make all whole. I am joined with no foot-land-rakers, no long-staff sixpenny strikers, none of these mad mustachio purple-hued malt worms; but with nobility and tranquileity, burgomasters and great oneyers, such as can hold in, such as will strike sooner than speak, and speak sooner than drink, and drink sooner than pray: and yet I lie, for they pray continually to their saint, the commonwealth, or rather, not pray to her, but prey on her, for they ride up and down on her and make her their boots."

These exuberant sketches are often purely fanciful, Shakespeare giving 'a local habitation and a name' to creatures of 'airy nothing', like Mercutio's account of Queen Mab and Robin Goodfellow's description of himself. More frequently they are based on exact observation: but even here the mode of presentation is all-important, for they must be made to appeal more to the imagination than to the memory or experience. Edgar, for instance, in *King Lear*, when he declares that he has been a serving-man, has no call to add a word further; but he backs up his lie with a brilliant 'character' of the type of domestic he chooses to be imagined, as though the opportunity were too good for the lightning-artist in Shakespeare to forego!

"A serving-man, proud in heart and mind, that curled my hair, wore gloves in my cap, served the lust of my mistress's heart, and did the act of darkness with her; swore as many oaths as I spake words, and broke them in the sweet face of heaven; one that slept in the contriving of lust and waked to do it. Wine loved I deeply, dice dearly, and in woman outparamoured the Turk: false of heart, light of ear, bloody of hand, hog in sloth, fox in stealth, wolf in greediness, dog in madness, lion in prey."

This 'serving-man' is as much alive as any character in the play: yet he is completely imaginary and unnecessary to the plot! He is part of Edgar's picture of the world, and he becomes part of ours. Shakespeare fills his world with such creatures, living, imaginary, or even dead: and it is the same to the end of his story. When the old shepherd, in *The Winter's Tale*—possibly the last of the plays—would stir his adopted daughter Perdita into greater activity, he does it by drawing a 'character' of his wife, now deceased.

"Fie, daughter! When my old wife liv'd, upon
This day she was both pantler, butler, cook,
Both dame and servant; welcom'd all, serv'd all,
Would sing her song and dance her turn; now here
At upper end o' the table, now i' the middle;

> On his shoulder, and his; her face o' fire
> With labour and the thing she took to quench it
> She would to each one sip. You are retir'd
> As if you were a feasted one, and not
> The hostess of the meeting."

Shakespeare's people live in just such a live world as is depicted here. They are sentient beings, quick to feel and to respond to feeling; and it does not seem to matter whether they are 'actual' or imaginary. When Iago describes Cassio as a 'countercaster', 'a mere arithmetician', or as 'a slipper and subtle knave' does it greatly matter whether the descriptions are authentic or not? They present vividly the interpretation of the lieutenant's character that Iago wishes Roderigo to accept, and they become at once part of his victim's conception of the real world by which he is surrounded.

Shakespeare peoples his plays with characters who seem to us to be alive, and to whom other characters are alive also. They re-act strongly to their world, and the strength of their reaction is the measure of their reality for us. They 'come alive' in a three-dimensional world of human relationships; they exist in one another's minds as well as ours. They are not moved like puppets, or dissected for an anatomical demonstration in 'charactery'; but are drawn to or rebound from one another like vital creatures. They live not by virtue of effective posing on the stage, but in their relationship to one another, and when that relationship has been 'hit-off' or established, further illustration is unnecessary.

> "This is a slight, unmeritable man,
> Meet to be sent on errands,"

says Antony of Lepidus—and we know at once the men and how they stand to one another. A single line,

> "When you sing, sweet, I'd have you do it ever."

is enough to characterize the singer and the listener. Such simplification, without the intrusive repetition of the author, gives a quality to the relationship that has something vital and untheatrical about it: more extensive description would merely blur the picture of something which is simple and direct and yet unfathomable, like the elemental passions of love or hate.

The superiority of Shakespeare's work in 'character' lies in its dramatic quality. Theophrastus, and his imitators, will define the trait of human nature they propose to discuss, and proceed to illustrate with tedious prolixity the ways in which it is exhibited in life: as thus, of *Stupidity.*

> "You may define Stupidity (says Theophrastus) as a slowness of mind in word or deed. But the Stupid man is one who, sitting at his counters, and having made all his calculations and worked out his sum, asks one who sits by him how much it comes to. When any one has a suit against him, and he has come to the day when the case must be decided, he forgets it and walks out into the field. Often also when he sits to see a play, the rest go out and he is left, fallen asleep in the theatre" . . . .

And so on, through another eight or ten examples of the same kind of conduct. It is as though a rubber doll were being bent a dozen ways before us to show the flexibility that was clear from the first twist!

Character-writing was almost as popular as sonneteering had been in its day, but not many 'characters' were written on the strictly Theophrastan model, and it will be obvious from the example quoted why that model was deserted, even by its first imitator, Hall. 'Characters' as Shakespeare uses them are not tediously repetitive, like something automatic, but convey a sense of life; they give life to those about them, as well as receive it from them; they live in and by one another. His sketches have all the merits that the best of the character-writers aimed at—force, brevity, lightness, picturesqueness, and consistency; but they have a merit which 'characters' rolled out flat for dissection, or made to dance alone to a set tune, can never have. They do not live and move in solitary worlds. How deep was Shakespeare's sense of their interdependence—and that of all of us—may be seen when we compare, say, the pictures of Henry V painted respectively by the Dauphin and by the Constable of France, in 'Two Characters in One King' (Group A15) or take the picture of Orlando that Oliver draws for Charles the Wrestler, and put it beside the one he draws for himself: or the twin accounts of Sir Andrew given by Sir Toby, to suit varying circumstances. Which is the real character —the one we spread abroad to become operative in people's minds and influence their actions, or the one we keep to ourselves? The 'honest blunt soldier' of Iago's acquaintances, or the 'cogging villain' whom his wife all unsuspectingly describes? Shakespeare was alive to the delicate balance of 'character' and 'reputation', of our opinions of ourselves and others' opinions of us, in a 'total' picture of reality. Are Antony's captains in the right—or Antony, the 'peerless lover'?

> Look where they come!
> Take but good note, and you shall see in him
> The triple pillar of the world transformed
> Into a strumpet's fool. Behold and see.
> CLEOP: If it be love indeed, tell me how much.
> ANT: There's beggary in the love that can be reckon'd.

Shall Cleopatra go down in Roman history, staged 'in the posture of a whore', or as the 'lass incomparable', whose 'infinite variety age could not wither nor custom stale'?

"The web of our life is of a mingled yarn", says the First Lord in *All's Well That End's Well*: "our virtues would be proud if our faults whipped them not; and our crimes would despair if they were not cherished by our virtues." If we look too closely or too carelessly, as with some kinds of geometrical pattern, what seemed to be one thing is transformed into another.

> "Virtue itself turns vice, being misapplied,
> And vice sometime's by action dignified",

reflects Father Lawrence in *Romeo and Juliet*, and it is clear from this andm any similar ponderings that Shakespeare was conscious of the relativity of values in human affairs, and in our knowledge of reality itself. That consciousness reveals itself repeatedly in his treatment of 'characters': as, for instance, in that of Helen of Troy, in *Troilus and Cressida*.

HECTOR: Brother, she is not worth what she doth cost
    The holding.
TROILUS: What is aught but as't is valued?
HECTOR: But value dwells not in particular will;
    It holds his estimate and dignity
    As well wherein 'tis precious of itself
    As in the prizer. 'Tis mad idolatry
    To make the service greater than the god.'

A strong sense—in spite of their vitality—of the uncertainty in which we stand runs through these 'characters' of Shakespeare, and touches the plays repeatedly with irony. Who shall say whether it is better to have, like Glendower,

"framed to the harp
Many an English ditty lovely well"

or to be like his rival Hotspur, who

"had rather be a kitten and cry mew
Than one of these same metre ballad-mongers"?

Nor are we constantly one thing: as may be seen from the way in which one type passes 'into' another. Love, as so often in the comedies, will make a man undergo such metamorphosis as to leave his friends wondering if he is the man indeed; and jealousy will transmute him utterly. Hatred and a change of circumstances will turn a courtier into a rebel. Nowhere is Falstaff (or Shakespeare) more observant than in his comment on Justice Shallow and his men.

"It is a wonderful thing to see the sensible coherence of his men's spirits and his: they, by observing him, do bear themselves like foolish justices; he, by conversing with them, is turned into a justice-like serving-man." Sir John himself, when it suits Ford to do so, is praised as Ophelia praises Hamlet, for his many "war-like, court-like, and learned preparations".

3

Here is 'the courtier's, soldier's, scholar's eye, tongue, sword' of Ophelia's description strangely placed, indeed! Yet how much unlike! Repeatedly Shakespeare juxtaposes the portraits— "Look here, upon this picture, and on this"—as though to question the nature of ourselves, to make us see how much we live in others' eyes and minds, as well as in our own.

"You that are old", cries Falstaff, "consider not the capacities of us that are young; you measure the heat of our livers with the bitterness of your galls; and we that are in the vaward of our youth, I must confess, are wags too."

The Chief Justice is indignant.

"Do you set down your name in the scroll of youth, that are written down with all the characters of age? Have you not a moist eye, a dry hand, a yellow cheek, a white beard, a decreasing leg, an increasing belly? Is not your voice broken, your mind short, your chin double, your wit single, and every part about you blasted with antiquity, and will you yet call yourself young? Fie, fie, fie, Sir John!"

"My lord", is the answer, "I was born about three of the clock in the afternoon, with a white head, and something a round belly. For my voice, I have lost it with halloaing and singing of anthems. . . . The truth is, I am old in judgment and understanding; and he that will caper with me for a thousand marks, let him lend me the money, and have at him."

Who shall say that the old man is worsted? Character, Shakespeare would seem to be saying, is a facet, only, of reality; and what it means to you depends very much upon where you stand. As an operative force it is as much what you are in people's minds as what you are in yourself, and it is the great merit of 'charactery' in drama to make this pluralism clear, to present a poly-sided reality, in character.

"What a piece of work is man", exclaims the poetic Hamlet. "How noble in reason! how infinite in faculty! in form, in moving, how express and admirable! in action how like an angel! in apprehension, how like a god!"

But that other, the more portly 'soldier, courtier, scholar' Falstaff, could present a different picture of the same *homo sapiens*. To him it was all too easy for Justice Shallow, or any other man, to be "like a man made after supper of a cheese paring. When 'a was naked, he was for all the world like a forked radish, with a head fantastically carved upon it with a knife!"

So much does the seeing eye colour and transform what it takes in! So much are we phantasms walking the stage of our own and other's imaginations! Nowhere does this become more apparent than in a study of Shakespeare's Charactery.

# GROUPS

# AND INDIVIDUAL

# CHARACTERS

1 *Great Place*

DUKE: O place and greatness! millions of false eyes
    Are stuck upon thee: volumes of report
    Run with these false and most contrarious quests
    Upon thy doings: thousand escapes of wit
    Make thee the father of their idle dream
    And rack thee in their fancies!

MEASURE FOR MEASURE, IV.i. 61–66

2 *A Saintly King*

QUEEN: I tell thee, Pole, when in the city Tours
    Thou ran'st a tilt in honour of my love,
    And stol'st away the ladies' hearts of France,
    I thought King Henry had resembled thee
    In courage, courtship, and proportion:
    But all his mind is bent to holiness,
    To number Ave-Maries on his beads;
    His champions are the prophets and apostles,
    His weapons holy saws of sacred writ;
    His study is his tilt-yard, and his loves
    Are brazen images of canonized saints.
    I would the college of the cardinals
    Would choose him pope, and carry him to Rome,
    And set the triple crown upon his head:
    That were a state fit for his holiness.

KING HENRY VI, PT. II, I. iii. 53–67

3 *A Gracious Monarch*

KING HENRY: That's not my fear; my meed hath got me fame:
    I have not stopp'd mine ears to their demands,
    Nor posted off their suits with slow delays;
    My pity hath been balm to heal their wounds,

My mildness hath allay'd their swelling griefs,
My mercy dried their water-flowing tears;
I have not been desirious of their wealth,
Nor much oppress'd them with great subsidies,
Nor forward of revenge, though they much err'd.
Then why should they love Edward more than me?
No, Exeter, these graces challenge grace:
And, when the lion fawns upon the lamb,
The lamb will never cease to follow him.

KING HENRY VI, PT. III, IV. viii, 38–50

### 4 A King-Maker—Fallen

WARWICK: Ah, who is nigh? come to me, friend or foe,
And tell me who is victor, York or Warwick?
Why ask I that? my mangled body shows,
My blood, my want of strength, my sick heart shows,
That I must yield my body to the earth,
And, by my fall, the conquest to my foe.
Thus yields the cedar to the axe's edge,
Whose arms gave shelter to the princely eagle,
Under whose shade the ramping lion slept,
Whose top branch overpeer'd Jove's spreading tree,
And kept low shrubs from winter's powerful wind.
These eyes, that now are dimm'd with death's black veil,
Have been as piercing as the mid-day sun
To search the secret treasons of the world:
The wrinkles in my brows, now fill'd with blood,
Were liken'd oft to kingly sepulchres;
For who liv'd king, but I could dig his grave?
And who durst smile when Warwick bent his brow?
Lo! now my glory smear'd in dust and blood;
My parks, my walks, my manors that I had,
Even now forsake me; and, of all my lands
Is nothing left me by my body's length.
Why, what is pomp, rule, reign, but earth and dust?
And, live we how we can, yet die we must.

KING HENRY VI, PT. III, V. ii. 5–28

### 5 A Meritorious Monarch

GLOUCESTER: England ne'er had a king until his time.
Virtue he had, deserving to command:
His brandish'd sword did blind men with his beams;
His arms spread wider than a dragon's wings;
His sparkling eyes, replete with wrathful fire,
More dazzled and drove back his enemies
Than mid-day sun fierce bent against their faces.
What should I say! his deeds exceed all speech:
He ne'er lift up his hand but conquered.

KING HENRY VI, PT. I, I. i. 8–16

### 6 A Pious Prince

BUCKINGHAM: Ah, ha, my lord, this prince is not an Edward!
He is not lolling on a lewd day-bed,
But on his knees at meditation;
Not dallying with a brace of courtezans,
But meditating with two deep divines;
Not sleeping, to engross his idle body,
But praying, to enrich his watchful soul:
Happy were England, would this gracious prince
Take on himself the sovereignty thereof:
But, sure, I fear, we shall ne'er win him to it.

KING RICHARD III, III.vii. 70–79

### 7 Seeker of Popular Favour

KING RICHARD: Ourself and Bushy, Bagot here and Green
Observed his courtship to the common people,
How he did seem to dive into their hearts
With humble and familiar courtesy,
What reverence he did throw away on slaves,
Wooing poor craftsmen with the craft of smiles
And patient underbearing of his fortune,
As 't were to banish their affects with him.
Off goes his bonnet to an oyster-wench;

A brace of draymen bid God speed him well
And had the tribute of his supple knee,
With 'Thanks, my countrymen, my loving friends';
As were our England in reversion his,
And he our subjects' next degree in hope.

KING RICHARD II, I. iv. 23–36

## 8 *A Patriotic Prince*

YORK: I am the last of noble Edward's sons,
Of whom thy father, Prince of Wales, was first;
In war was never lion raged more fierce,
In peace was never gentle lamb more mild,
Than was that young and princely gentleman.
His face thou hast, for even so look'd he,
Accomplish'd with the number of thy hours;
But when he frown'd, it was against the French,
And not against his friends; his noble hand
Did win what he did spend and spent not that
Which his triumphant father's hand had won;
His hands were guilty of no kindred blood,
But bloody with the enemies of his kin.

KING RICHARD II, II. i. 172–184

## 9 *Majesty Outfaced*

KING RICHARD: Was this face the face
That every day under his household roof
Did keep ten thousand men? was this the face
That, like the sun, did make beholders wink?
Was this the face that faced so many follies,
And was at last out-fac'd by Bolingbroke?
A brittle glory shineth in this face:
As brittle as the glory is the face;
For there it is, crack'd in a hundred shivers.

KING RICHARD II, IV. i. 281–289

10 *Popular Usurper*

YORK: Then, as I said, the duke, great Bolingbroke,
    Mounted upon a hot and fiery steed
    Which his aspiring rider seem'd to know,
    With slow but stately pace kept on his course,
    Whilst all tongues cried, 'God save thee, Bolingbroke!'
    You would have thought the very windows spake,
    So many greedy looks of young and old
    Through casements darted their desiring eyes
    Upon his visage, and that all the walls
    With painted imagery had said at once
    'Jesu preserve thee! welcome, Bolingbroke!'
    Whilst he, from the one side to the other turning,
    Bareheaded, lower than his proud steed's neck,
    Bespake them thus, 'I thank you, countrymen':
    And thus still doing, thus he pass'd along.

                         KING RICHARD II, V. ii. 7–21


11 *A King Outcast*

YORK: As in a theatre, the eyes of men,
    After a well-grac'd actor leaves the stage,
    Are idly bent on him that enters next,
    Thinking his prattle to be tedious;
    Even so, or with much more contempt, men's eyes
    Did scowl on gentle Richard; no man cried 'God save him!'
    No joyful tongue gave him his welcome home:
    But dust was thrown upon his sacred head;
    Which with such gentle sorrow he shook off,
    His face still combating with tears and smiles,
    The badges of his grief and patience,
    That had not God, for some strong purpose, steel'd
    The hearts of men, they must perforce have melted
    And barbarism itself have pitied him.

                         KING RICHARD II, V. ii. 23–36

## 12 *Politic Prudence and Imprudence*

KING HENRY: God pardon thee! yet let me wonder, Harry,
    At thy affections, which do hold a wing
    Quite from the flight of all thy ancestors.
    Thy place in council thou hast rudely lost,
    Which by thy younger brother is supplied,
    And art almost an alien to the hearts
    Of all the court and princes of my blood.
    The hope and expectation of thy time
    Is ruin'd, and the soul of every man
    Prophetically do forethink thy fall.
    Had I so lavish of my presence been,
    So common-hackney'd in the eyes of men,
    So stale and cheap to vulgar company,
    Opinion, that did help me to the crown,
    Had still kept loyal to possession
    And left me in reputeless banishment,
    A fellow of no mark nor likelihood.
    By being seldom seen, I could not stir
    But like a comet I was wonder'd at;
    That men would tell their children 'This is he';
    Others would say, 'Where? which is Bolingbroke?'
    And then I stole all courtesy from heaven,
    And dress'd myself in such humility
    That I did pluck allegiance from men's hearts,
    Loud shouts and salutations from their mouths,
    Even in the presence of the crowned king.
    Thus did I keep my person fresh and new;
    My presence, like a robe pontifical,
    Ne'er seen but wonder'd at; and so my state,
    Seldom but sumptuous, showed like a feast,
    And won by rareness such solemnity.
    The skipping king, he ambled up and down
    With shallow jesters and rash bavin wits,
    Soon kindled and soon burnt; carded his state,
    Mingled his royalty with cap'ring fools,
    Had his great name profaned with their scorns

And gave his countenance, against his name,
To laugh at gibing boys and stand the push
Of every beardless vain comparative,
Grew a companion to the common streets,
Enfeoff'd himself to popularity;
That, being daily swallow'd by men's eyes,
They surfeited with honey and began
To loathe the taste of sweetness, whereof a little
More than a little is by much too much.
So when he had occasion to be seen,
He was but as the cuckoo is in June,
Heard, not regarded; seen, but with such eyes
As, sick and blunted with community,
Afford no extraordinary gaze,
Such as is bent on sun-like majesty
When it shines seldom in admiring eyes;
But rather drows'd and hung their eyelids down,
Slept in his face, and rend'red such aspect
As cloudy men use to their adversaries,
Being with his presence glutted, gorg'd and full.
And in that very line, Harry, standest thou;
For thou has lost thy princely privilege
With vile participation: not an eye
But is a-weary of thy common sight,
Save mine, which hath desir'd to see thee more;
Which now doth that I would not have it do,
Make blind itself with foolish tenderness.

HENRY IV, PT. I, III. ii. 29–91

13 *A Rebel Bishop*

LANCASTER: My Lord of York, it better show'd with you,
When that your flock, assembled by the bell,
Encircled you to hear with reverence
Your exposition on the holy text,
Than now to see you here an iron man,
Cheering a rout of rebels with your drum,

Turning the word to sword and life to death.
That man that sits within a monarch's heart,
And ripens in the sunshine of his favour,
Would he abuse the countenance of the king,
Alack, what mischief might he set abroach
In shadow of such greatness! With you, lord bishop,
It is even so. Who hath not heard it spoken
How deep you were within the books of God?
To us the speaker in his parliament;
To us the imagin'd voice of God himself;
The very opener and intelligencer
Between the grace, the sanctities of heaven,
And our dull workings. O, who shall believe
But you misuse the reverence of your place,
Employ the countenance and grace of heaven,
As a false favourite doth his prince's name,
In deeds dishonourable? You have taken up,
Under the counterfeited zeal of God,
The subjects of his substitute, my father;
And both against the peace of heaven and him
Have here up-swarm'd them.

HENRY IV, PT. II, IV. ii. 4–30

14 *Humouring a Humoursome Prince*

KING: Thou hast a better place in his affection
Than all thy brothers: cherish it, my boy,
And noble offices thou mayst effect
Of mediation, after I am dead,
Between his greatness and thy other brethren:
Therefore omit him not; blunt not his love,
Nor lose the good advantage of his grace
By seeming cold or careless of his will;
For he is gracious, if he be observe'd:
He hath a tear for pity and a hand
Open as day for melting charity:
Yet notwithstanding, being incens'd, he's flint,

As humorous as winter and as sudden
As flaws congealed in the spring of day.
His temper, therefore, must be well observ'd:
Chide him for faults, and do it reverently,
When you perceive his blood inclin'd to mirth;
But, being moody, give him line and scope,
Till that his passions, like a whale on ground,
Confound themselves with working. Learn this, Thomas,
And thou shalt prove a shelter to thy friends,
A hoop of gold to bind they brothers in,
That the united vessel of their blood,
Mingled with venom of suggestion—
As, force perforce, the age will pour it in—
Shall never leak, though it do work as strong
As aconitum or rash gunpowder.

HENRY IV, PT. II, IV. iv. 22–48

15 *Two Characters of One King*

DAUPHINE: And let us do it with no show of fear;
No, with no more than if we heard that England
Were busied with a Whitsun morris-dance:
For, my good liege, she is so idly king'd,
Her sceptre so fantastically borne
By a vain, giddy, shallow, humorous youth,
That fear attends her not.

CONSTABLE:                    O peace, Prince Dauphin!
You are too much mistaken in this king,
Question your grace the late ambassadors,
With what great state he heard their embassy,
How well supplied with noble counsellors,
How modest in exception, and withal
How terrible in constant resolution,
And you shall find his vanities forespent
Were but the outside of the Roman Brutus,
Covering discretion with a coat of folly;

As gardeners do with ordure hide those roots
That shall first spring and be most delicate.

KING HENRY V, II. iv. 23–40

### 16 *A King Commander*

CHORUS:                      O now, who will behold
The royal captain of this ruin'd band
Walking from watch to watch, from tent to tent,
Let him cry 'Praise and glory on his head!'
For forth he goes and visits all his host,
Bids them good morrow with a modest smile
And calls them brothers, friends and countrymen.
Upon his royal face there is no note
How dread an army hath enrounded him;
Nor doth he dedicate one jot of colour
Unto the weary and all-watched night:
But freshly looks and over-bears attaint
With cheerful semblance and sweet majesty;
That every wretch, pining and pale before,
Beholding him, plucks comfort from his looks.
A largess universal like the sun
His liberal eye doth give to every one,
Thawing cold fear, that mean and gentle all
Behold, as may unworthiness define,
A little touch of Harry in the night.

KING HENRY V, IV. CHORUS. 28–47

### 17 *The King but a Man*

KING HENRY: For, though I speak it to you, I think the king is
but a man, as I am: the violet smells to him as it doth to
me; the element shows to him as it doth to me; all his
senses have but human conditions: his ceremonies laid by,
in his nakedness he appears but a man; and though his
affections are higher mounted than ours, yet when they
stoop, they stoop with the like wing. Therefore when he

sees reason of fears, as we do, his fears, out of doubt, be of the same relish as ours are: yet, in reason, no man should posssess him with any appearance of fear, lest he, by showing it, should dishearten his army.

KING HENRY V, IV. i. 106–118

## 18 *Oppressive Greatness*

CASSIUS: Why, man, he doth bestride the narrow world
Like a Colossus, and we petty men
Walk under his huge legs, and peep about
To find ourselves dishonourable graves.
Men at some time are masters of their fates:
The fault, dear Brutus, is not in our stars,
But in ourselves, that we are underlings.

JULIUS CAESAR, I. ii. 134–140

## 19 *A Fixed and Constant Man*

CAESAR: I could be well mov'd, if I were as you;
If I could pray to move, prayers would move me:
But I am constant as the northern star,
Of whose true-fix'd and resting quality
There is no fellow in the firmament.
The skies are painted with unnumber'd sparks,
They are all fire and every one doth shine,
But there's but one in all doth hold his place:
So, in the world: 'tis furnish'd well with men,
And men are flesh and blood, and apprehensive;
Yet in the number I do know but one
That unassailable holds on his rank,
Unshak'd of motion: and that I am he,
Let me a little show it, even in this;
That I was constant Cimber should be banish'd,
And constant do remain to keep him so.

JULIUS CAESAR, III. i. 58–73

4

20 *A Godlike Monarch*

HAMLET: Look here, upon this picture, and on this;
    The counterfeit presentment of two brothers.
    See, what a grace was seated on this brow;
    Hyperion's curls, the front of Jove himself,
    An eye like Mars, to threaten and command,
    A station like the herald Mercury
    New-lighted on a heaven-kissing hill,
    A combination and a form indeed,
    Where every god did seem to set his seal,
    To give the world assurance of a man.
    This was your husband.

                       HAMLET, III. iv. 53–63

21 *A Vice of Kings*

HAMLET:                   A murderer and a villain!
    A slave that is not twentieth part the tithe
    Of your precedent lord! A vice of kings!
    A cutpurse of the empire and the rule,
    That from a shelf the precious diadem stole,
    And put it in his pocket!
QUEEN:                No more!
HAMLET: A king of shreds and patches,—

                       HAMLET, III. iv. 96–102

22 *Retiring Greatness*

DUKE:                  Give me your hand;
    I'll privily away: I love the people,
    But do not like to stage me to their eyes.
    Though it do well, I do not relish well
    Their loud applause and Aves vehement,
    Nor do I think the man of safe discretion
    That does affect it.

            MEASURE FOR MEASURE, I. i. 66–72

*23 A Just Deputy*

PROVOST:                                    It is a bitter deputy.
DUKE: Not so, not so: his life is parallel'd
    Even with the stroke and line of his great justice:
    He doth with holy abstinence subdue
    That in himself which he spurs on his power
    To qualify in others: were he meal'd with that
    Which he corrects, then were he tyrannous;
    But this being so, he's just.

               MEASURE FOR MEASURE, IV. ii. 81–88


*24 Old Majesty Distraught*

KENT: Who's there, beside foul weather?
GENT: One minded like the weather, most unquietly.
KENT: I know you. Where's the King?
GENT: Contending with the fretful elements;
    Bids the wind blow the earth into the sea,
    Or swell the curled waters 'bove the main,
    That things might change or cease; tears his white hair,
    Which the impetuous blasts, with eyeless rage,
    Catch in their fury, and make nothing of;
    Strives in his little world of man to out-scorn
    The to-and-fro conflicting wind and rain.
    This night, wherein the cub-drawn bear would couch,
    The lion and the belly-pinched wolf
    Keep their fur dry, unbonneted he runs,
    And bids what will take all.
KENT:                                    But who is with him?
GENT: None but the fool, who labours to outjest
    His heart-struck injuries.

               KING LEAR, III. i. 1–17


*25 Mad King*

CORDELIA: Alack, 'tis he! Why, he was met even now
    As mad as the vex'd sea, singing aloud,
    Crown'd with rank fumiter and furrow weeds,

With hardocks, hemlock, nettles, cuckoo, flow'rs,
Darnel, and all the idle weeds that grow
In our sustaining corn.

KING LEAR, IV. iv. 1–6

## 26 *Scrupulous Ambition*

LADY MACBETH:                                    yet do I fear thy nature;
It is too full o' the milk of human kindness
To catch the nearest way; thou wouldst be great,
Art not without ambition, but without
The illness should attend it: what thou wouldst highly,
That wouldst thou holily; wouldst not play false,
And yet wouldst wrongly win: thou'dst have, great
     Glamis,
That which cries 'Thus thou must do, if thou have it';
And that which rather thou dost fear to do
Than wishest should be undone.

MACBETH, I. V. 17–26

## 27 *A Royal Nature*

MACBETH:                                    Our fears in Banquo
Stick deep; and in his royalty of nature
Reigns that which would be fear'd: 'tis much he dares:
And, to that dauntless temper of his mind,
He hath a wisdom that doth guide his valour
To act in safety. There is none but he
Whose being I do fear: and under him
My Genius is rebuked; as, it is said,
Mark Antony's was by Caesar.

MACBETH, III. i. 49–57

## 28 *A Prince Simply Virtuous*

MALCOLM:                                    I am yet
Unknown to love, never was forsworn,
Scarcely have coveted what was mine own;
At no time broke my faith, would not betray

The devil to his fellow, and delight
No less in truth than life: my first false speaking
Was this upon myself: what I am truly,
Is thine and my poor country's to command:

MACBETH, IV. iii. 125–132

## 29 *An Incomparable Emperor*

CLEOPATRA: I dreamt there was an Emperor Antony:
 O, such another sleep, that I might see
 But such another man!
DOLABELLA:       If it might please ye,—
CLEOPATRA: His face was as the heavens; and therein stuck
 A sun and moon, which kept their course, and lighted
 The little O, the earth.
DOLABELLA:       Mose sovereign creature,—
CLEOPATRA: His legs bestrid the ocean: his rear'd arm
 Crested the world: his voice was propertied
 As all the tuned spheres, and that to friends;
 But when he meant to quail and shake the orb,
 He was as rattling thunder. For his bounty,
 There was no winter in 't; an autumn 'twas
 That grew the more by reaping: his delights
 Were dolphin-like; they show'd his back above
 The element they lived in: in his livery
 Walk'd crowns and crownets; realms and islands were
 As plates dropp'd from his pocket.

ANTONY AND CLEOPATRA, V. ii. 76–92

## 30 *Character of the Tribunes of the People*

MENENIUS: You know neither me, yourselves, nor any thing.
 You are ambitious for poor knaves' caps and legs: you
 wear out a good wholesome forenoon in hearing a cause
 between an orange-wife and a forest-seller, and then
 rejourn the controversy of three-pence to a second day of
 audience. When you are hearing a matter between party

and party, if you chance to be pinched with the colic, you make faces like mummers, set up the bloody flag against all patience, and, in roaring for a chamber-pot, dismiss the controversy bleeding, the more entangled by your hearing: all the peace you may in their cause is, calling both the parties knaves. You are a pair of strange ones.

BRUTUS: Come, come, you are well understood to be a perfecter giber for the table than a necessary bencher in the Capitol.

MENENIUS: Our very priests must become mockers if they shall encounter such ridiculous subjects as you are. When you speak best unto the purpose it is not worth the wagging of your beards; and your beards deserve not so honourable a grave as to stuff a botcher's cushion, or to be entombed in an ass's pack-saddle. Yet you must be saying Marcius is proud; who, in a cheap estimation, is worth all your predecessors since Deucalion, though peradventure some of the best of 'em were hereditary hangmen.

CORIOLANUS, II. i. 76–104

### 31 *A Self-Dependent Spider of a Man*

NORFOLK: All this was order'd by the good discretion
    Of the right reverend Cardinal of York.

BUCKINGHAM: The devil speed him! no man's pie is freed
    From his ambitious finger. What had he
    To do in these fierce vanities? I wonder
    That such a keech can with his very bulk
    Take up the rays o' the beneficial sun,
    And keep it from the earth.

NORFOLK:                   Surely, sir,
    There's in him stuff that puts him to these ends;
    For, being not propp'd by ancestry, whose grace
    Chalks successors their way, nor call'd upon
    For high feats done to the crown; neither allied
    To eminent assistants; but, spider-like,
    Out of his self-drawing web, he gives us note,

The force of his own merit makes his way;
A gift that heaven gives for him, which buys
A place next to the king.

KING HENRY VIII, I. i. 50–66

### 32 *A Man of Power and Malice*

NORFOLK:                                    I advise you—
And take it from a heart that wishes towards you
Honour and plenteous safety—that you read
The cardinal's malice and his potency
Together; to consider further that
What his high hatred would effect wants not
A minister in his power. You know his nature,
That he's revengeful, and I know his sword
Hath a sharp edge; it's long and 't may be said
It reaches far, and where 't will not extend,
Thither he darts it. Bosom up my counsel;
You'll find it wholesome. Lo, where comes that rock
That I advise your shunning.

KING HENRY VIII, I. i. 102–114

### 33 *Two Characters of One Great Man*

KATHERINE: So, may he rest; his faults lie gently on him!
Yet thus far, Griffith, give me leave to speak him,
And yet with charity. He was a man
Of an unbounded stomach, ever ranking
Himself with princes; one that by suggestion
Tied all the kingdom: simony was fair-play:
His own opinion was his law: i' the presence
He would say untruths, and be ever double
Both in his words and meaning: he was never,
But where he meant to ruin, pitiful:
His promises were, as he then was, mighty;
But his performance, as he is now, nothing:
Of his own body he was ill, and gave
The clergy ill example.

GRIFFITH:                    Noble madam,
Men's evil manners live in brass; their virtues
We write in water. May it please your highness
To hear me speak his good now?
KATHERINE:                          Yes, good Griffith;
I were malicious else.
GRIFFITH:                This cardinal,
Though from an humble stock, undoubtedly
Was fashion'd to much honour from his cradle.
He was a scholar, and a ripe and good one;
Exceeding wise, fair-spoken, and persuading:
Lofty and sour to them that loved him not,
But to those men that sought him, sweet as summer.
And though he were unsatisfied in getting,
Which was a sin, yet in bestowing, madam,
He was most princely; ever witness for him
Those twins of learning that he raised in you,
Ipswich and Oxford! one of which fell with him,
Unwilling to outlive the good that did it;
The other, though unfinish'd, yet so famous
So excellent in art, and still so rising,
That Christendom shall ever speak his virtue.
His overthrow heap'd happiness upon him;
For then, and not till then, he felt himself,
And found the blessedness of being little:
And, to add greater honours to his age
Than man could give him, he died fearing God.
KATHERINE: After my death I wish no other herald,
No other speaker of my living actions,
To keep mine honour from corruption,
But such an honest chronicler as Griffith.
Whom I most hated living, thou has made me,
With thy religious truth and modesty,
Now in his ashes honour: peace be with him!

KING HENRY VIII, IV. ii. 31-75

### 1 *A Gracious Queen*

PERICLES: See, where she comes apparell'd like the spring,
    Graces her subjects, and her thoughts the king
    Of every virtue gives renown to men!
    Her face the book of praises, where is read
    Nothing but curious pleasures, as from thence
    Sorrow were ever raz'd, and testy wrath
    Could never be her mild companion.

                    PERICLES, I. i. 12–18

### 2 *A Queen of Curds and Cream*

POLITENES: This is the prettiest low-born lass that ever
    Ran on the green-sward: nothing she does or seems
    But smacks of something greater than herself,
    Too noble for this place.
CAMILLO:             He tells her something
    That makes her blood look out: good sooth, she is
    The queen of curds and cream.

             THE WINTER'S TALE, IV. iii. 156–161

### 3 *A Queen of Earthly Queens*

KING:                 Go thy ways, Kate:
    That man i' the world who shall report he has
    A better wife, let him in nought be trusted,
    For speaking false in that: thou art, alone,
    If thy rare qualities, sweet gentleness,
    Thy meekness saint-like, wife-like government,
    Obeying in commanding, and thy parts
    Sovereign and pious else, could speak thee out,
    The queen of earthly queens. She's noble born,

And like her true nobility she has
Carried herself towards me.

KING HENRY VIII, II. iv. 131–141

## 4 *A Pattern of All Princes*

CRANMER: This royal infant—heaven still move about her!—
Though in her cradle, yet now promises
Upon this land a thousand thousand blessings,
Which time shall bring to ripeness: she shall be—
But few now living can behold that goodness—
A pattern to all princes living with her,
And all that shall succeed: Saba was never
More covetous of wisdom and fair virtue
Than this pure soul shall be: all princely graces,
That mould up such a mighty piece as this is,
With all the virtues that attend the good,
Shall still be doubled on her: truth shall nurse her,
Holy and heavenly thoughts shall counsel her:
She shall be loved and fear'd: her own shall bless her;
Her foes shake like a field of beaten corn,
And hang their heads with sorrow. Good grows with her:
In her days every man shall eat in safety,
Under his own vine, what he plants, and sing
The merry songs of peace to all his neighbours:
God shall be truly known; and those about her
From her shall read the perfect ways of honour,
And by those claim their greatness, not by blood.

KING HENRY VIII, V. V. 18–39

## (a) Warriors

### 1 War and Peace

SECOND SERV: Why, then we shall have a stirring world again. This peace is nothing but to rust iron, increase tailors, and breed ballad-makers.

FIRST SERV: Let me have war, say I: it exceeds peace as far as day does night; it's spritely, waking, audible, and full of vent. Peace is a very apoplexy, lethargy; mulled, deaf, sleepy, insensible; a getter of more bastard children than war's a destroyer of men.

SECOND SERV: 'Tis so: and as war, in some sort, may be said to be a ravisher, so it cannot be denied but peace is a great maker of cuckolds.

FIRST SERV: Ay, and it makes men hate one another.

THIRD SERV: Reason: because they then less need one another. The wars for my money. I hope to see Romans as cheap as Volscians. They are rising, they are rising.

BOTH FIRST AND SECOND SERV: In, in, in, in!

CORIOLANUS, IV. V. 234–252

### 2 Futile Valour

MOROCCO:                          By this scimitar
That slew the Sophy and a Persian prince
That won three fields of Sultan Solyman,
It would outstare the sternest eyes that look,
Outbrave the heart most daring on the earth,
Pluck the young sucking cubs from the she-bear,
Yea, mock the lion when he roars for prey,
To win thee, lady. But, alas the while!
If Hercules and Lichas play at dice

Which is the better man? The greater throw
May turn by fortune from the weaker hand:
So is Alcides beaten by his page;
And so may I, blind fortune leading me,
Miss that which one unworthier may attain,
And die with grieving.

THE MERCHANT OF VENICE, II. i. 24–38

### 3 *Stout Warrior!*

PRINCE HENRY: I am not yet of Percy's mind, the Hotspur of the
north; he that kills me some six or seven dozen of Scots at
Breakfast, washes his hands, and says to his wife 'Fie upon
this quiet life! I want work'. 'O my sweet Harry', says she,
'how many hast thou killed today?' 'Give my roan horse a
drench', says he; and answers 'Some fourteen', an hour
after; 'a trifle, a trifle.' I prithee, call in Falstaff; I'll play
Percy, and that damn'd brawn shall play Dame Mortimer
his wife.

HENRY IV, PT. I, II. iv. 116–126

### 4 *Model for a Prince*

KING HENRY: For all the world
As thou art to this hour was Richard then
When I from France set foot at Ravenspurgh,
And even as I was then is Percy now.
Now, by my sceptre and my soul to boot,
He hath more worthy interest to the state
Than thou the shadow of succession;
For of no right, nor colour like to right,
He doth fill fields with harness in the realm,
Turns head against the lion's armed jaws,
And, being no more in debt to years than thou,
Leads ancient lords and reverend bishops on
To bloody battles and to bruising arms.

What never-dying honour hath he got
Against renowned Douglas! whose high deeds,
Whose hot incursions and great name in arms
Holds from all soldiers chief majority
And military title capital
Through all the kingdoms that acknowledge Christ:
Thrice hath this Hotspur, Mars in swathling clothes,
This infant warrior, in his enterprizes,
Discomfited great Douglas, ta'en him once,
Enlarged him and made a friend of him,
To fill the mouth of deep defiance up
And shake the peace and safety of our throne.

HENRY IV, PT. I, III. ii. 93–117

## 5 Golden Youth in Arms

HOTSPUR:                        Where is his son,
The nimble-footed madcap Prince of Wales,
And his comrades, that daff'd the world aside,
And bid it pass?

VERNON:                All furnish'd, all in arms;
All plum'd like estridges that with the wind
Bated like eagles having lately bath'd;
Glittering in golden coats, like images;
As full of spirit as the month of May,
And gorgeous as the sun at midsummer;
Wanton as youthful goats, wild as young bulls.
I saw young Harry, with his beaver on,
His cuisses on his thighs, gallantly arm'd,
Rise from the ground like feathered Mercury,
And vaulted with such ease into his seat,
As if an angel dropp'd down from the clouds,
To turn and wind a fiery Pegasus
And witch the world with noble horsemanship.

HENRY IV, PT. I, IV. i. 94–110

6 *An Active-Valiant Gentleman*

PRINCE OF WALES:                    Tell your nephew,
    The Prince of Wales doth join with all the world
    In praise of Henry Percy: by my hopes,
    This present enterprise set off his head,
    I do not think a braver gentleman,
    More active-valiant or more valiant-young,
    More daring or more bold, is now alive
    To grace this latter age with noble deeds.

                                    HENRY IV, PT. I, V. i. 85–92


7 *A Modest Young Warrior*

HOTSPUR: O, would the quarrel lay upon our heads,
    And that no man might draw short breath today
    But I and Harry Monmouth! Tell me, tell me,
    How show'd his tasking? seem'd it in contempt?
VERNON: No, by my soul; I never in my life
    Did hear a challenge urg'd more modestly,
    Unless a brother should a brother dare
    To gentle exercise and proof of arms.
    He gave you all the duties of a man;
    Trimm'd up your praises with a princely tongue,
    Spoke your deservings like a chronicle,
    Making you ever better than his praise
    By still dispraising praise valued with you;
    And, which became him like a prince indeed,
    He made a blushing cital of himself;
    And chid his truant youth with such a grace
    As if he master'd there a double spirit
    Of teaching and of learning instantly.
    There did he pause: but let me tell the world,
    If he outlive the envy of this day,
    England did never owe so sweet a hope,
    So much misconstrued in his wantonness.

                                    HENRY IV, PT. I, V. ii. 47–68

8 *Model for Youth*

LADY PERCY: There were two honours lost, yours and your son's.
For yours, the God of heaven brighten it!
For his, it stuck upon him as the sun
In the grey vault of heaven, and by his light
Did all the chivalry of England move
To do brave acts: he was indeed the glass
Wherein the noble youth did dress themselves:
He had no legs that practis'd not his gait;
And speaking thick, which nature made his blemish,
Became the accents of the valiant;
For those that could speak low and tardily
Would turn their own perfection to abuse,
To seem like him: so that in speech, in gait,
In diet, in affections of delight,
In military rules, humours of blood,
He was the mark and glass, copy and book,
That fashion'd others.

HENRY IV, PT. II, II. iii. 16–32

9 *A Youth of Promise*

LEON: I find here that Don Pedro hath bestowed much honour
on the young Florentine called Claudio.

MESS: Much deserved on his part and equally remembered by
Don Pedro: he hath borne himself beyond the promise of
his age, doing, in the figure of a lamb, the feats of a lion:
he hath indeed better bettered expectation that you must
expect of me to tell you how.

MUCH ADO ABOUT NOTHING, I. i. 9–17

10 *Insubordination Imitated*

NESTOR: Ajax is grown self-will'd, and bears his head
In such a rein, in full as proud a place
As broad Achilles; keeps his tent like him;
Makes factious feasts; rails on our state of war,
Bold as an oracle, and sets Thersites,

A slave whose gall coins slanders like a mint,
To match us in comparisons with dirt;
To weaken and discredit our exposure,
How rank soever rounded in with danger.

TROILUS AND CRESSIDA, I. iii. 188–196


11 *Provoking Challenger*

AENEAS:                              Kings, princes, lords!
If there be one among the fair'st of Greece
That holds his honour higher than his ease,
That seeks his praise more than he fears his peril,
That knows his valour, and knows not his fear,
That loves his mistress more than in confession,
With truant vows to her own lips he loves,
And dare avow her beauty and her worth
In other arms than hers—to him this challenge.
Hector, in view of Trojans and of Greeks,
Shall make it good, or do his best to do it,
He hath a lady, wiser, fairer, truer,
Than ever Greek did compass in his arms;
And will to-morrow with his trumper call,
Midway between your tents and walls of Troy,
To rouse a Grecian that is true in love:
In any come, Hector shall honour him;
If none, he'll say in Troy when he retires,
The Grecian dames are sunburnt, and not worth
The splinter of a lance. Even so much.

TROILUS AND CRESSIDA, I. iii. 264–283


12 *A Stupid Vain Warrior*

THERSITES: Ajax goes up and down the field, asking for himself.
ACHILLES: How so?
THERSITES: He must fight singly to-morrow with Hector, and is
    so prophetically proud of an heroical cudgelling that he
    raves in saying nothing.

ACHILLES: How can that be?

THERSITES: Why, he stalks up and down like a peacock, a stride and a stand; ruminates like a hostess that hath no arithmetic but her brain to set down her reckoning; bites his lip with a politic regard, as who should say 'There were wit in this head, an 'twould out'; and so there is, but it lies as coldly in him as fire in flint, which will not show without knocking. The man's undone for ever; for if Hector break not his neck i' the combat, he'll break 't himself in vain-glory. He knows not me: I said 'Good morrow, Ajax'; and he replies 'Thanks, Agamemnon'. What think you of this man that takes me for the general? He's grown a very land-fish, languageless, a monster. A plague of opinion! a man may wear it on both sides, like a leather jerkin.

ACHILLES: Thou must be my ambassador to him, Thersites.

THERSITES: Who, I? why, he'll answer nobody; he professes not answering; speaking is for beggars; he wears his tongue in 's arms.

TROILUS AND CRESSIDA, III. iii. 245–274

## 13 A True Knight

AGAMEMNON: What Trojan is that same that looks so heavy?

ULYSSES: The youngest son of Priam, a true knight;
Not yet mature, yet matchless; firm of word,
Speaking in deeds and deedless in his tongue;
Not soon provok'd nor being provok'd soon calm'd:
His heart and hand both open and both free;
For what he has he gives, what thinks he shows;
Yet gives he not till judgment guide his bounty,
Nor dignifies an impare thought with breath.
Manly as Hector, but more dangerous;
For Hector, in his blaze of wrath, subscribes
To tender objects; but he in heat of action
Is more vindicative than jealous love.
They call him Troilus, and on him erect
A second hope, as fairly built as Hector.

5

Thus says Æneas; one that knows the youth
Even to his inches, and with private soul
Did in great Ilion thus translate him to me.

TROILUS AND CRESSIDA, IV. V. 95–112

### 14 *A False Character of a Captain*

FIRST SOLD: We'll see what may be done, so you confess freely:
therefore, once more to this Captain Dumain. You have
answered to his reputation with the duke and to his valour:
what is his honesty?

PAROLLES: He will steal, sir, an egg out of a cloister; for rapes
and ravishments he parallels Nessus; he professes not keeping oaths; in breaking 'em he is stronger than Hercules;
he will lie, sir, with such volubility, that you would think
truth were a fool; drunkenness is his best virtue, for he will
be swine-drunk, and in his sleep he does little harm, save to
his bed-clothes about him; but they know his conditions,
and lay him in straw. I have but little more to say, sir, of his
honesty: he has every thing that an honest man should not
have; what an honest man should have, he has nothing.

FIRST LORD: I begin to love him for this.

BERTRAM: For this description of thine honesty? A pox upon
him for me! he is more and more a cat.

FIRST SOLD: What say you to his expertness in war?

PAROLLES: Faith, sir, has led the drum before the English
tragedians,—to belie him I will not,—an more of his
soldiership I know not; except, in that country he had the
honour to be the officer at a place there called Mile-end, to
instruct for the doubling of files: I would do the man what
honour I can, but of this I am not certain.

FIRST LORD: He hath out-villained villany so far that the rarity
redeems him.

BERTRAM: A pox on him! he's a cat still.

FIRST SOLD: His qualities being at this poor price, I need not
ask you if gold will corrupt him to revolt.

PAROLLES: Sir, for a cardecue he will sell the fee-simple of his salvation, the inheritance of it; and cut the entail from all remainders, and a perpetual succession for it perpetually.

FIRST SOLD: What's his brother, the other Captain Dumain?

SECOND LORD: Why does he ask him of me?

FIRST SOLD: What's he?

PAROLLES: E'en a crow o' the same nest; not altogether so great as the first in goodness, but greater a great deal in evil. He excels his brother for a coward, yet his brother is reputed one of the best that is. In a retreat he outruns any lackey; marry, in coming on he has the cramp.

ALL'S WELL THAT ENDS WELL, IV. iii. 277–328

### 15 *A Worthy Foe*

MARCIUS:                              They have a leader,
Tullus Aufidius, that will put you to 't.
I sin in envying his nobility,
And were I any thing but what I am,
I would wish me only he.

COMINIUS:                              You have fought together.

MARCIUS: Were half to half the world by the ears, and he
Upon my party, I'd revolt, to make
Only my wars with him: he is a lion
That I am proud to hunt.

CORIOLANUS, I. i. 234–242

### 16 *An Awe-Inspiring Soldier*

LARTIUS: What is become of Marcius?

ALL:                              Slain, sir, doubtless.

FIRST SOLD: Following the fliers at the very heels,
With them he enters; who, upon the sudden,
Clapp'd-to their gates; he is himself alone,
To answer all the city.

LARTIUS:                              O noble fellow!
Who sensibly outdares his senseless sword,
And, when it bows, stand'st up. Thou art left, Marcius!

A carbuncle entire, as big as thou art,
Were not so rich a jewel. Thou wast a soldier
Even to Cato's wish, not fierce and terrible
Only in strokes; but, with thy grim looks and
The thunder-like percussion of thy sounds,
Thou mad'st thine enemies shake, as if the world
Were feverous and did tremble.

CORIOLANUS, I. iv. 48–61

## 17 *Hero into Suppliant*

CORIOLANUS:                  Well, I must do 't,
Away, my disposition, and possess me
Some harlot's spirit! my throat of war be turn'd,
Which quired with my drum, into a pipe
Small as an eunuch, or the virgin voice
That babies lulls asleep! the smiles of knaves
Tent in my cheeks, and school-boys' tears take up
The glasses of my sight! a beggar's tongue
Make motion through my lips, and my arm'd knees,
Who bow'd but in my stirrup, bend like his
That hath receiv'd an alms! I will not do 't,
Lest I surcease to honour mine own truth,
And by my body's action teach my mind
A most inherent baseness.

CORIOLANUS, III. ii. 110–123

## 18 *An Inspiring Leader*

COMINIUS: He is their god: he leads them like a thing
Made by some other deity than Nature,
That shapes man better; and they follow him,
Against us brats, with no less confidence
Than boys pursuing summer butterflies,
Or butchers killing flies.

CORIOLANUS, IV. vi. 91–96

## (b) Courtly Princes

### 1 A Sweet Prince

GLOUCESTER: Hath she forgot already that brave prince,
 Edward, her lord, whom I, some three months since,
 Stabb'd in my angry mood at Tewksbury?
 A sweeter and a lovelier gentleman,
 Framed in the prodigality of nature,
 Young, valiant, wise, and, no doubt, right royal,
 The spacious world cannot again afford:
 And will she yet debase her eyes on me,
 That cropp'd the golden prime of this sweet prince,
 And made her widow to a woful bed?

       KING RICHARD III, I. ii. 241–250

### 2 A Ripe Young Man

VALENTINE: I know him as myself; for from our infancy
 We have conversed and spent our hours together:
 And though myself have been an idle truant,
 Omitting the sweet benefit of time
 To clothe mine age with angel-like perfection,
 Yet hath Sir Proteus, for that's his name,
 Made use and fair advantage of his days;
 His years but young, but his experience old;
 His head unmellow'd, but his judgment ripe;
 And, in a word, for far behind his worth
 Comes all the praises that I know bestow,
 He is complete in feature and in mind
 With all good grace to grace a gentleman.

    THE TWO GENTLEMEN OF VERONA, II. iv. 63–75

### 3 A Riotous Prince

BOLINGBROKE: Can no man tell me of my unthrifty son?
 'T is full three months since I did see him last:
 If any plague hang over us, 't is he.

I would to God, my lords, he might be found:
Inquire at London, 'mongst the taverns there,
For there, they say, he daily doth frequent,
With unrestrained loose companions,
Even such, they say, as stand in narrow lanes,
And beat our watch, and rob our passengers;
Which he, young wanton and effeminate boy,
Takes on the point of honour to support
So dissolute a crew.

KING RICHARD II, V. iii. 1–12

## 4 Princes Well-Matched

FIRST CIT: That daughter there of Spain, the Lady Blanch,
Is niece to England: look upon the years
Of Lewis the Dauphin and that lovely maid:
If lusty love should go in quest of beauty,
Where should he find it fairer than in Blanch?
If zealous love should go in search of virtue,
Where should he find it purer than in Blanch?
If love ambitious sought a match of birth,
Whose veins bound richer blood than Lady Blanch?
Such as she is, in beauty, virtue, birth,
Is the young Dauphin every way complete:
If not complete, O, say he is not she;
And she again wants nothing, to name want,
If want it be not that she is not he:
He is the half part of a blessed man,
Left to be finished by such as she;
And she a fair divided excellence,
Whose fulness of perfection lies in him.
O, two such silver currents, when they join,
Do glorify the banks that bound them in;
And two such shores to two such streams made one,
Two such controlling bounds shall you be, kings,
To these two princes, if you marry them.

KING JOHN, II, i. 423–445

## 5 A Politic Offender

PRINCE OF WALES: I know you all, and will awhile uphold
    The unyok'd humour of your idleness:
    Yet herein will I imitate the sun,
    Who doth permit the base contagious clouds
    To smother up his beauty from the world,
    That, when he please again to be himself,
    Being wanted, he may be more wonder'd at,
    By breaking through the foul and ugly mists
    Of vapours that did seem to strangle him.
    If all the year were playing holidays,
    To sport would be as tedious as to work;
    But when they seldom come, they wish'd for come,
    And nothing pleaseth but rare accidents.
    So, when this loose behaviour I throw off,
    And pay the debt I never promised,
    By how much better than my word I am,
    By so much shall I falsify men's hopes;
    And like bright metal on a sullen ground,
    My reformation, glitt'ring o'er my fault,
    Shall show more goodly and attract more eyes
    Than that which hath no foil to set it off.
    I'll so offend, to make offence a skill;
    Redeeming time when men think least I will.

HENRY IV, PT. I, I. ii. 217–239

## 6 A Good Mixer

POINS: Where hast been, Hal?

PRINCE HENRY: With three or four loggerheads amongst three
or four score hogsheads. I have sounded the very base-
string of humility. Sirrah, I am sworn brother to a leash of
drawers; and can call them all by their christen names, as
Tom, Dick, and Francis. They take it already upon their salvation, that though I be but Prince of Wales, yet I am the
king of courtesy; and tell me flatly I am no proud Jack, like
Falstaff, but a Corinthian, a lad of mettle, by the Lord, so

they call me, and when I am king of England, I shall command all the good lads in Eastcheap. They call drinking
deep, dyeing scarlet; and when you breathe in your water-
ing, they cry 'hem'! and bid you play it off. To conclude,
I am so good a proficient in one quarter of an hour, that I
can drink with any tinker in his own language during my
life. I tell thee, Ned, thou hast lost much honour, that thou
wert not with me in this action.

HENRY IV, PT. I, II. iv. 3–20

### 7 A Rough Warrior Schooled

WORCESTER: In faith, my lord, you are too wilfulblame;
   And since your coming hither have done enough
   To put him quite beside his patience.
   You must needs learn, lord, to amend this fault:
   Though sometimes it show greatness, courage, blood,—
   And that's the dearest grace it renders you,—
   Yet often times it doth present harsh rage,
   Defect of manners, want of government,
   Pride, haughtiness, opinion and disdain:
   The least of which haunting a nobleman
   Loseth men's hearts and leaves behind a stain
   Upon the beauty of all parts besides,
   Beguiling them of commendation.
HOTSPUR: Well, I am school'd: good manners be your speed!
   Here come our wives, and let us take our leave.

HENRY IV, PT. I, II. i. 176–190

### 8 Sudden Scholar

CANTERBURY: The king is full of grace and fair regard.
ELY: And a true lover of the holy church.
CANTERBURY: The courses of his youth promised it not.
   The breath no sooner left his father's body,
   But that his wildness, mortified in him,
   Seem'd to die too; yea, at that very moment

Consideration, like an angel, came
And whipp'd the offending Adam out of him,
Leaving his body as a paradise,
To envelope and contain celestial spirits.
Never was such a sudden scholar made;
Never came reformation in a flood,
With such a heady currance, scouring faults;
Nor never Hydra-headed wilfulness
So soon did lose his seat and all at once
As in this king.

ELY:                    We are blessed in the change.

CANTERBURY: Hear him but reason in divinity,
      And, all—admiring, with an inward wish
      You would desire the king were made a prelate:
      Hear him debate of commonwealth affairs,
      You would say it hath been all in all his study:
      List his discourse of war, and you shall hear
      A fearful battle render'd you in music:
      Turn him to any cause of policy,
      The Gordian knot of it he will unloose,
      Familiar as his garter: that, when he speaks,
      The air, a charter'd libertine, is still,
      And the mute wonder lurketh in men's ears,
      To steal his sweet and honey'd sentences;
      So that the art and practic part of life
      Must be the mistress to this theoric:
      Which is a wonder how his grace should glean it,
      Since his addiction was to courses vain,
      His companies unletter'd, rude and shallow
      His hours fill'd up with riots, banquets, sports,
      And never noted in him any study,
      Any retirement, any sequestration
      From open haunts and popularity.

ELY: The strawberry grows underneath the nettle,
      And wholesome berries thrive and ripen best
      Neighbour'd by fruit of baser quality:
      And so the prince obscured his contemplation

Under the veil of wildness; which, no doubt,
Grew like the summer grass, fastest by night,
Unseen, yet crescive in his faculty.
CANTERBURY: It must be so; for miracles are ceased;
And therefore we must needs admit the means
How things are perfected.

HENRY V, I. i. 22–69

## 9 *A Gentleman Basely Bred*

ORLANDO: As I remember, Adam, it was upon this fashion bequeathed me by will but poor a thousand crowns, and, as
thou sayest, charged my brother, on his blessing, to breed
me well: and there begins my sadness. My brother Jaques
he keeps at school, and report speaks goldenly of his profit:
for my part, he keeps me rustically at home, or, to speak
more properly, stays me here at home unkept; for call you
that keeping for a gentleman of my birth, that differs not
from the stalling of an ox? His horses are bred better; for,
besides that they are fair with their feeding, they are taught
their manage, and to that end riders dearly hired: but I, his
brother, gain nothing under him but growth; for the
which his animals on his dunghills are as much bound to
him as I. Besides this nothing that he so plentifully gives
me, the something that nature gave me his countenance
seems to take from me: he lets me feed with his hinds, bars
me the place of a brother, and, as much as in him lies,
mines my gentility with my education. This is it, Adam,
that grieves me; and the spirit of my father, which I think
is within me, begins to mutiny against this servitude: I will
no longer endure it, though yet I know no wise remedy
how to avoid it.

AS YOU LIKE IT, I. i. 1–27

## 10 *Two Characters in One*

OLIVER: I had myself notice of my brother's purpose herein and
have by underhand means laboured to dissuade him from

it, but he is resolute. I'll tell thee, Charles: it is the stub-
bornest young fellow of France, full of ambition, an
envious emulator of every man's good parts, a secret and
villainous contriver against me his natural brother: there-
for use thy discretion; I had as lief thou didst break his neck
as his finger. And thou were best look to 't; for if thou
dost him any slight disgrace or if he do not mightily grace
himself on thee, he will practise against thee by poison,
entrap thee by some treacherous device and never leave
thee till he hath ta'en thy life by some indirect means or
other; for, I assure thee, and almost with tears I speak it,
there is not one so young and so villainous this day living.
I speak but brotherly of him; but should I anatomize him
to thee as he is, I must blush and weep and thou must look
pale and wonder.

CHARLES: I am heartily glad I came hither to you. If he come
to-morrow, I'll give him his payment: if ever he go alone
again, I'll never wrestle for prize more: and so God keep
your worship!

OLIVER: Farewell, good Charles. (Exit Charles) Now will I stir
this gamester: I hope I shall see an end of him; for my soul,
yet I know not why, hates nothing more than he. Yet he's
gentle, never schooled and yet learned, full of noble
device, of all sorts enchantingly beloved, and indeed so
much in the heart of the world, and especially of my own
people, who best know him, that I am altogether mis-
prised: but it shall not be so long; this wrestler shall clear
all: nothing remains but that I kindle the boy thither;
which now I'll go about.

AS YOU LIKE IT, I. i. 147-182

11 *A Low-Spirited Youth*

ORLANDO: But let your fair eyes and gentle wishes go with me
to my trial: Wherein if I be foiled, there is but one shamed
that was never gracious; if killed, but one dead that is
willing to be so: I shall do my friends no wrong, for I have

none to lament me, the world no injury, for in it I have nothing; only in the world I fill up a place, which may be better supplied when I have made it empty.

AS YOU LIKE IT, I. ii. 200–208

### 12 A Swashing Young Man

ROSALIND:                                    Were it not better,
    Because that I am more than common tall,
    That I did suit me all points like a man?
    A gallant curtle-axe upon my thigh,
    A boar-spear in my hand, and—in my heart
    Lie there what hidden woman's fear there will—
    We'll have a swashing and a martial outside,
    As many other mannish cowards have
    That do outface it with their semblances.

AS YOU LIKE IT, I. iii. 117–125

### 13 A Noble Suitor Answered

OLIVIA: Your lord does know my mind; I cannot love him:
    Yet I suppose him virtuous, know him noble,
    Of great estate, of fresh and stainless youth;
    In voices well divulg'd, free, learn'd, and valiant;
    And in dimension and the shape of nature
    A gracious person: but yet I cannot love him;
    He might have took his answer long ago.

TWELFTH NIGHT, I. v. 278–284

### 14 Paragon of Princes—Blasted

OPHELIA: O, what a noble mind is here o'erthrown!
    The courtier's, scholar's, soldier's, eye, tongue, sword;
    The expectancy and rose of the fair state,
    The glass of fashion and the mould of form,
    The observed of all observers, quite, quite down!
    And I, of ladies most deject and wretched,

That sucked the honey of his music vows,
Now see that noble and most sovereign reason,
Like sweet bells jangled, out of tune and all harsh;
That unmatched form and feature of blown youth
Blasted with ecstasy. O, woe is me,
To have seen what I have seen, see what I see!

HAMLET, III. i. 159–170

## 15 *The Horseman*

KING:                  Two months since,
Here was a gentleman of Normandy;—
I've seen myself, and served against, the French,
And they can well on horseback; but this gallant
Had witchcraft in 't. He grew unto his seat,
And to such wondrous doing brought his horse,
As had he been incorpsed and demi-natured
With the brave beast. So far he topped my thought,
That I, in forgery of shapes and tricks,
Come short of what he did.
LAERTES:              A Norman, was 't?
KING: A Norman.
LAERTES: Upon my life, Lamond.
KING:                The very same.

HAMLET, IV. VII. 81–92

## 16 *A Rival Measured*

CLOTEN: I dare speak it to myself—for it is not vain-glory for a
man and his glass to confer in his own chamber—I mean,
the lines of my body are as well drawn as his; no less young,
more strong, not beneath him in fortunes, beyond him in
the advantage of the time, above him in birth, alike
conversant in general services, and more remarkable in
single oppositions: yet this imperceiverant thing loves him
in my despite. What mortality is!

CYMBELINE, IV. i. 7–17

### 17 *A Competent Sad Youth*

BELARIUS:  This youth, howe'er distress'd, appears he hath had
    Good ancestors.
ARVIRAGUS:         How angel-like he sings!
GUIDESIUS: But his neat cookery! he cut our roots in characters;
    And sauced our broths, as Juno had been sick,
    And he her dieter.
ARVIRAGUS:        Nobly he yokes
    A smiling with a sigh, as if the sigh
    Was that it was, for not being such a smile;
    The smile mocking the sigh, that it would fly
    From so divine a temple, to commix
    With winds that sailors rail at.

                  CYMBELINE, IV. ii. 47–56


### 18 *The Nature of Princes*

BELARIUS:                O thou goddess,
    Thou divine Nature, how thyself thou blazon'st
    In these two princely boys! They are as gentle
    As zephyrs blowing below the violet,
    Not wagging his sweet head; and yet as rough,
    Their royal blood enchafed, as the rud'st wind
    That by the top doth take the mountain pine
    And make him stoop to the vale. 'Tis wonder
    That an invisible instinct should frame them
    To royalty unlearn'd, honour untaught,
    Civility not seen from other, valour
    That wildly grows in them, but yields a crop
    As if it had been sow'd.

                  CYMBELINE, IV.ii.169–181

# D. COURTIERS

### 1 *Courtier into Rebel*

KING: I muse my Lord of Gloucester is not come:
    'Tis not his wont to be the hindmost man,
    Whate'er occasion keeps him from us now.
QUEEN: Can you not see? or will ye not observe
    The strangeness of his altered countenance?
    With what a majesty he bears himself,
    How insolent of late he is become,
    How proud, how peremptory, and unlike himself?
    We know the time since he was mild and affable,
    And if we did but glance a far-off look,
    Immediately he was upon his knee,
    That all the court admired him for submission:
    But meet him now, and, be it in the morn,
    When every one will give the time of day,
    He knits his brow and shows an angry eye,
    And passeth by with stiff unbowed knee,
    Disdaining duty that to us belongs.
    Small curs are not regarded when they grin,
    But great men tremble when the lion roars;
    And Humphrey is no little man in England.

                 KING HENRY VI, PT. II, III. i. 1–20

### 2 *A Fallen Favourite*

KING: Ay, Margaret; my heart is drowned with grief,
    Whose flood begins to flow within mine eyes,
    My body round engirt with misery,
    For what's more miserable than discontent?
    Ah! uncle Humphrey, in thy face I see
    The map of honour, truth, and loyalty;
    And yet, good Humphrey, is the hour to come

That e'er I proved thee false, or feared thy faith.
What low'ring star now envies thy estate,
That these great lords, and Margaret our queen,
Do seek subversion of thy harmless life?
Thou never didst them wrong, nor no man wrong;
And as the butcher takes away the calf,
And binds the wretch, and beats it when it strays,
Bearing it to the bloody slaughter-house;
Even so, remorseless, have they borne him hence;
And as the dam runs lowing up and down,
Looking the way her harmless young one went,
And can do nought but wail her darling's loss;
Even so myself bewails good Gloucester's case,
With sad unhelpful tears, and with dimmed eyes
Look after him, and cannot do him good;
So mighty are his vowed enemies.
His fortunes I will weep; and 'twixt each groan
Say 'Who's a traitor? Gloucester he is none.'

KING HENRY VI, PT. II, III. i. 198–222

3 *Sly Silken Courtiers*

GLOUCESTER: They do me wrong, and I will not endure it:
Who are they that complain unto the king,
That I, forsooth, am stern and love them not?
By holy Paul, they love his grace but lightly
That fill his ears with such dissentious rumours.
Because I cannot flatter and speak fair,
Smile in men's faces, smooth, deceive and cog,
Duck with French nods and apish courtesy,
I must be held a rancorous enemy.
Cannot a plain man live and think no harm,
But thus his simple truth must be abused
By silken, sly, insinuating Jacks?

KING RICHARD III, I. iii. 42–53

## 4 A Covert Traitor

LOVEL: Here is the head of that ignoble traitor,
The dangerous and unsuspected Hastings.
GLOUCESTER: So dear I loved the man that I must weep.
I took him for the plainest harmless creature
That breathed upon this earth a Christian;
Made him my book, wherein my soul recorded
The history of all her secret thoughts:
So smooth he daub'd his vice with slow of virtue,
That, his apparent open guilt omitted,
I mean, his conversation with Shore's wife,
He lived from all attainder of suspect.
BUCKINGHAM: Well, well, he was the covert'st shelter'd traitor
That ever lived.

KING RICHARD III, III. V. 21–33


## 5 A Courtly Mocker

FIRST LORD: Lord Longaville is one.
PRINCESS:                           Know you the man?
MARIA: I know him, madam: at a marriage-feast,
Between Lord Perigort and the beauteous heir
Of Jaques Falconbridge, solemnized
In Normandy, saw I this Longaville:
A man of sovereign parts he is esteem'd;
Well fitted in arts, glorious in arms:
Nothing becomes him ill that he would well.
The only soil of his fair virtue's gloss,
If virtue's gloss will stain with any soil,
Is a sharp wit match'd with too blunt a will;
Whose edge hath power to cut, whose will still wills
It should none spare that come within his power.
PRINCESS: Some merry mocking lord, belike; is 't so?
MARIA: They say so most that most his humours know.
PRINCESS: Such short-lived wits do wither as they grow.

LOVE'S LABOUR'S LOST, II. i. 37–54

6

## 6 *Wit, Beauty, and Simplicity*

KATHERINE: The young Dumain, a well-accomplished youth,
    Of all that virtue love for virtue loved:
    Most power to do most harm, least knowing ill;
    For he hath wit to make an ill shape good,
    And shape to win grace though he had no wit.
    I saw him at the Duke Alencon's once;
    And much too little of that good I saw
    Is my report to his great worthiness.

                    LOVE'S LABOUR'S LOST, II. i. 56–63

## 7 *An Eloquent Jesting Courtier*

ROSALINE: Another of these students at that time
    Was there with him, as I have heard a truth.
    Biron they call him; but a merrier man,
    Within the limit of becoming mirth,
    I never spent an hour's talk withal:
    His eye begets occasion for his wit;
    For every object that the one doth catch
    The other turns to a mirth-moving jest,
    Which his fair tongue, conceit's expositor,
    Delivers in such apt and gracious words
    That aged ears play truant at his tales
    And younger hearings are quite ravished;
    So sweet and voluble is his discourse.

                    LOVE'S LABOUR'S LOST, II. i. 64–76

## 8 *A Courtly Tell-Tale*

BIRON: Neither of either; I remit both twain.
    I see the trick on't: here was a consent,
    Knowing aforehand of our merriment,
    To dash it like a Christmas comedy:
    Some carry-tale, some please-man, some slight zany,
    Some mumble-news, some trencher-knight, some Dick,
    That smiles his cheek in years and knows the trick

To make my lady laugh when she's disposed,
Told our intents before; which once disclosed,
The ladies did change favours: and then we,
Following the signs, woo'd but the sign of she.

LOVE'S LABOUR'S LOST, v. ii. 460–470


9 *Brisk Courtier Out of his Element*
HOTSPUR: My liege, I did deny no prisoners.
But I remember, when the fight was done,
When I was dry with rage and extreme toil,
Breathless and faint, leaning upon my sword,
Came there a certain lord, neat, and trimly dress'd,
Fresh as a bridegroom; and his chin new reap'd
Show'd like a stubble-land at harvest-home;
He was perfumed like a milliner;
And 'twixt his finger and his thumb he held
A pouncet-box, which ever and anon
He gave his nose and took't away again;
Who therewith angry, when it next came there,
Took it in snuff; and still he smil'd and talk'd,
And as the soldiers bore dead bodies by,
He call'd them untaught knaves, unmannerly,
To bring a slovenly unhandsome corse
Betwixt the wind and his nobility.
With many holiday and lady terms
He question'd me; amongst the rest, demanded
My prisoners in your majesty's behalf.
I then, all smarting with my wounds being cold,
To be so pest'red with a popinjay,
Out of my grief and my impatience,
Answer'd neglectingly, I know not what,
He should, or he should not; for he made me mad
To see him shine so brisk and smell so sweet
And talk so like a waiting-gentlewoman
Of guns and drums and wounds,—God save the mark!—
And telling me the sovereign'st thing on earth

Was parmaceti for an inward bruise;
And that it was great pity, so it was,
This villainous salt-petre should be digg'd
Out of the bowels of the harmless earth,
Which many a good tall fellow had destroy'd
So cowardly; and but for these vile guns,
He would himself have been a soldier.

HENRY IV, PT. I, I. iii. 29–64

10 *A Mere Traitor*

KING HENRY:                                    But, O,
What shall I say to thee, Lord Scroop? thou cruel,
Ingrateful, savage and inhuman creature!
Thou that didst bear the key of all my counsels,
That knew'st the very bottom of my soul,
That almost mightst have coin'd me into gold,
Wouldst thou have practised on me for thy use!
May it be possible, that foreign hire
Could out of thee extract one spark of evil
That might annoy my finger? 'tis so strange,
That, though the truth of it stands off as gross
As black and white, my eye will scarcely see it.
Treason and murder ever kept together,
As two yoke-devils sworn to either's purpose,
Working so grossly in a natural cause,
That admiration did not hoop at them:
But thou, 'gainst all proportion, didst bring in
Wonder to wait on treason and on murder:
And whatsoever cunning fiend it was
That wrought upon thee so preposterously
Hath got the voice in hell for excellence:
All other devils that suggest by treasons
Do botch and bungle up damnation
With patches, colours, and with forms being fetch'd
From glistering semblances of piety;
But he that temper'd thee bade thee stand up,

Gave thee no instance why thou shouldst do treason,
Unless to dub thee with the name of traitor.
If that same demon that hath gull'd thee thus
Should with his lion gait walk the whole world,
He might return to vasty Tartar back,
And tell the legions 'I can never win
A soul so easy as that Englishman's'.
O, how hast thou with jealousy infected
The sweetness of affiance! Show men dutiful?
Why, so didst thou: seem they grave and learned?
Why, so didst thou: come they of noble family?
Why, so didst thou: seem they religious?
Why, so didst thou: or are they spare in diet,
Free from gross passion or of mirth or anger,
Constant in spirit, not swerving with the blood,
Garnish'd and deck'd in modest complement,
Not working with the eye without the ear,
And but in purged judgement trusting neither?
Such and so finely boulted didst thou seem:
And thus thy fall hath left a kind of blot,
To mark the full-fraught man and best indued
With some suspicion. I will weep for thee;
For this revolt of thine, methinks, is like
Another fall of man. Their faults are open:
Arrest them to the answer of the law;
And God acquit them of their practices!

HENRY V, II. ii. 93–144


11 *The Inventory of a Handsome Youth*

PHEBE: Think not I love him though I ask for him;
    'T is but a peevish boy; yet he talks well;
    But what care I for words? yet words do well
    When he that speaks them pleases those that hear.
    It is a pretty youth: not very pretty:
    But sure he's proud, and yet his pride becomes him:
    He'll make a proper man: the best thing in him

Is his complexion; and faster than his tongue
Did make offence his eye did heal it up.
He is not very tall; yet for his years he's tall:
His leg is but so so; and yet 't is well:
There was a pretty redness in his lip,
A little riper and more lusty red
Than that mix'd in his cheek; 't was just the difference
Betwixt the constant red and mingled damask.
There be some women, Silvius, had they mark'd him
In parcels as I did, would have gone near
To fall in love with him; but, for my part,
I love him not nor hate him not; and yet
I have more cause to hate him than to love him:
For what had he to do to chide at me?
He said mine eyes were black and my hair black:
And, now I am remember'd, scorn'd at me:
I marvel why I answer'd not again:
But that's all one: omittance is no quittance;
I'll write to him a very taunting letter,
And thou shalt bear it: wilt thou, Silvius?

SILVIUS: Phebe, with all my heart.

AS YOU LIKE IT, III. V. 109–136

## 12 *Character of a Courtier and his Quarrel*

JAQUES: Good my lord, bid him welcome: this is the motley-
minded gentleman that I have so often met in the forest:
he hath been a courtier, he swears.

TOUCHSTONE: If any man doubt that, let him put me to my
purgation. I have trod a measure; I have flattered a lady;
I have been politic with my friend, smooth with mine
enemy; I have undone three tailors; I have had four
quarrels, and like to have fought one.

JAQUES: And how was that ta'en up?

TOUCHSTONE: Faith, we met, and found the quarrel was upon
the seventh cause.

JAQUES: How seventh cause? Good my lord, like this fellow.

. . . . .

TOUCHSTONE: Upon a lie seven times removed:—bear your body more seeming, Audrey:—as thus, sir. I did dislike the cut of a certain courtier's beard: he sent me word, if I said his beard was not cut well, he was in the mind it was: this is called the Retort Courteous. If I sent him word again 'it was not well cut', he would send me word, he cut it to please himself: this is called the Quip Modest. If again 'it was not well cut', he disabled my judgment: this is called the Reply Churlish. If again 'it was not well cut', he would answer, I spake not true: this is called the Reproof Valiant. If again 'it was not well cut', he would say I lied: this is called the Countercheck Quarrelsome: and so to the Lie Circumstantial and the Lie Direct.

JAQUES: And how often did you say his beard was not well cut?

TOUCHSTONE: I durst go no further than the Lie Circumstantial, nor he durst not give me the Lie Direct; and so we measured swords and parted.

AS YOU LIKE IT, V. iv. 40–54, 71–91

## 13 *A Persistent Young Man*

MALVOLIO: Madam, yond young fellow swears he will speak with you. I told him you were sick; he takes on him to understand so much, and therefore comes to speak with you: I told him you were asleep; he seems to have a fore-knowledge of that too, and therefore comes to speak with you. What is to be said to him, lady? he's fortified against any denial.

OLIVIA: Tell him he shall not speak with me.

MALVOLIO: He has been told so; and he says, he'll stand at your door like a sheriff's post, and be the supporter to a bench, but he'll speak with you.

OLIVIA: What kind o' man is he?

MALVOLIO: Why, of mankind.

OLIVIA: What manner of man?

MALVOLIO: Of very ill manner; he'll speak with you, will you or no.

OLIVIA: Of what personage and years is he?

MALVOLIO: Not yet old enough for a man, nor young enough for a boy; as a squash is before 'tis a peascod, or a codling when 'tis almost an apple: 'tis with him in standing water, between boy and man. He is very well-favoured, and he speaks very shrewishly; one would think his mother's milk were scarce out of him.

OLIVIA: Let him approach: call in my gentlewoman.

MALVOLIO: Gentlewoman, my lady calls.

TWELFTH NIGHT, I. V. 147–175

## 14 Court Sponge

HAMLET: That I can keep your counsel and not mine own. Besides, to be demanded of a sponge! What replication should be made by the son of a king?

ROSENCRANTZ: Take you me for a sponge, my lord?

HAMLET: Ay, sir, that soaks up the King's countenance, his rewards, his authorities. But such officers do the King best service in the end. He keeps them, as an ape doth nuts, in the corner of his jaw; first mouthed, to be last swallowed. When he needs what you have gleaned, it is but squeezing you, and, sponge, you shall be dry again.

HAMLET, IV. II. 11–23

## 15. The Absolute Card of Gentility

OSRIC: Sir, here is newly come to court Laertes, believe me, an absolute gentleman, full of most excellent differences, of very soft society and great showing; indeed to speak feelingly of him, he is the card or calendar of gentry, for you shall find in him the continent of what part a gentleman would see.

HAMLET: Sir, his definement suffers no perdition in you; though, I know, to divide him inventorially would dizzy the arithmetic of memory, and yet but yaw neither, in respect of his quick sail. But, in the verity of extolment, I take him to be a soul of great article; and his infusion of such dearth and nearness, as, to make true diction of him, his semblance is his mirror; and who else would trace him, his umbrage, nothing more.

OSRIC: Your lordship speaks most infallibly of him.

HAMLET, V. ii. 111–128

## 16 *Soldier, Courtier, Scholar*

FORD: Now, Sir John, here is the heart of my purpose: you are a gentleman of excellent breeding, admirable discourse, of great admittance, authentic in your place and person, generally allowed for your many war-like, court-like, and learned preparations.

THE MERRY WIVES OF WINDSOR, II. ii. 238–243

## 17 *Model Courtier*

KING: I would I had that corporal soundness now,
As when thy father and myself in friendship
First tried our soldiership! He did look far
Into the service of the time and was
Discipled of the bravest: he lasted long;
But on us both did haggish age steal on,
And wore us out of act. It much repairs me
To talk of your good father. In his youth
He had the wit, which I can well observe
To-day in our young lords; but they may jest
Till their own scorn return to them unnoted
Ere they can hide their levity in honour.
So like a courtier, contempt nor bitterness
Were in his pride or sharpness; if they were
His equal had awak'd them; and his honour,

Clock to itself, knew the true minute when
Exception bid him speak, and at this time
His tongue obey'd his hand: who were below him
He us'd as creatures of another place,
And bow'd his eminent top to their low ranks,
Making them proud of his humility,
In their poor praise he humbled. Such a man
Might be a copy to these younger times,
Which, followed well, would demonstrate them now
But goers backward.

ALL'S WELL THAT ENDS WELL, I. ii. 24–48


18 *The Courtier Coached*

PAROLLES: Use a more spacious ceremony to the noble lords;
    you have restrained yourself within the list of too cold an
    adieu: be more expressive to them; for they wear them-
    selves in the cap of time, there do muster true gait, eat,
    speak, and move under the influence of the most received
    star; and though the devil lead the measure, such are to be
    followed. After them, and take a more dilated farewell.

ALL'S WELL THAT ENDS WELL, II. i. 51–59


19 *A Declared Traitor*

EDGAR: Behold, it is the privilege of mine honours,
    My oath, and my profession. I protest—
    Maugre thy strength, youth, place, and eminence,
    Despite thy victor sword and fire-new fortune,
    Thy valour and thy heart—thou art a traitor;
    False to thy gods, thy brother, and thy father;
    Conspirant 'gainst this high illustrious prince;
    And from th' extremest upward of thy head
    To the descent and dust beneath thy foot,
    A most toad-spotted traitor.

KING LEAR, V. iii. 131–140

### 20 *Penitent Traitor*

DUNCAN: Is execution done on Cawdor? Are not
 Those in commission yet return'd?
MALCOLM:         My liege,
 They are not yet come back. But I have spoke
 With one that saw him die; who did report
 That very frankly he confess'd his treasons,
 Implored your highness' pardon, and set forth
 A deep repentance: nothing in his life
 Became him like the leaving it; he died
 As one that had been studied in his death,
 To throw away the dearest thing he owed,
 As 'twere a careless trifle.
DUNCAN:        There's no art
 To find the mind's construction in the face:
 He was a gentleman on whom I built
 An absolute trust.

             MACBETH, I. iv. 1–14


### 21 *Cold Ungrateful Men*

FLAVIUS: They answer, in a joint and corporate voice,
 That now they are at fall, want treasure, cannot
 Do what they would; are sorry—you are honourable—
 But yet they could have wish'd—they know not—
 Something hath been amiss—a noble nature
 May catch a wrench—would all were well—'tis pity;—
 And so, intending other serious matters,
 After distasteful looks and these hard fractions,
 With certain half-caps and cold-moving nods
 They froze me into silence.
TIMON:         You gods, reward them!
 Prithee, man, look cheerly. These old fellows
 Have their ingratitude in them hereditary;
 Their blood is cak'd, 'tis cold, it seldom flows;
 'Tis lack of kindly warmth they are not kind;

And nature, as it grows again toward earth,
Is fashion'd for the journey, dull and heavy.

TIMON OF ATHENS, II. ii. 214–229

## 22 Ungrateful Flatterer

FIRST STRANGER: Why, this is the world's soul: and just of the
     same piece
Is every flatterer's spirit. Who can call him
His friend that dips in the same dish? for, in
My knowing, Timon has been this lord's father,
And kept his credit with his purse;
Supported his estate; nay, Timon's money
Has paid his men their wages: he ne'er drinks
But Timon's silver treads upon his lip;
And yet—O, see the monstrousness of man,
When he looks out in an ungrateful shape!
He does deny him, in respect of his,
What charitable men afford to beggars.

TIMON OF ATHENS, III. ii. 72–83

## 23 A Rare Courtier

FIRST GENT:                    The king he takes the babe
To his protection; calls him Posthumus Leonatus;
Breeds him and makes him of his bed-chamber;
Puts to him all the learnings that his time
Could make him the receiver of: which he took,
As we do air, fast as 'twas minister'd,
And in 's spring became a harvest: lived in court—
Which rare it is to do—most praised, most loved;
A sample to the youngest, to the more mature
A glass that feated them, and to the graver
A child that guided dotards; to his mistress,
For whom he now is banish'd, her own price
Proclaims how she esteem'd him and his virtue;
By her election may be truly read
What kind of man he is.

SECOND GENT: I honour him
Even out of your report. But, pray you, tell me,
Is she sole child to the king?

CYMBELINE, I. i. 40–56

### 24 *Court Life and Country Life*

BELARIUS: Consider,
When you above perceive me like a crow,
That it is place which lessens and sets off:
And you may then revolve what tales I have told you
Of courts of princes, of the tricks in war:
This service is not service, so being done,
But being so allow'd: to apprehend thus,
Draws us a profit from all things we see;
And often, to our comfort, shall we find
The sharded beetle in a safer hold
Than is the full-wing'd eagle. O, this life
Is nobler than attending for a check,
Richer than doing nothing for a bribe,
Prouder than rustling in upaid-for silk:
Such gain the cap of him that makes 'em fine,
Yet keeps his book uncross'd: no life to ours.

GUIDERIUS: Out of your proof you speak: we, poor unfledged,
Have never wing'd from view o' the nest, nor know not
What air's from home. Haply this life is best
If quiet life be best, sweeter to you
That have a sharper known, well corresponding
With your stiff age: but unto us it is
A cell of ignorance, travelling a-bed,
A prison of a debtor that not dares
To stride a limit.

ARVIRAGUS: What should we speak of
When we are old as you? when we shall hear
The rain and wind beat dark December, how
In this our pinching cave shall we discourse
The freezing hours away? We have seen nothing:

We are beastly; subtle as the fox for prey,
Like warlike as the wolf for what we eat:
Our valour is to chase what flies; our cage
We make a quire, as doth the prison'd bird,
And sing our bondage freely.

BALARIUS:　　　　　　　　　　　How you speak!
Did you but know the city's usuries,
And felt them knowingly: the art o' the court,
As hard to leave as keep, whose top to climb
Is certain falling, or so slippery that
The fear's as bad as falling: the toil o' the war,
A pain that only seems to seek out danger
I' the name of fame and honour, which dies i' the search,
And hath as oft a slanderous epitaph
As record of fair act; nay, many times,
Doth ill deserve by doing well; what's worse,
Must court'sy at the censure:

CYMBELINE, III. iii. 11–55.

### 25 Cut-Purse Courtier

AUTOLYCUS: Whether it like me or no, I am a courtier. Seest
thou the air of the court in these enfoldings? hath not my
gait in it the measure of the court? receives not thy nose
court-odour from me? reflect I not on thy baseness court-
contempt? Thinkest thou, for that I insinuate, or toaze
from thee thy business, I am therefore no courtier? I am
courtier cap-a-pe; and one that will either push on or
pluck back thy business there: whereupon I command thee
to open thy affair.

THE WINTER'S TALE, IV. iii. 757–767

## (a) Soldiers

### 1 Lion into Calf

CONSTANCE: War! war! no peace! peace is to me a war.
O Lymoges! O Austria! thou dost shame
That bloody spoil: thou slave, thou wretch, thou coward!
Thou little valiant, great in villany!
Thou ever strong upon the stronger side!
Thou Fortune's champion that dost ever fight
But when her humourous ladyship is by
To teach thee safety! thou art perjured too,
And soothest up greatness. What a fool art thou,
A ramping fool, to brag and stamp and swear
Upon my party! Thou cold-blooded slave,
Hast thou not spoke like thunder on my side,
Been sworn my soldier, bidding me depend
Upon thy stars, thy fortune and thy strength,
And dost thou now fall over to my foes?
Thou wear a lion's hide! doff it for shame,
And hang a calf's-skin on those recreant limbs.

KING JOHN, III. i. 113–129

### 2 Troubled Soldier

L. PERCY: O, my good lord, why are you thus alone?
For what offence have I this fortnight been
A banish'd woman from my Harry's bed?
Tell me, sweet lord, what is't that takes from thee
Thy stomach, pleasure and thy golden sleep?
Why dost thou bend thine eyes upon the earth,
And start so often when thou sit'st alone?
Why hast thou lost the fresh blood in thy cheeks;
And given my treasures and my rights of thee

To thick-eyed musing and curs'd melancholy?
In thy faint slumbers I by thee have watch'd,
And heard thee murmur tales of iron wars;
Speak terms of manage to thy bounding steed;
Cry 'Courage! to the field!' and thou hast talk'd
Of sallies and retires, of trenches, tents,
Of palisadoes, frontiers, parapets,
Of basilisks, of cannon, culverin,
Of prisoners' ransom and of soldiers slain,
And all the currents of a heady fight.
Thy spirit within thee hath been so at war
And thus hath so bestirr'd thee in thy sleep,
That beads of sweat have stood upon thy brow,
Like bubbles in a late-disturbed stream;
And in thy face strange motions have appear'd,
Such as we see when men restrain their breath
On some great sudden hest. O, what portents are these?
Some heavy business hath my lord in hand,
And I must know it, else he loves me not.

HENRY IV, PT. I, II. iii. 42–69

### 3 *A Recruiting Officer*

FALSTAFF: If I be not asham'd of my soldiers, I am a sous'd
gurnet. I have misus'd the king's press damnably. I have
got, in exchange of a hundred and fifty soldiers, three
hundred and odd pounds. I press me none but good house-
holders, yeoman's sons; inquire me out contracted bache-
lors, such as had been ask'd twice on the banns; such a
commodity of warm slaves, as had as lieve hear the devil
as a drum; such as fear the report of a caliver worse than a
struck fowl or a hurt wild-duck. I press'd me none but such
toasts-and-butter, with hearts in their bellies no bigger
than pins' heads, and they have bought out their services;
and now my whole charge consists of ancients, corporals,
lieutenants, gentlemen of companies, slaves as ragged as
Lazarus in the painted cloth, where the glutton's dogs

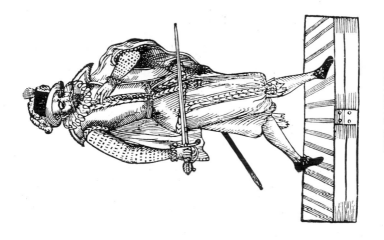

THE CAPTAIN

THE PEDLAR

# A
# FOOLES BOLT
## is foone shott.

Imprinted at London for *George Loftus*, and are to be
fold at the figne of the White Horfe at the Steps
of the North doore of *Paules.* 1614.

THE FOOL

lick'd his sores; and such as indeed were never soldiers, but discarded unjust serving-men, youngster sons to younger brothers, revolted tapsters and ostlers trade-fallen, the cankers of a calm world and a long peace, ten times more dishonourable ragged than an old fac'd ancient: and such have I, to fill up the rooms of them that have bought out their services, that you would think that I had a hundred and fifty tatter'd prodigals lately come from swine-keeping, from eating draff and husks. A mad fellow met me on the way and told me I had unloaded all the gibbets and press'd the dead bodies. No eye hath seen such scarecrows. I'll not march through Coventry with them, that's flat: nay, and the villains march wide betwixt the legs, as if they had gyves on; for indeed I had the most of them out of prison. There's but a shirt and a half in all my company; and the half shirt is two napkins tack'd together and thrown over the shoulders like a herald's coat without sleeves; and the shirt, to say the truth, stolen from my host at Saint Alban's or the red-nose innkeeper of Daventry. But that's all one; they'll find linen enough on every hedge.

HENRY IV, PT. I, IV. ii. 12–53

4 *A Captain—Forsooth!*

HOSTESS: No, good Captain Pistol; not here, sweet captain.
DOLL: Captain! thou abominable damn'd cheater, art thou not asham'd to be call'd captain? And captains were of my mind, they would truncheon you out, for taking their names upon you before you have earn'd them. You a Captain! you slave, for what? He a captain! hang him, rogue! he lives upon mouldy stewed prunes and dried cakes. A captain! God's light, these villains will make the word as odious as the word 'occupy'; which was an excellent good word before it was ill sorted: therefore captains had need look to 't.

HENRY IV, PT. II, II. iv. 148–161

## 5 *Soldier into Lover*

BENEDICK: I do much wonder that one man, seeing how much
another man is a fool when he dedicates his behaviours to
love, will, after he hath laughed at such shallow follies in
others, become the argument of his own scorn by falling in
love: and such a man is Claudio. I have known when there
was no music with him but the drum and the fife; and now
had he rather hear the tabor and the pipe: I have known
when he would have walked ten mile afoot to see a good
armour; and now will he lie ten nights awake, carving the
fashion of a new doublet. He was wont to speak plain and
to the purpose, like an honest man and a soldier, and now is
he turned orthography; his words are a very fantastical
banquet, just so many strange dishes.

MUCH ADO ABOUT NOTHING, II. iii. 7–23

## 6 *Counterfeit Soldier*

GOWER: Why, this is an arrant counterfeit rascal; I remember
him now; a bawd, a cutpurse.

FLUELLEN: I'll assure you, a' uttered as prave words at the pridge
as you shall see in a summer's day. But it is very well; what
he has spoke to me, that is well, I warrant you, when time
is serve.

GOWER: Why, 'tis a gull, a fool, a rogue, that now and then goes
to the wars, to grace himself at his return to London under
the form of a soldier. And such fellows are perfect in the
great commanders' names; and they will learn you by rote
where services were done; at such and such a sconce, at
such a breach, at such a convoy; who came off bravely, who
was shot, who was disgraced, what terms the enemy stood
on; and this they can perfectly in the phrase of war, which
they trick up with new-tuned oaths: and what a beard of
the general's cut and a horrid suit of the camp will do among
foaming bottles and ale-washed wits, is wonderful to be
thought on. But you must learn to know such slanders
of the age, or else you may be marvellously mistook.

FLUELLEN: I tell you what, Captain Gower; I do perceive he is
not the man that he would gladly make show to the world
he is: if I find a hole in his coat, I will tell him my mind.

KING HENRY V, III. vi. 64–92

## 7 Old Soldier

KING HENRY: This day is call'd the feast of Crispian:
He that outlives this day, and comes safe home,
Will stand a tip-tow when this day is named,
And rouse him at the name of Crispian.
He that shall live this day, and see old age,
Will yearly on the vigil feast his neighbours,
And say 'To-morrow is Saint Crispian':
Then will he strip his sleeve and show his scars,
And say 'These wounds I had on Crispin's day'.
Old men forget; yet all shall be forgot,
But he'll remember with advantages
What feats he did that day: then shall our names,
Familiar in his mouth as household words,
Harry the king, Bedford and Exeter,
Warwick and Talbot, Salisbury and Gloucester,
Be in their flowing cups freshly remember'd.
This story shall the good man teach his son;
And Crispin Crispian shall ne'er go by,
From this day to the ending of the world,
But we in it shall be remembered;
We few, we happy few, we band of brothers;
For he to-day that sheds his blood with me
Shall be my brother; be he ne'er so vile,
This day shall gentle his condition:
And gentlemen in England now a-bed
Shall think themselves accursed they were not here,
And hold their manhoods cheap whiles any speaks
That fought with us upon Saint Crispin's day.

KING HENRY V, IV. iii. 40–67

## 8 *Counter-Casting Soldier*

IAGO: Forsooth a great arithmetician,
    One Michael Cassio, a Florentine,
    A fellow almost damn'd in a fair wife;
    That never set a squadron in the field,
    Nor the division of a battle knows
    More than a spinster; unless the bookish theoric,
    Wherein the toged consuls can propose
    As masterly as he: mere prattle without practice
    Is all his soldiership. But he, sir, had the election;
    And I, of whom his eyes had seen the proof
    At Rhodes, at Cyprus, and on other grounds
    Christian and heathen, must be be-lee'd and calm'd
    By debitor and creditor: this counter-caster,
    He, in good time, must his lieutenant be,
    And I—God bless the mark!—his Moorship's ancient.

OTHELLO, I. i. 19–33

## 9 *Tough Soldier*

CAESAR:                                 Antony,
    Leave thy lascivious wassails. When thou once
    Was beaten from Modena, where thou slew'st
    Hirsius and Pansa, consuls at thy heel
    Did famine follow; who thou fought'st against,
    Though daintily brought up, with patience more
    Than savages could suffer: thou didst drink
    The stale of horses, and gilded puddle
    Which beasts would cough at: thy palate then did deign
    The roughest berry on the rudest hedge;
    Yea, like the stag, when snow the pasture sheets,
    The barks of trees thou browsed'st. On the Alps
    It is reported thou didst eat strange flesh,
    Which some did die to look on: and all this—
    It wounds thine honour that I speak it now—
    Was borne so like a soldier that thy cheek
    So much as lank'd not.

ANTONY AND CLEOPATRA, I. iv. 55–71

10 *Rough and Ready Soldier*

MENENIUS: Consider this: he has been bred i' the wars
    Since 'a could draw a sword, and is ill school'd
    In bolted language; meal and bran together
    He throws without distinction.

CORIOLANUS, III. i. 318–322

(b) Servants

1 *Old Faithful*

ADAM:                      Let me be your servant:
    Though I look old, yet I am strong and lusty;
    For in my youth I never did apply
    Hot and rebellious liquors in my blood,
    Nor did not with unbashful forehead woo
    The means of weakness and debility;
    Therefore my age is as a lusty winter,
    Frosty, but kindly: let me go with you;
    I'll do the service of a younger man
    In all your business and necessities.
ORLANDO: O good old man, how well in thee appears
    The constant service of the antique world,
    When service sweat for duty, not for meed!
    Thou art not for the fashion of these times,
    Where none will sweat but for promotion,
    And having that, do choke their service up
    Even with the having: it is not so with thee.

AS YOU LIKE IT, II. iii. 46–62

2 *An Honest Servant*

QUICKLY: An honest, willing kind fellow, as ever servant shall
come in house withal; and, I warrant you, no tell-tale nor
no breedbate: his worst fault is, that he is given to prayer;
he is something peevish that way: but nobody but has his
fault; but let that pass.

THE MERRY WIVES OF WINDSOR, I. iv. 10–16

### 3 *A Courtly Serving Man*

LEAR: What hast thou been?

EDGAR: A servingman, proud in heart and mind; that curl'd my hair, wore gloves in my cap; serv'd the lust of my mistress' heart and did the act of darkness with her; swore as many oaths as I spake words, and broke them in the sweet face of heaven; one that slept in the contriving of lust, and wak'd to do it. Wine lov'd I deeply, dice dearly; and in woman out-paramour'd the Turk. False of heart, light of ear, bloody of hand; hog in sloth, fox in stealth, wolf in greediness, dog in madness, lion in prey. Let not the creaking of shoes nor the rustling of silks betray thy poor heart to woman. Keep thy foot out of brothel, thy hand out of placket, thy pen from lender's book, and defy the foul fiend.

KING LEAR, III. iv. 84–99

### 4 *Selfish Service*

IAGO: O, sir, content you;
I follow him to serve my turn upon him:
We cannot all be masters, nor all masters
Cannot be truly follow'd. You shall mark
Many a duteous and knee-crooking knave,
That doting on his own obsequious bondage
Wears out his time, much like his master's ass,
For nought but provender, and when he's old, cashier'd;
Whip me such honest knaves. Others there are
Who, trimm'd in forms and visages of duty,
Keep yet their hearts attending on themselves,
And throwing but shows of service on their lords,
Do well thrive by them, and when they have lined their
    coats
Do themselves homage: these fellows have some soul,
And such a one do I profess myself.

OTHELLO, I, i, 41–55

## (c) Actors

### 1 The Actor

HAMLET: O, what a rogue and peasant slave am I!
 Is it not monstrous that this player here,
 But in a fiction, in a dream of passion,
 Could force his soul so to his own conceit
 That from her working all his visage wanned,
 Tears in his eyes, distraction in 's aspect,
 A broken voice, and his whole function suiting
 With forms to his conceit? And all for nothing!
 For Hecuba!
 What's Hecuba to him, or he to Hecuba,
 That he should weep for her? What would he do,
 Had he the motive and the cue for passion
 That I have?

         HAMLET, II. ii. 584–596

### 2 The Deep Tragedian

GLOUCESTER: Come, cousin, canst thou quake, and change thy
  colour,
 Murder thy breath in middle of a word,
 And then begin again, and stop again,
 As if thou wert distraught and mad with terror?
BUCKINGHAM: Tut, I can counterfeit the deep tragedian;
 Speake and look back, and pry on every side,
 Tremble and start at wagging of a straw,
 Intending deep suspicion: ghastly looks
 Are at my service, like enforced smiles;
 And both are ready in their offices,
 At any time, to grace my stratagems.

       KING RICHARD III, III. V. I–II

### 3 The 'Ham' Actor (a)

HAMLET: Speak the speech, I pray you, as I pronounced it to you,
 trippingly on the tongue; but if you mouth it, as many of

your players do, I had as lief the town-crier spoke my lines.
Nor do not saw the air too much with your hand, thus, but
use all gently; for in the very torrent, tempest and, as I may
say, whirlwind of your passion, you must acquire and beget
a temperance that may give it smoothness. O, if offends
me to the soul to hear a robustious periwig-pated fellow
tear a passion to tatters, to very rags, to split the ears of the
groundlings, who for the most part are capable of nothing
but inexplicable dumb-shows and noise. I would have such
a fellow whipped for o'erdoing Termagant. It out-herods
Herod. Pray you, avoid it.

HAMLET, III. ii. 1–17

### 3  *The 'Ham' Actor (b)*

HAMLET: O, there be players that I have seen play, and heard
others praise, and that highly, not to speak it profanely,
neither having the accent of Christians nor the gait of
Christian, pagan, nor man, have so strutted and bellowed
that I have thought some of nature's journeymen had
made men and not made them well, they imitated humanity so abominably.

HAMLET, III. ii. 33–40

### (d) The Fool and Jester

### 1 *The Fool*

JAQUES: A fool, a fool! I met a fool i' the forest,
    A motley fool; a miserable world!
    As I do live by food, I met a fool;
    Who laid him down and bask'd him in the sun,
    And rail'd on Lady Fortune in good terms,
    In good set terms and yet a motley fool.
    'Good-morrow, fool', quoth I. 'No, sir', quoth he,
    'Call me not fool till heaven hath sent me fortune':
    And then he drew a dial from his poke,
    And, looking on it with lack-lustre eye,

Says very wisely, 'It is ten o'clock:
Thus we may see,' quoth he, 'how the world wags:
'T is but an hour ago since it was nine,
And after one hour more 't will be eleven;
And so, from hour to hour, we ripe and ripe,
And then, from hour to hour, we rot and rot;
And thereby hangs a tale.' When I did hear
The motley fool thus moral on the time,
My lungs began to crow like chanticleer,
That fools should be so deep-contemplative,
And I did laugh sans intermission
An hour by his dial. O noble fool!
A worthy fool! Motley's the only wear.

DUKE SENIOR: What fool is this?

JAQUES: A worthy fool! One that hath been a courtier
And says, if ladies be but young and fair,
They have the gift to know it: and in his brain
Which is as dry as the remainder biscuit
After a voyage, he hath strange places cramm'd
With observation, the which he vents
In mangled forms. O that I were a fool!
I am ambitious for a motley coat.

DUKE SENIOR: Thou shalt have one.

JAQUES:                              It is my only suit;
Provided that you weed your better judgements
Of all opinion that grows rank in them
That I am wise. I must have liberty
Withal, as large a charter as the wind,
To blow on whom I please; for so fools have;
And they that are most galled with my folly,
They most must laugh. And why, sir, must they so?
The 'why' is plain as way to parish church:
He that a fool doth very wisely hit
Doth very foolishly, although he smart,
Not to seem senseless of the bob: if not,
The wise man's folly is anatomized

Even by the squandering glances of the fool.
Invest me in my motley; give me leave
To speak my mind, and I will through and through
Cleanse the foul body of the infected world,
If they will patiently receive my medicine.

AS YOU LIKE IT, II. vii. 12–61

## 2 *The Fool and his Zanies*

OLIVIA: What think you of this fool, Malvolio? doth he not
mend?

MALVOLIO: Yes, and shall do till the pangs of death shake him:
infirmity, that decays the wise, doth ever make the better
fool.

CLOWN: God send you, sir, a speedy infirmity, for the better
increasing your folly! Sir Toby will be sworn that I am no
fox; but he will not pass his word for twopence that you
are no fool.

OLIVIA: How say you to that, Malvolio?

MALVOLIO: I marvel your ladyship takes delight in such a barren
rascal: I saw him put down the other day with an ordinary
fool that has no more brain than a stone. Look you now,
he's out of his guard already; unless you laugh and minister
occasion to him, he is gagged. I protest, I take these wise
men, that crow so at these set kind of fools, no better than
the fools' zanies.

OLIVIA: O, you are sick of self-love, Malvolio, and taste with a
distempered appetite. To be generous, guiltless, and of free
disposition, is to take those things for bird-bolts that you
deem cannon-bullets: there is no slander in an allowed
fool, though he do nothing but rail; nor no railing in a
known discreet man, although he do nothing but reprove.

CLOWN: Now Mercury endue thee with leasing, for thou
speakest well of fools!

TWELFTH NIGHT, I. V. 78–105

### 3 *The Wit of the Fool*

VIOLA: This fellow's wise enough to play the fool;
    And to do that well craves a kind of wit:
    He must observe their mood on whom he jests,
    The quality of persons, and the time;
    And, like the haggard, check at every feather
    That comes before his eye. This is a practice
    As full of labour as a wise man's art:
    For folly that he wisely shows is fit;
    But wise men, folly-fall'n, quite taint their wit.

                    TWELFTH NIGHT, III. i. 68–76

### 4 *Dead Jester*

HAMLET: (Let me see.) Alas, poor Yorick! I knew him, Horatio; a fellow of infinite jest, of most excellent fancy. He hath borne me on his back a thousand times. And now how abhorred in my imagination it is! My gorge rises at it. Here hung those lips that I have kissed I know not how oft. Where be your gibes now, your gambols, your songs, your flashes of merriment, that were wont to set the table on a roar? Not one now, to mock your own grinning? Quite chop-fallen? Now get you to my lady's chamber, and tell her, let her paint an inch thick, to this favour she must come. Make her laugh at that.

                    HAMLET, V. i. 201–215

## (e) *Miscellaneous*

### 1 *Schoolmaster Exorcist*

ANTIPHOLUS OF EPHESUS:       . . . by the way we met
    My wife, her sister, and a rabble more
    Of vile confederates; along with them
    They brought one Pinch, a hungry lean-faced villain,
    A mere anatomy, a mountebank,

A threadbare juggler and a fortune-teller,
A needy, hollow-eyed, sharp-looking wretch,
A living dead man: this pernicious slave
Forsooth, took on him as a conjurer;
And, gazing in mine eyes, feeling my pulse,
And with no face, as 'twere, outfacing me,
Cries out, I was possess'd. Then, all together
They fell upon me, bound me, bore me thence,
And in a dark and dankish vault at home
There left me and my man, both bound together;

COMEDY OF ERRORS, V. i. 235–249


## 2 *A Sergeant*

ADRIANA: Where is thy master, Dromio? Is he well?
DROMIO OF SYRACUSE: No, he's in Tartar limbo, worse than
    hell:
    A devil in an everlasting garment hath him by the heel,
    One whose hard heart is buttoned up with steel;
    A fiend, a fury, pitiless and rough;
    A wolf, nay, worse; a fellow all in buff;
    A back-friend, a shoulder-clapper, one that countermands
    The passages of alleys, creeks, and narrow lands:
    A hound that runs counter, and yet draws dry-foot well;
    One that before the judgement, carries poor souls to
    hell.
ADRIANA: Why, man, what is the matter?
DROMIO OF SYRACUSE: I do not know the matter: he is rested
    on the case.
ADRIANA: What, is he arrested? tell me at whose suit.
DROMIO OF SYRACUSE: I know not at whose suit he is arrested
    well;
    But he's in a suit of buff which 'rested him, that can I
    tell'.

COMEDY OF ERRORS, IV. ii. 31–45

### 3 *Sergeant Again*

DROMIO OF SYRACUSE: Master, here's the gold you sent me for. What, have you got rid of the picture of old Adam new-apparelled?

ANTIPHOLUS OF SYRACUSE: What gold is this? What Adam dost thou mean?

DROMIO OF SYRACUSE: Not that Adam that kept the Paradise, but that Adam that keeps the prison: he that goes in the calf's skin that was killed for the Prodigal: he that came behind you, sir, like an evil angel, and bid you forsake your liberty.

ANTIPHOLUS OF SYRACUSE: I understand thee not.

DROMIO OF SYRACUSE: No? why, 'tis a plain case: he that went, like a base-viol, in a case of leather; the man, sir, that, when gentlemen are tired, gives them a bob and rests them; he, sir, that takes pity on decayed men, and gives them suits of endurance; he that sets up his rest to do more exploits with his mace than a morris-pike.

ANTIPHOLUS OF SYRACUSE: What, thou mean'st an officer?

DROMIO OF SYRACUSE: Ay, sir, the sergeant of the band; he that brings any man to answer it that breaks his band; one that thinks a man always going to bed, and says, 'God give you good rest!'

ANTIPHOLUS OF SYRACUSE: Well, sir, there rest in your foolery.

COMEDY OF ERRORS, IV. iii. 12–33

### 4 *A Bold Bad Priest*

GLOUCESTER: Presumptuous priest! this place commands my patience
Or thou should'st find thou hast dishonour'd me.
Think not, although in writing I preferr'd
The manner of thy vile outrageous crimes,
That therefore I have forged, or am not able
Verbatim to rehearse the method of my pen:
No, prelate; such is thy audacious wickedness,

Thy lewd, pestiferous, and dissentious pranks,
As very infants prattle of thy pride.
Thou art a most pernicious usurer,
Froward by nature, enemy to peace;
Lascivious, wanton, more than well beseems
A man of thy profession and degree:
And for thy treachery, what's more manifest?
In that thou laid'st a trap to take my life,
As well at London Bridge as at the Tower.
Beside, I fear me, if thy thoughts were sifted,
The king, thy sovereign, is not quite exempt
From envious malice of thy swelling heart.

KING HENRY VI, PT. I, III. i. 8–26

### 5 A Tailor

KATHERINA: I never saw a better-fashion'd gown,
More quaint, more pleasing, nor more commendable:
Belike you mean to make a puppet of me.
PETRUCHIO: Why, true; he means to make a puppet of thee.
TAILOR: She says your worship means to make a puppet of
her.
PETRUCHIO: O monstrous arrogance! Thou liest, thou thread,
thou thimble,
Thou yard, three-quarters, half-yard, quarter, nail!
Thou flea, thou nit, thou winter-cricket thou!
Braved in mine own house with a skein of thread?
Away, thou rag, thou quantity, thou remnant;
Or I shall so be-mete thee with thy yard,
As thou shalt think on prating whilst thou livest!
I tell thee, that thou hast marr'd her gown.
TAILOR: Your worship is deceived; the gown is made
Just as my master had directions:
Grumio gave order how it should be done.

THE TAMING OF THE SHREW, IV. iii. 101–118

## 6 An Apothecary

ROMEO: I do remember an apothecary,
And hereabouts he dwells, which late I noted
In tatter'd weeds, with overwhelming brows,
Culling of simples; meagre were his looks,
Sharp misery had worn him to the bones:
And in his needy shop a tortoise hung,
An alligator stuff'd and other skins
Of ill-shaped fishes; and about his shelves
A beggarly account of empty boxes,
Green earthen pots, bladders and musty seeds,
Remnants of packthread, and old cakes of roses,
Were thinly scatter'd to make up a show.
Noting this penury, to myself I said,
An if a man did need a poison now,
Whose sale is present death in Mantua,
Here lives a caitiff wretch would sell it him.
O, this same thought did but forerun my need,
And this same needy man must sell it me.

ROMEO AND JULIET, V. i. 37–54

## 7 The Nun

THESEUS: Therefore, fair Hermia, question your desires,
Know of your youth, examine well your blood,
Whether, if you yield not to your father's choice,
You can endure the livery of a nun:
For aye to be in shady cloister mew'd,
To live a barren sister all your life,
Chanting faint hymns to the cold fruitless moon.
Thrice blessed they, that master so their blood,
To undergo such maiden pilgrimage;
But earthlier happy is the rose distill'd,
Than that which, withering on the virgin thorn,
Grows, lives, and dies, in single blessedness.

A MIDSUMMER-NIGHT'S DREAM, I. i. 67–78

8 *Troubled Trader*

SALANIO: Believe me, sir, had I such venture forth,
       The better part of my affections would
       Be with my hopes abroad. I should be still
       Plucking the grass, to know where sits the wind,
       Peering in maps for ports and piers and roads;
       And every object that might make me fear
       Misfortune to my ventures, out of doubt
       Would make me sad.

SALARINO                  My wind cooling my broth
       Would blow me to an angle, when I thought
       What harm a wind too great at sea might do.
       I should not see the sandy hour-glass run,
       But I should think of shallows and of flats,
       And see my wealthy Andrew dock'd in sand,
       Vailing her high-top lower than her ribs
       To kiss her burial. Should I go to church
       And see the holy edifice of stone,
       And not bethink me straight of dangerous rocks,
       Which touching but my gentle vessel's side,
       Would scatter all her spices on the stream,
       Enrobe the roaring waters with my silks,
       And, in a word, but even now worth this,
       And now worth nothing? Shall I have the thought
       To think on this, and shall I lack the thought
       That such a thing bechanced would make me sad?
       But tell not me; I know, Antonio
       Is sad to think upon his merchandise.

                          THE MERCHANT OF VENICE, I. i. 15–40


9 *A Drawer at an Inn*

PRINCE HENRY: What's o'clock, Francis?
FRANCIS: Anon, Anon, sir.
PRINCE HENRY: That ever this fellow should have fewer words
       than a parrot, and yet the son of a woman! His industry is

# THE BELMAN
## OF LONDON.

Bringing to light the moſt notorious
villanies that are now practiſed
in the K I N G D O M E.

Profitable for Gentlemen, Lawyers, Merchants, Citizens, Farmers,
Maſters of Houſholds, and all ſortes of ſeruants, to marke,
and delightfull for all men to Reade.

*Lege, Perlege, Relege.*

Printed at London for N A T H A N I E L  B V T T E R. 1 6 0 8.

THE BELLMAN

THE MAGICIAN — DR. FAUSTUS

up-stairs and down-stairs; his eloquence the parcel of a reckoning.

HENRY IV, PT. I, II. iv. 109–115

## 10 *A True Labourer*

CORIN: Sir, I am a true labourer: I earn that I eat, get that I wear, owe no man hate, envy no man's happiness, glad of other men's good, content with my harm, and the greatest of my pride is to see my ewes graze and my lambs suck.

AS YOU LIKE IT, III. ii. 78–82

## 11 *Dead Lawyer*

HAMLET: There's another. Why may not that be the skull of a lawyer? Where be his quiddities now, his quillets, his cases, his tenures, and his tricks? Why does he suffer this rude knave now to knock him about the sconce with a dirty shovel, and will not tell him of his action of battery? Hum! This fellow might be in 's time a great buyer of land, with his statutes, his recognizances, his fines, his double vouchers, his recoveries; is this the fine of his fines and the recovery of his recoveries, to have his fine pate full of fine dirt? Will his vouchers vouch him no more of his purchases, and double ones too, than the length and breadth of a pair of indentures? The very conveyances of his lands will scarcely lie in this box, and must the inheritor himself have no more, ha?

HORATIO: Not a jot more, my lord.

HAMLET: Is not parchment made of sheep-skins?

HORATIO: Ay, my lord, and of calf-skins too.

HAMLET: They are sheep and calves which seek out assurance in that.

HAMLET, V. I. 104–125

## 12 *Door-Keeper in a Brothel*

MARINA: Thou hold'st a place, for which the paind'st fiend
Of hell would not in reputation change;
Thou art the damned door-keeper to every

8

Coistrel that comes inquiring for his Tib;
To the choleric fisting of every rogue
Thy ear is liable; thy food is such
As hath been belch'd on by infected lungs.

PERICLES, IV. vi. 178–184

13 *A Pedlar of Ballads*

SERVANT: O master, if you did but hear the pedlar at the door, you would never dance again after a tabor and pipe; no, the bagpipe could not move you: he sings several tunes faster than you'll tell money; he utters them as he had eaten ballads and all men's ears grew to his tunes.

CLOWN: He could never come better; he shall come in. I love a ballad but even too well, if it be doleful matter merrily set down, or a very pleasant thing indeed and sung lamentably.

SERVANT: He hath songs for man or woman, of all sizes; no milliner can so fit his customers with gloves: he has the prettiest love-songs for maids; so without bawdry, which is strange; with such delicate burthens of dildos and fadings, 'jump her and thump her'; and where some stretch-mouthed rascal would, as it were, mean misch'ef and break a foul gap into the matter, he makes the maid to answer 'Whoop, do me no harm, good man'; puts him off, slights him, with 'Whoop, do me no harm, good man.'

POLIXENES: This is a brave fellow.

CLOWN: Believe me, thou talkest of an admirable conceited fellow. Has he any unbraided wares?

SERVANT: He hath ribbons of all the colours i' the rainbow; points more than all the lawyers in Bohemia can learnedly handle, though they come to him by the gross: inkles, caddisses, cambrics, lawns: why, he sings 'em over as they were gods or goddesses; you would think a smock were a she-angel, he so chants to the sleeve-hand and the work about the square on't.

CLOWN: Prithee bring him in; and let him approach singing.

PERDITA: Forewarn him that he use no scurrilous words in 's tunes.

THE WINTER'S TALE, IV. iii. 181–215


## 14 *The Magician*

PROSPERO: (makes a magic circle with his staff) Ye elves of hills, brooks, standing lakes, and groves,
And ye that on the sands with printless foot
Do chase the ebbing Neptune, and do fly him
When he comes back; you demi-puppets that
By moonshine do the green sour ringlets make,
Whereof the ewe not bites; and you whose pastime
Is to make midnight mushrumps, that rejoice
To hear the solemn curfew; by whose aid
(Weak masters though ye be) I have bedimm'd
The noontide sun, call'd forth the mutinous winds,
And 'twixt the green sea and the azur'd vault
Set roaring war; to the dread rattling thunder
Have I given fire and rifted Jove's stout oak
With his own bolt; the strong-bas'd promontory
Have I made shake and by the spurs pluck'd up
The pine and cedar; graves at my command
Have wak'd their sleepers, op'd, and let 'em forth
By my so potent art. But this rough magic
I here abjure; and when I have requir'd
Some heavenly music (which even now I do)
To work mine end upon their senses that
This airy charm is for, I'll break my staff,
Bury it certain fadoms in the earth,
And deeper than did ever plummet sound
I'll drown my book.

THE TEMPEST, V. i. 33–57

### 1 Solemn Teuton

NERISSA: Then there is the County Palatine.

PORTIA: He doth nothing but frown, as who should say 'If you will not have me, choose': he hears merry tales and smiles not: I fear he will prove the weeping philosopher when he grows old, being so full of unmannerly sadness in his youth. I had rather be married to a death's-head with a bone in his mouth than to either of these. God defend me from these two!

THE MERCHANT OF VENICE, I. ii. 48–57

### 2 Chameleon Frenchman

NERISSA: How say you by the French lord, Monsieur Le Bon?

PORTIA: God made him, and therefore let him pass for a man. In truth, I know it is a sin to be a mocker: but, he! why, he hath a horse better than the Neapolitan's, a better bad habit of frowning than the Count Palatine; he is every man in no man; if a throstle sing, he falls straight a capering: he will fence with his own shadow: if I should marry him, I I should marry twenty husbands. If he would despise me, I would forgive him, for if he love me to madness, I shall never requite him.

THE MERCHANT OF VENICE, I. ii. 58–69

### 3 Illiterate Englishman

NERISSA: What say you, then, to Falconbridge, the young baron of England?

PORTIA: You know I say nothing to him, for he understands not me, nor I him: he hath neither Latin, French, nor Italian, and you will come into the court and swear that I have a poor pennyworth in the English. He is a proper man's picture, but, alas, who can converse with a dumb-show? How oddly he is suited! I think he bought his doublet in Italy, his round hose in France, his bonnet in Germany and his behaviour every where.

THE MERCHANT OF VENICE, I. ii. 70–81

### 4 *Drunken German*

NERISSA: How like you the young German, the Duke of Saxony's nephew?

PORTIA: Very vilely in the morning, when he is sober, and most vilely in the afternoon, when he is drunk: when he is best, he is a little worse than a man, and when he is worst, he is little better than a beast: and the worst fall that ever fell, I hope I shall make shift to go without him.

THE MERCHANT OF VENICE, I. ii. 90–96

### 5 *The Stubborn Jew*

ANTONIO: I pray you, think you question with the Jew:
You may as well go stand upon the beach
And bid the main flood bate his usual height;
You may as well use question with the wolf
Why he hath made the ewe bleat for the lamb;
You may as well forbid the mountain pines
To wag their high tops and to make no noise,
When they are fretten with the gusts of heaven;
You may as well do any thing most hard,
As seek to soften that—than which what's harder?—
His Jewish heart: therefore, I do beseech you,
Make no more offers, use no further means,
But with all brief and plain conveniency
Let me have judgement and the Jew his will.

THE MERCHANT OF VENICE, IV. i. 70–83

6 *The Knowledgeable Scot*

GOWER. Here a' comes; and the Scots captain, Captain Jamy,
    with him.

FLUELLEN: Captain Jamy is a marvellous falorous gentleman,
    that is certain; and of great expedition and knowledge in
    th' aunchient wars, upon my particular knowledge of his
    directions: by Cheshu, he will maintain his argument as
    well as any military man in the world, in the disciplines of
    the pristine wars of the Romans.

KING HENRY V, III. ii. 83–91

## (a) Marriage

### 1 *The Character of Marriage*

PETRUCHIO: Katharine, I charge thee, tell these headstrong
 women
 What duty they do owe their lords and husbands.
WIDOW: Come, come, you're mocking: we will have no telling.
PETRUCHIO: Come on, I say; and first begin with her.
WIDOW: She shall not.
PETRUCHIO: I say she shall: and first begin with her.
KATHARINA: Fie, fie! unkit that threatening unkind brow;
 And dart not scornful glances from those eyes.
 To wound thy lord, thy king, thy governor:
 It blots thy beauty as frosts do bite the meads,
 Confounds thy fame as whirlwinds shake fair buds,
 And in no sense is meet or amiable.
 A woman moved is like a fountain troubled,
 Muddy, ill-seeming, thick, bereft of beauty;
 And while it is so, none so dry or thirsty
 Will deign to sip or touch one drop of it.
 Thy husband is thy lord, thy life, thy keeper,
 Thy head, thy sovereign; one that cares for thee,
 And for thy maintenance commits his body
 To painful labour both by sea and land,
 To watch the night in storms, the day in cold,
 Whilst thou liest warm at home, secure and safe;
 And craves no other tribute at thy hands
 But love, fair looks and true obedience;
 Too little payment for so great a debt.
 Such duty as the subject owes the prince
 Even such a woman oweth to her husband;
 And when she is froward, peevish, sullen, sour,
 And not obedient to his honest will,

What is she but a foul contending rebel,
And graceless traitor to her loving lord?
I am ashamed that women are so simple
To offer war where they should kneel for peace,
Or seek for rule, supremacy and sway,
When they are bound to serve, love, and obey.
Why are our bodies soft, and weak, and smooth,
Unapt to toil and trouble in the world,
But that our soft conditions and our hearts
Should well agree with our external parts?
Come, come, you froward and unable worms!
My mind hath been as big as one of yours,
My heart as great, my reason haply more,
To bandy word for word and frown for frown;
But now I see our lances are but straws,
Our strength as weak, our weakness past compare,
That seeming to be most which we indeed least are.
Then vail your stomachs, for it is no boot,
And place your hands below your husband's foot:
In token of which duty, if he please,
My hand is ready, may it do him ease.

THE TAMING OF THE SHREW, V. ii. 131–180

### (b) Husbands and Fathers

### 1 A Fair Disloyal Husband

LUCIANA: And may it be that you have quite forgot
 A husband's office? Shall, Antipholus,
 Even in the spring of love thy love-springs rot?
 Shall love in building grow so ruinous?
 If you did wed my sister for her wealth,
 Then for her wealth's sake use her with more kindness:
 Or if you like elsewhere, do it by stealth;
 Muffle your false love with some show of blindness;
 Let not my sister read it in your eye;
 Be not thy tongue thy own shame's orator;

Look sweet, speak fair, become disloyalty;
Apparel vice like virtue's harbinger;
Bear a fair presence, though your heart be tainted;
Teach sin the carriage of a holy saint;
Be secret-false: what need she be acquainted?
What simple thief brags of his own attaint?
'Tis double wrong, to truant with your bed
And let her read it in thy looks at board:
Shame hath a bastard fame, well managed;
Ill deeds are doubled with an evil word.
Alas, poor women! make us but believe,
Being compact of credit, that you love us;
Though others have the arm, show us the sleeve;
We in your motion turn and you may move us.
Then, gentle brother, get you in again:
Comfort my sister, cheer her, call her wife;
'Tis holy sport, to be a little vain,
When the sweet breath of flattery conquers strife.

COMEDY OF ERRORS, III. ii. 1–28


## 2 *A Tamer of Shrews*

PETRUCHIO: Thus have I politicly begun my reign,
And 'tis my hope to end successfully.
My falcon now is sharp and passing empty;
And till she stoop she must not be full-gorged,
For then she never looks upon her lure.
Another way I have to man my haggard,
To make her come and know her keeper's call,
That is, to watch her, as we watch these kites
That bate and beat and will not be obedient.
She eat no meat to-day, nor none shall eat;
Last night she slept not, nor to-night she shall not;
As with the meat, some undeserved fault
I'll find about the making of the bed;
And here I'll fling the pillow, there the bolster,
This way the coverlet, another way the sheets:

Ay, and amid this hurly I intend
That all is done in reverend care of her;
And in conclusion she shall watch all night:
And if she chance to nod, I'll rail and brawl,
And with the clamour keep her still awake.
This is a way to kill a wife with kindness;
And thus I'll curb her mad and headstrong humour.
He that knows better how to tame a shrew,
Now let him speak: 'tis charity to show.

THE TAMING OF THE SHREW, IV. i. 191–214

### 3 Fathers Over-Careful

KING:                    See, sons, what things you are!
How quickly nature falls into revolt
When gold becomes her object!
For this the foolish over-careful fathers
Have broke their sleep with thoughts, their brains with care,
Their bones with industry;
For this they have engross'd and piled up
The cank'red heaps of strange-achieved gold;
For this they have been thoughtful to invest
Their sons with arts and martial exercises:
When, like the bee, culling from every flower
The virtuous sweets,
Our thighs pack'd with wax, our mouths with honey,
We bring it to the hive, and, like the bees,
Are murder'd for our pains. This bitter taste
Yields his engrossments to the ending father.

HENRY IV, PT. II, IV. V. 63–78

### 4 Contented Cuckold

CLOWN: I am out o' friends, madam; and I hope to have friends
for my wife's sake.
COUNT: Such friends are thine enemies, knave.
CLOWN: You're shallow, madam; e'en great friends; for the
knaves come to do that for me which I am aweary of. He

that ears my land spares my team, and gives me leave to in
the crop: if I be his cuckold, he's my drudge. He that
comforts my wife is the cherisher of my flesh and blood;
he that cherishes my flesh and blood loves my flesh and
blood; he that loves my flesh and blood is my friend: *ergo*,
he that kisses my wife is my friend. If men could be contented to be what they are, there were no fear in marriage;
for young Charbon the puritan, and old Poysam the
papist, howsome'er their hearts are severed in religion, their
heads are both one; they may jowl horns together, like
any deer i' the herd.

ALL'S WELL THAT ENDS WELL, I. iii. 43–60

## 5 Father and Son Matched

PAULINA:                                    It is yours;
And, might we lay the old proverb to your charge,
So like you, 'tis the worse. Behold, my lords,
Although the print be little, the whole matter
And copy of the father, eye, nose, lip;
The trick of's frown; his forehead; nay, the valley,
The pretty dimples of his chin and cheek; his smiles;
The very mould and frame of hand, nail, finger:
And thou, good goddess Nature, which hast made it
So like to him that got it, if thou hast
The ordering of the mind too, 'mongst all colours
No yellow in't, lest she suspect, as he does,
Her children not her husband's!

THE WINTER'S TALE, II. iii. 95–107

## (c) Wives and Mothers

### 1 A Jealous Railing Wife

ADRIANA: To none of these, except it be the last;
Namely, some love that drew him oft from home.
ABBESS: You should for that have reprehended him.
ADRIANA: Why, so I did.

ABBESS:　　　　　　　　　Ay, but not rough enough.
ADRIANA: As roughly as my modesty would let me.
ABBESS: Haply, in private.
ADRIANA:　　　　　　　　And in assemblies too.
ABBESS: Ay, but not enough.
ADRIANA: It was the copy of our conference:
　　In bed, he slept not for my urging it;
　　At board, he fed not for my urging it;
　　Alone, it was the subject of my theme;
　　In company, I often glanced it;
　　Still did I tell him it was vile and bad.
ABBESS: And therefore came it that the man was mad.
　　The venom clamours of a jealous woman
　　Poisons more deadly than a mad dog's tooth.
　　It seems, his sleeps were hinder'd by thy railings:
　　And thereof comes it that his head is light.
　　Thou say'st his meat was sauced by thy upbraidings:
　　Unquiet meals make ill digestions;
　　Thereof the raging fire of fever bred;
　　And what's a fever but a fit of madness?
　　Thou say'st his sports were hinder'd by thy brawls:
　　Sweet recreation barred, what doth ensue
　　But moody, heavy and dull melancholy,
　　Kinsman to grim and comfortless despair;
　　And at her heels a huge infectious troop
　　Of pale distemperatures and foes to life?
　　In food, in sport, and life-preserving rest
　　To be disturb'd, would mad or man or beast;
　　The consequence is, then, thy jealous fits
　　Hath scar'd thy husband from the use of wits.

COMEDY OF ERRORS, V. i. 55–86

2 *A Cut Loaf*

DEMETRIUS: She is a woman, therefore may be woo'd;
　　She is a woman, therefore may be won;
　　She is Lavinia, therefore must be lov'd.

What, man! more water glideth by the mill
Than wots the miller of; and easy it is
Of a cut loaf to steal a shive, we know:
Though Bassianus be the emperor's brother,
Better than he have worn Vulcan's badge.

TITUS ANDRONICUS, II. i. 82–89

### 3 *A Gold-Gilt Wife*

PETRUCHIO: Signior Hortensio, 'twixt such friends as we
Few words suffice; and therefore, if thou know
One rich enough to be Petruchio's wife,
As wealth is burden of my wooing dance,
Be she as foul as was Florentius' love,
As old as Sibyl, and as curst and shrewd
As Socrates' Xanthippe, or a worse,
She moves me not, or not removes, at least,
Affection's edge in me, were she as rough
As are the swelling Adriatic seas:
I come to wive it wealthily in Padua;
If wealthily, then happily in Padua.

THE TAMING OF THE SHREW, I. ii. 65–76

### 4 *A Rich and Biddable Bride*

PORTIA: You see me, Lord Bassanio, where I stand,
Such as I am: though for myself alone
I would not be ambitious in my wish,
To wish myself much better; yet, for you
I would be trebled twenty times myself;
A thousand times more fair, ten thousand times
More rich;
That only to stand high in your account
I might in virtues, beauties, livings, friends,
Exceed account; but the full sum of me
Is sum of something, which, to term in gross
Is an unlesson'd girl, unschool'd, unpractised;

Happy in this, she is not yet so old
But she may learn; happier then in this,
She is not bred so dull but she can learn;
Happiest of all in that her gentle spirit
Commits itself to yours to be directed,
As from her lord, her governor, her king.
Myself and what is mine to you and yours
Is now converted: but now I was the lord
Of this fair mansion, master of my servants,
Queen o'er myself; and even now, but now,
This house, these servants, and this same myself
Are yours, my lord: I give them with this ring;
Which when you part from, lose, or give away,
Let it presage the ruin of your love
And be my vantage to exclaim on you.

THE MERCHANT OF VENICE, III. ii. 149–175

## 5 Trusty Wife!

HOTSPUR:                          But hark you, Kate;
I must not have you henceforth question me
Whither I go, nor reason whereabout:
Whither I must, I must; and, to conclude,
This evening must I leave you, gentle Kate.
I know you wise, but yet no farther wise
Than Harry Percy's wife: constant you are,
But yet a woman: and for secrecy,
No lady closer; for I well believe
Thou wilt not utter what thou dost not know;
And so far will I trust thee, gentle Kate.

HENRY IV, PT. I, II. iii. 107–117

## 6 A Constant Noble Woman

PORTIA: I grant I am a woman; but withal
A woman that Lord Brutus took to wife:
I grant I am a woman; but withal

A woman well-reputed, Cato's daughter.
Think you I am no stronger than my sex,
Being so father'd and so husbanded?
Tell me your counsels, I will not disclose 'em:
I have made strong proof of my constancy,
Giving myself a voluntary wound
Here in the thigh: can I bear that with patience,
And not my husband's secrets?
BRUTUS:                          O ye gods,
Render me worthy of this noble wife!

> JULIUS CAESAR, II. i. 292–303

## 7 *An Incomparable Bride*

MONTANO: But, good lieutenant, is your general wived?
CASSIO: Most fortunately: he hath achieved a maid
That paragons description and wild fame;
One that excels the quirks of blazoning pens,
And in the essential vesture of creation
Does tire the ingener.

> OTHELLO, II. i. 60–65

## 8 *A Vexatious Wife*

DESDEMONA: Do not doubt that; before Emilia here
I give thee warrant of thy place: assure thee,
If I do vow a friendship, I'll perform it
To the last article: my lord shall never rest;
I'll watch him tame and talk him out of patience;
His bed shall seem a school, his board a shrift;
I'll intermingle every thing he does
With Cassio's suit: therefore be merry, Cassio;
For thy solicitor shall rather die
Than give thy cause away.

> OTHELLO, III. iii. 19–28

### 9 *A Goodly Mother Matched*

PERICLES: I am great with woe, and shall deliver weeping.
My dearest wife was like this maid, and such a one
My daughter might have been: my queen's square brows;
Her stature to an inch; as wand-like straight;
As silver-voic'd; her eyes as jewel-like,
And cas'd as richly; in pace another Juno;
Who starves the ears she feeds, and makes them hungry,
The more she gives them speech.

PERICLES, V. i. 107–114


### 10 *A True and Humble Wife*

QUEEN KATHERINE: Sir, I desire you do me right and justice,
And to bestow your pity on me; for
I am a most poor woman, and a stranger,
Born out of your dominions; having here
No judge indifferent, nor no more assurance
Of equal friendship and proceeding. Alas, sir,
In what have I offended you? what cause
Hath my behaviour given to your displeasure,
That thus you should proceed to put me off,
And take your good grace from me? Heaven witness,
I have been to you a true and humble wife,
At all times to your will conformable,
Ever in fear to kindle your dislike,
Yea, subject to your countenance, glad or sorry
As I saw it inclined: when was the hour
I ever contradicted your desire,
Or made it not mine too? Or which of your friends
Have I not strove to love, although I knew
He were mine enemy? what friend of mine
That had to him derived your anger, did I
Continue in my liking? nay, gave notice
He was from thence discharged? Sir, call to mind
That I have been your wife, in this obedience,

Upward of twenty years, and have been blest
With many children by you: if in the course
And process of this time you can report,
And prove it too, against mine honour aught,
My bond to wedlock, or my love and duty,
Against your sacred person, in God's name,
Turn me away, and let the foul'st contempt
Shut door upon me, and so give up
To the sharp'st kind of justice.

KING HENRY VIII, II. iv. 11–42

## 11 *A Patient Constant Wife*

QUEEN KATHERINE: Have I lived thus long—let me speak myself,
    Since virtue finds no friends—a wife, a true one?
    A woman, I dare say without vain-glory,
    Never yet branded with suspicion?
    Have I with all my full affections
    Still met the king? loved him next heaven? obey'd him?
    Been, out of fondness, superstitious to him?
    Almost forgot my prayers to content him?
    And am I thus rewarded? 't is not well, lords.
    Bring me a constant woman to her husband,
    One that ne'er dream'd a joy beyond his pleasure,
    And to that woman, when she has done most,
    Yet will I add an honour, a great patience.

KING HENRY VIII, III. i. 124–136

## (d) *Sons and Daughters*

### 1 *Boys Eternal*

HERMIONE:                Come, I'll question you
  Of my lord's tricks and yours when you were boys:
  You were pretty lordings then?
POLIXENES:             We were, fair queen,
  Two lads that thought there was no more behind,

9

But such a day to-morrow as to-day,
And to be boy eternal.
HERMIONE:                    Was not my lord
The verier wag o' the two?
POLIXENES: We were as twinn'd lambs that did frisk i' the sun,
And bleat the one at the other: what we changed
Was innocence for innocence; we knew not
The doctrine of ill-doing, nor dream'd
That any did. Had we pursued that life,
And our weak spirits ne'er been higher rear'd
With stronger blood, we should have answer'd heaven
Boldly 'not guilty'; the imposition clear'd
Hereditary ours.

THE WINTER'S TALE, I. ii. 60–75

## 2 *Child in the House*

LEONTES: You will! why, happy man be's dole! My brother,
Are you so fond of your young prince, as we
Do seem to be of ours?
POLIXENES:                    If at home, sir,
He's all my exercise, my mirth, my matter:
Now my sworn friend, and then mine enemy;
My parasite, my soldier, statesman, all:
He makes a July's day short as December;
And with his varying childness cures in me
Thoughts that would thick my blood.

THE WINTER'S TALE, I. ii. 163–171

## 3 *A Sensitive Lad*

LEONTES: How does the boy?
FIRST SERV:                    He took good rest to-night;
'Tis hoped his sickness is discharged.
LEONTES: To see his nobleness!
Conceiving the dishonour of his mother,
He straight declined, droop'd, took it deeply,

Fasten'd and fix'd the shame on't in himself,
Threw off his spirit, his appetite, his sleep,
And downright languish'd.

THE WINTER'S TALE, II. iii. 9–17

### 4 *A Perfect Page*

LUCIUS:                          This one thing only
I will entreat; my boy, a Briton born,
Let him be ransom'd: never master had
A page so kind, so duteous, diligent,
So tender over his occasions, true,
So feat, so nurse-like:

CYMBELINE, V. v. 83–88

### 5 *Unnatural Child*

ALBANY:                          O Goneril.
You are not worth the dust which the rude wind
Blows in your face! I fear your disposition.
That nature which contemns it origin
Cannot be bordered certain in itself.
She that herself will sliver and disbranch
From her material sap, perforce must wither
And come to deadly use.

KING LEAR, IV. ii. 29–36

### 6 *Two Unspeakable Loves* (a)

GONERIL: Sir, I love you more than words can wield the matter;
Dearer than eyesight, space, and liberty;
Beyond what can be valued, rich or rare;
No less than life, with grace, health, beauty, honour;
As much as child e'er lov'd, or father found;
A love that makes breath poor, and speech unable.
Beyond all manner of so much I love you.

KING LEAR, I. i. 57–63

6 *Two Unspeakable Loves* (*b*)

REG: Sir, I am made
    Of the self-same metal that my sister is,
    And prize me at her worth. In my true heart
    I find she names my very deed of love;
    Only she comes too short, that I profess
    Myself an enemy to all other joys
    Which the most precious square of sense possesses,
    And find I am alone felicitate
    In your dear Highness' love.

                                KING LEAR, I. i. 70–78


7 *A Daughter Cursed*

LEAR: Hear, Nature, hear! dear goddess, hear!
    Suspend thy purpose, if thou didst intend
    To make this creature fruitful.
    Into her womb convey sterility;
    Dry up in her the organs of increase;
    And from her derogate body never spring
    A babe to honour her! If she must teem,
    Create her child of spleen, that it may live
    And be a thwart disnatur'd torment to her.
    Let it stamp wrinkles in her brow of youth,
    With cadent tears fret channels in her cheeks,
    Turn all her mother's pains and benefits
    To laughter and contempt, that she may feel
    How sharper than a serpent's tooth it is
    To have a thankless child! Away, away!

                                KING LEAR, I. iv. 299–313

## (a) Major

### 1 The Several Ages of Villainy

DUCHESS OF YORK: No, by the holy rood, thou know'st it well,
Thou camest on earth to make the earth my hell.
A grievous burthen was thy birth to me;
Tetchy and wayward was thy infancy;
Thy school-days frightful, desperate, wild, and furious,
Thy prime of manhood daring, bold, and venturous,
Thy age confirm'd, proud, subtle, bloody, treacherous,
More mild, but yet more harmful, kind in hatred:
What comfortable hour canst thou name
That ever graced me in thy company?

KING RICHARD III, IV. iv. 166–175

### 2 A Monstrous Villain

GLOUCESTER: But I, that am not shaped for sportive tricks,
Nor made to court an amorous looking-glass;
I, that am rudely stamp'd, and want love's majesty
To strut before a wanton ambling nymph;
I, that am curtail'd of this fair proportion,
Cheated of feature by dissembling nature,
Deform'd, unfinish'd, sent before my time
Into this breathing world, scarce half made up,
And that so lamely and unfashionable
That dogs bark at me as I halt by them;
Why, I, in this weak piping time of peace,
Have no delight to pass away the time,
Unless to spy my shadow in the sun
And descant on mine own deformity:
And therefore, since I cannot prove a lover,

To entertain these fair well-spoken days,
I am determined to prove a villain
And hate the idle pleasures of these days.

KING RICHARD III, I. i. 14–31


### 3 An Accursed Villain—Cursed

QUEEN MARGARET: And leave out thee! stay, dog, for thou shalt
    hear me.
If heaven have any grievous plague in store
Exceeding those that I can wish upon thee,
O, let them keep it till thy sins be ripe,
And then hurl down their indignation
On thee, the troubler of the poor world's peace!
The worm of conscience still begnaw thy soul!
Thy friends suspect for traitors while thou livest,
And take deep traitors for thy dearest friends!
No sleep close up that deadly eye of thine,
Unless it be whilst some tormenting dream
Affrights thee with a hell of ugly devils!
Thou elvish-mark'd, abortive, rooting hog!
Thou that wast seal'd in thy nativity
The slave of nature and the son of hell!
Thou rag of honour!

KING RICHARD III, I. iii. 216–231


### 4 A Fawning Venomous Dog

QUEEN MARGARET: O Buckingham, take heed of yonder dog!
Look, when he fawns, he bites; and when he bites,
His venom tooth will rankle to the death:
Have not to do with him, beware of him;
Sin, death, and hell have set their marks on him,
And all their ministers attend on him.

KING RICHARD III, I. iii. 289–294

*5 A Carnal Cur*

QUEEN MARGARET: From forth the kennel of thy womb hath
      crept
    A hell-hound that doth hunt us all to death:
    That dog, that had his teeth before his eyes,
    To worry lambs and lap their gentle blood,
    That foul defacer of God's handiwork,
    That excellent grand tyrant of the earth,
    That reigns in galled eyes of weeping souls,
    Thy womb let loose, to chase us to our graves.
    O upright, just, and true-disposing God,
    How do I thank thee, that this carnal cur
    Preys on the issue of his mother's body,
    And makes her pew-fellow with others' moan!

                KING RICHARD III, IV iv. 47–58


*6 A Notorious Active Villain*

AARON: Ay, that I had not done a thousand more.
    Even now I curse the day, and yet, I think,
    Few come within the compass of my curse,
    Wherein I did not some notorious ill:
    As kill a man, or else devise his death;
    Ravish a maid, or plot the way to do it;
    Accuse some innocent, and forswear myself;
    Set deadly enmity between two friends;
    Make poor men's cattle break their necks;
    Set fire on barns and hay-stacks in the night,
    And bid the owners quench them with their tears.
    Oft have I digg'd up dead men from their graves,
    And set them upright at their dear friends' doors,
    Even when their sorrows almost were forgot;
    And on their skins, as on the bark of trees,
    Have with my knife carved in Roman letters,
    'Let not your sorrow die, though I am dead.'
    Tut! I have done a thousand dreadful things

As willingly as one would kill a fly,
And nothing grieves me heartily indeed
But that I cannot do ten thousand more.

TITUS ANDRONICUS, V. i. 124–144


### 7 A Cankered Villain

DON JOHN: I had rather be a canker in a hedge than a rose in his grace, and it better fits my blood to be disdained of all than to fashion a carriage to rob love from any: in this, though I cannot be said to be a flattering honest man, it must not be denied but I am a plain-dealing villain. I am trusted with a muzzle and enfranchised with a clog; therefore I have decreed not to sing in my cage. If I had my mouth, I would bite; if I had my liberty, I would do my liking: in the mean time, let me be that I am, and seek not to alter me.

MUCH ADO ABOUT NOTHING, I. iii. 28–39


### 8 A Slipper and Subtle Young Knave

IAGO: Now, sir, this granted—as it is a most pregnant and unforced position—who stands so eminently in the degree of this fortune as Cassio does? a knave very voluble; no further conscionable than in putting on the mere form of civil and humane seeming, for the better compassing of his salt and most hidden loose affection? why, none; why, none: a slipper and subtle knave; a finder out of occasions; that has an eye can stamp and counterfeit advantages, though true advantage never present itself: a devilish knave! Besides, the knave is handsome, young, and hath all those requisites in him that folly and green minds look after: a pestilent complete knave; and the woman hath found him already.

OTHELLO, II. i. 240–255

9 *A Cogging Villain*

EMILIA: I will be hang'd, if some eternal villain,
　　Some busy and insinuating rogue,
　　Some cogging, cozening slave, to get some office,
　　Have not devised this slander; I'll be hang'd else.

　　　　　　　　　　　　OTHELLO, IV. ii. 130–133

10 *The Parricide*

GLOUCESTER: Now, Edmund, where's the villain?
EDMUND: Here stood he in the dark, his sharp sword out,
　　Mumbling of wicked charms, conjuring the moon
　　To stand's auspicious mistress.
GLOUCESTER:　　　　　　　　　But where is he?
EDMUND: Look, sir, I bleed.
GLOUCESTER:　　　　　　　　Where is the villain, Edmund?
EDMUND: Fled this way, sir. When by no means he could . . .
GLOUCESTER: Pursue him, ho! Go after. (*Exeunt some Servants*)
　　By no means what?
EDMUND: Persuade me to the murther of your lordship;
　　But that I told him the revenging gods
　　'Gainst parricides did all their thunders bend;
　　Spoke with how manifold and strong a bond
　　The child was bound to th' father—sir, in fine,
　　Seeing how loathly opposite I stood
　　To his unnatural purpose, in fell motion
　　With his prepared sword he charges home
　　My unprovided body, lanch'd mine arm;
　　But when he saw my best alarum'd spirits,
　　Bold in the quarrel's right, rous'd to th'encounter,
　　Or whether gasted by the noise I made,
　　Full suddenly he fled.

　　　　　　　　　　　　KING LEAR, II. i. 39–58

11 *A Superserviceable Knave*

KENT: Fellow, I know thee.
OSWALD: What dost thou know me for?

KENT: A knave: a rascal; an eater of broken meats; a base, proud, shallow, beggarly, three-suited, hundred-pound, filthy, worsted-stocking knave; a lily-liver'd, action-taking, whoreson, glass-gazing, superserviceable, finical rogue; one-trunk-inheriting slave; one that wouldst be a bawd in way of good service, and art nothing but the composition of a knave, beggar, coward, pander, and the son and heir of a mongrel bitch; one whom I will beat into clamorous whining, if thou deny the least syllable of thy addition.

KING LEAR, II. ii. 11–26

### 12 Halcyon Rogues

KENT: Yes, sir, but anger hath a privilege.
CORNWALL: Why art thou angry?
KENT: That such a slave as this should wear a sword,
Who wears no honesty. Such smiling rogues as these,
Like rats, oft bite the holy cords atwain
Which are too intrinse t'unloose; smooth every passion
That in the natures of their lords rebel,
Bring oil to fire, snow to their colder moods;
Renege, affirm, and turn their halcyon beaks
With every gale and vary of their masters,
Knowing naught (like dogs) but following.
A plague upon your epileptic visage!
Smile you my speeches, as I were a fool?
Goose, an I had you upon Sarum Plain,
I'ld drive ye cackling home to Camelot.

KING LEAR, II. ii. 75–89

### 13 Woman into Fiend

LADY MACBETH:                     The raven himself is hoarse
That croaks the fatal entrance of Duncan
Under my battlements. Come, you spirits
That tend on mortal thoughts, unsex me here,

And fill me, from the crown to the toe, top-full
Of direst cruelty! make thick my blood,
Stop up the access and passage to remorse,
That no compunctious visitings of nature
Shake my fell purpose, nor keep peace between
The effect and it! Come to my woman's breasts,
And take my milk for gall, you murdering ministers,
Wherever in your sightless substances
You wait on nature's mischief! Come, thick night,
And pall thee in the dunnest smoke of hell,
That my keen knife see not the wound it makes,
Nor heaven peep through the blanket of the dark,
To cry 'Hold, hold!'

MACBETH, I. V. 39–55

### (b) Minor

#### 1 Gentlemen of the Shade

FALSTAFF: Marry, then, sweet wag, when thou art king, let not
us that are squires of the night's body be called thieves of
the day's beauty: let us be Diana's foresters, gentlemen of
the shade, minions of the moon; and let men say we be men
of good government, being governed, as the sea is, by our
noble and chaste mistress the moon, under whose countenance we steal.

PRINCE OF WALES: Thou say'st well, and it holds well too; for
the fortune of us that are the moon's men doth ebb and
flow like the sea, being governed, as the sea is, by the
moon. As, for proof, now: a purse of gold most resolutely
snatch'd on Monday night and most dissolutely spent on
Tuesday morning; got with swearing 'Lay by' and spent
with crying 'Bring in'; now in as low an ebb as the foot
of the ladder and by and by in as high a flow as the ridge
of the gallows.

HENRY IV, PT. I, I. ii. 26–43

## 2 *Exalted Thuggery*

GADSHILL: What talkest thou to me of the hangman? if I hang, I'll make a fat pair of gallows; for if I hang, old Sir John hangs with me, and thou know'st he is no starveling. Tut! there are other Trojans that thou dream'st not of, the which for sport sake are content to do the profession some grace; that would, if matters should be look'd into, for their own credit sake, make all whole. I am join'd with no foot land-rakers, no long-staff sixpenny strikers, none of these mad mustachio purple-hued malt-worms; but with nobility and tranquillity, burgomasters and great oneyers, such as can hold in, such as will strike sooner than speak, and speak sooner than drink, and drink sooner than pray: and yet 'zounds, I lie; for they pray continually to their saint, the commonwealth; or rather, not pray to her, but prey on her, for they ride up and down on her and make her their boots.

CHAMBERLAIN: What, the commonwealth their boots? will she hold out water in foul way?

GADSHILL: She will, she will; justice hath liquor'd her. We steal as in a castle, cock-sure; we have the receipt of fern-seed, we walk invisible.

HENRY IV, PT. I, II. i. 73–99

## 3 *A Bottle-Ale Rascal*

PISTOL: Then to you, Mistress Dorothy; I will charge you.

DOLL: Charge me! I scorn you, scurvy companion. What! you poor, base, rascally, cheating, lack-linen mate! Away, you mouldy rogue, away!

PISTOL: I know you, Mistress Dorothy.

DOLL: Away, you cut-purse rascal! you filthy bung, away! by this wine, I'll thrust my knife in your mouldy chaps and you play the saucy cuttle with me. Away, you bottle-ale rascal! you basket-hilt stale juggler, you! Since when, I pray you, sir? God's light, with two points on your shoulder? much!

HENRY IV, PT. II, II. iv. 129–141

### 4 *Villainous Jester*

BEATRICE: Why, he is the prince's jester: a very dull fool; only
his gift is in devising impossible slanders: none but
libertines delight in him; and the commendation is not in
his wit, but in his villainy; for he both pleases men and
angers them, and then they laugh at him and beat him. I
am sure he is in the fleet: I would he had boarded me.

MUCH ADO ABOUT NOTHING, II. i. 144–151

### 5 *An Affected Plain Knave*

CORNWALL: Why dost thou call him knave? What is his fault?
KENT: His countenance likes me not.
CORNWALL: No more perchance does mine, or his, or hers.
KENT: Sir, 'tis my occupation to be plain.
    I have seen better faces in my time
    Than stands on any shoulder that I see
    Before me at this instant.
CORNWALL:              This is some fellow
    Who, having been prais'd for bluntness, doth affect
    A saucy roughness, and constrains the garb
    Quite from his nature. He cannot flatter, he!
    An honest mind and plain—he must speak truth!
    An they will take it, so: if not, he's plain.
    These kind of knaves I know which in this plainness
    Harbour more craft and more corrupter ends
    Than twenty silly-ducking observants
    That stretch their duties nicely.

KING LEAR, II. ii. 94–110

### 6 *A Snapper-Up of Unconsidered Trifles*

AUTOLYCUS: My traffic is sheets; when the kite builds, look to
lesser linen. My father named me Autolycus; who being,
as I am, littered under Mercury, was likewise a snapper-up
of unconsidered trifles. With die and drab I purchased this

caparison, and my revenue is the silly cheat. Gallows and knock are too powerful on the highway: beating and hanging are terrors to me: for the life to come, I sleep out the thought of it. A prize! a prize!

THE WINTER'S TALE, IV. ii. 23–32

## 7 A Thriving Cut-Purse

AUTOLYCUS: I understand the business, I hear it: to have an open ear, a quick eye, and a nimble hand, is necessary for a cut-purse; a good nose is requisite also, to smell out work for the other senses. I see this is the time that the unjust man doth thrive. What an exchange had this been without boot! What a boot is here with this exchange! Sure the gods do this year connive at us, and we may do any thing extempore. The prince himself is about a piece of iniquity, stealing away from his father with his clog at his heels: if I thought it were a piece of honesty to acquaint the king withal, I would not do't: I hold it the more knavery to conceal it; and therein am I constant to my profession.

THE WINTER'S TALE, IV. iv. 687–701

### 1 *One Marked for Villainy*

KING JOHN: How oft the sight of means to do ill deeds
 Make deeds ill done! Hadst not thou been by,
 A fellow by the hand of nature mark'd,
 Quoted and sign'd to do a deed of shame,
 This murder had not come into my mind:
 But taking note of thy abhorr'd aspect,
 Finding thee fit for bloody villany,
 Apt, liable to be employ'd in danger,
 I faintly broke with thee of Arthur's death;
 And thou to be endeared to a king;
 Made it no conscience to destroy a prince.

KING JOHN, IV. ii. 219–229

### 2 *Man Without Music*

LORENZO: The man that hath no music in himself,
 Nor is not moved with concord of sweet sounds,
 Is fit for treasons, stratagems and spoils;
 The motions of his spirit are dull as night
 And his affections dark as Erebus;
 Let no such man be trusted. Mark the music.

THE MERCHANT OF VENICE, V. i. 83–88

### 3 *The Fat and Lean*

PRINCE HENRY: I'll be no longer guilty of this sin; this sanguine
 coward, this bed-presser, this horse-back-breaker, this huge
 hill of flesh,—

FALSTAFF: 'Sblood, you starveling, you elf-skin, you dried neat's
 tongue, you stock-fish! O for breath to utter what is like
 thee! you tailor's-yard, you sheath, you bow-case, you vile
 standing-tuck,—

PRINCE HENRY: Well, breathe awhile, and then to it again: and
when thou hast tir'd thyself in base comparisons, hear me
speak but this.

HENRY IV, PT. I, II. iv. 271–281

### 4 One not Unnecessarily Virtuous

FALSTAFF: I was as virtuously given as a gentleman need to be;
virtuous enough; swore little; dic'd not above seven times
a week; went to a bawdy-house not above once in a quarter of an hour; liv'd well and in good compass: and now I
live out of all order, out of all compass.

HENRY IV, PT. I, III. iii. 16–23

### 5 Knight of the Burning Lamp

FALSTAFF: Do thou amend thy face, and I'll amend my life: thou
art our admiral, thou bearest the lantern in the poop, but
'tis in the nose of thee; thou art the Knight of the Burning
Lamp.

BARDOLPH: Why, Sir John, my face does you no harm.

FALSTAFF: No, I'll be sworn; I make as good use of it as many a
man doth of a Death's-head or a memento mori: I never
see thy face but I think upon hell-fire and Dives that liv'd
in purple; for there he is in his robes, burning, burning. If
thou wert any way given to virtue, I would swear by thy
face; my oath should be 'By this fire, that's God's angel':
but thou art altogether given over; and wert indeed, but
for the light in thy face, the son of utter darkness. When
thou ran'st up Gadshill in the night to catch my horse, if I
did not think thou hadst been an ignis fatuus or a ball of
wildfire, there's no purchase in money. O, thou art a
perpetual triumph, an everlasting bonfire-light! Thou has
saved me a thousand marks in links and torches, walking
with thee in the night betwixt tavern and tavern: but the
sack that thou hast drunk me would have bought me lights

as good cheap at the dearest chandler's in Europe. I have maintain'd that salamander of yours with fire any time this two and thirty years; God reward me for it!

BARDOLPH: 'Sblood, I would my face were in your belly!

FALSTAFF: God-a-mercy! so should I be sure to be heart-burn'd.

HENRY IV, PT. I, III. iii. 27–59


### 6 Twin Characters of Falstaff

PRINCE HENRY: Thou art violently carried away from grace: there is a devil haunts thee in the likeness of an old fat man; a tun of man is thy companion. Why dost thou converse with that trunk of humours, that bolting-hutch of beastliness, that swollen parcel of dropsies, that huge bombard of sack, that stuff'd cloak-bag of guts, that roasted Manningtree ox with the pudding in his belly, that reverend vice, that grey iniquity, that father ruffian, that vanity in years? Wherein is he good, but to taste sack and drink it? wherein neat and cleanly, but to carve a capon and eat it? wherein cunning, but in craft? wherein crafty, but in villainy? wherein villainous, but in all things? wherein worthy, but in nothing?

FALSTAFF: I would your grace would take me with you: whom means your grace?

PRINCE HENRY: That villainous abominable misleader of youth, Falstaff, that old white-bearded Satan.

FALSTAFF: My lord, the man I know.

PRINCE HENRY: I know thou dost.

FALSTAFF: But to say I know more harm in him than in myself, were to say more than I know. That he is old, the more the pity, his white hairs do witness it. If sack and sugar be a fault, God help the wicked! if to be old and merry be a sin, then many an old host that I know is damned: if to be fat be to be hated, then Pharaoh's lean kine are to be loved. No, my good lord; banish Peto, banish Bardolph, banish

10

Poins: but for sweet Jack Falstaff, kind Jack Falstaff, true Jack Falstaff, valiant Jack Falstaff, and therefore more valiant, being, as he is, old Jack Falstaff, banish not him thy Harry's company: banish plump Jack, and banish all the world.

PRINCE HENRY: I do, I will.

HENRY IV, PT. I, II. iv. 497–536

## 7 *Falstaff Young and Falstaff Old*

FALSTAFF: You that are old consider not the capacities of us that are young; you do measure the heat of your livers with the bitterness of your galls: and we that are in the vaward of our youth, I must confess, are wags, too.

CHIEF JUSTICE: Do you set down your name in the scroll of youth, that are written down old with all the characters of age? Have you not a moist eye? a dry hand? a yellow cheek? a white beard? a decreasing leg? an increasing belly? is not your voice broken? your wind short? your chin double? your wit single? and every part about you blasted with antiquity? and will you yet call yourself young? Fie, fie, fie, Sir John!

FALSTAFF: My lord, I was born about three of the clock in the afternoon, with a white head and something a round belly. For my voice, I have lost it with halloing and singing of anthems. To approve my youth further, I will not: the truth is, I am only old in judgment and understanding; and he that will caper with me for a thousand marks, let him lend me the money, and have at him! For the box of the ear that the prince gave you, he gave it like a rude prince, and you took it like a sensible lord. I have check'd him for it, and the young lion repents; marry, not in ashes and sackcloth, but in new silk and old sack.

HENRY IV, PT. II, I. ii. 198–226

8 *Character of a Good Companion*

DOLL: They say Poins has a good wit.

FALSTAFF: He a good wit? hang him, baboon! his wit's as thick
as Tewksbury mustard; there's no more conceit in him
than is in a mallet.

DOLL: Why does the prince love him so, then?

FALSTAFF: Because their legs are both of a bigness, and a plays at
quoits well, and eats conger and fennel, and drinks off
candles' ends for flap-dragons, and rides the wild-mare
with the boys, and jumps upon join'd-stools, and swears
with a good grace, and wears his boots very smooth, like
unto the sign of The Leg, and breeds no bate with telling
of discreet stories; and such other gambol faculties a has,
that show a weak mind and an able body, for the which the
prince admits him: for the prince himself is such another;
the weight of a hair will turn the scales between their
avoirdupois.

HENRY IV, PT. II, II. iv. 260–277

9 *Like Justice Like Man*

FALSTAFF: If I were saw'd into quantities, I should make four
dozen of such bearded hermit staves as Master Shallow. It
is a wonderful thing to see the semblable coherence of his
men's spirits and his: they, by observing of him, do bear
themselves like foolish justices; he, by conversing with
them, is turned into a justice-like serving-man: their spirits
are so married in conjunction with the participation of
society that they flock together in consent, like so many
wild-geese. If I had a suit to Master Shallow, I would
humour his men, I would curry with Master Shallow that
no man could better command his servants. It is certain
that either wise bearing or ignorant carriage is caught,
as men take diseases, one of another: therefore let men
take heed of their company.

HENRY IV, PT. I, V. i. 68–86

10 *A Man in his Humours*

DON JOHN: I wonder that thou, being—as thou sayest thou art
—born under Saturn, goest about to apply a moral medicine to a mortifying mischief. I cannot hide what I am: I
must be sad when I have cause, and smile at no man's jests;
eat when I have stomach, and wait for no man's leisure;
sleep when I am drowsy, and tend on no man's business;
laugh when I am merry, and claw no man in his humour.

MUCH ADO ABOUT NOTHING, I. iii. 10–19

11 *A Man Hard to Please*

BENEDICT: I will not be sworn but love may transform me to an
oyster: but I'll take my oath on it, till he have made an
oyster of me, he shall never make me such a fool. One
woman is fair, yet I am well; another is wise, yet I am
well; another virtuous, yet I am well; but till all graces be
in one woman, one woman shall not come in my grace.
Rich she shall be, that's certain; wise, or I'll none; virtuous,
or I'll never cheapen her; fair, or I'll never look on her;
mild, or come not near me; noble, or not I for an angel;
of good discourse, an excellent musician, and her hair shall
be of what colour it please God.

MUCH ADO ABOUT NOTHING, II. iii. 24–37

12 *The Humour of Hate*

SHYLOCK: You'll ask me, why I rather choose to have
A weight of carrion flesh than to receive
Three thousand ducats: I'll not answer that:
But, say, it is my humour: is it answer'd?
What if my house be trouble with a rat
And I be pleased to give ten thousand ducats
To have it baned? What, are you answer'd yet?
Some men there are love not a gaping pig;
Some, that are mad if they behold a cat;
And others, at the bagpipe; for affection,

Mistress of passion, sways it to the mood
Of what it likes or loathes. Now, for your answer:
As there is no firm reason to be render'd,
Why he cannot abide a gaping pig;
Why he, a harmless necessary cat;
Why he, a wollen bagpipe;
So can I give no reason, nor I will not,
More than a lodged hate and a certain loathing
I bear Antonio, that I follow thus
A losing suit against him. Are you answer'd?

THE MERCHANT OF VENICE, IV. i. 40–62

## 13 *A Humour of Perversity*

HERO: Why, you speak truth. I never yet saw man,
    How wise, how noble, young, how rarely featured,
    But she would spell him backward: if fair-faced,
    She would swear the gentleman should be her sister;
    If black, why, nature, drawing of an antique,
    Made a foul blot; if tall, a lance ill-headed;
    If low, an agate very vildly cut;
    If speaking, why, a vane blown with all winds;
    If silent, why, a block moved with none.
    So turns she every man the wrong side out,
    And never gives to truth and virtue that
    Which simpleness and merit purchaseth.

MUCH ADO ABOUT NOTHING, III. i. 59–70

## 14 *Wit Discredited*

BENEDICT: Sir, you wit ambles well; it goes easily.
DON PEDRO: I'll tell thee how Beatrice praised thy wit the other
    day. I said, thou hadst a fine wit: 'True', said she, 'a fine
    little one.' 'No', said I, 'a great wit': 'Right', says she, 'a
    great gross one.' 'Nay', said I, 'a good wit': 'Just', said she,
    'it hurts nobody.' 'Nay', said I, 'the gentleman is wise':
    'Certain', said she, 'a wise gentleman.' 'Nay', said I, 'he

hath the tongues': 'That I believe', said she, 'for he swore
a thing to me on Monday night, which he foreswore on
Tuesday morning; there's a double tongue; there's two
tongues.' Thus did she, an hour together, trans-shape thy
particular virtues: yet at last she concluded with a sigh,
thou was the properest man in Italy.

MUCH ADO ABOUT NOTHING, V. i. 162–178


15 *The Lean Thinker*

CAESAR: Let me have men about me that are fat:
　　　Sleek-headed men and such as sleep o'nights:
　　　Yond Cassius has a lean and hungry look;
　　　He thinks too much: such men are dangerous.
ANTONY: Fear him not, Caesar; he's not dangerous;
　　　He is a noble Roman and well given.
CAESAR: Would he were fatter! But I fear him not:
　　　Yet if my name were liable to fear,
　　　I do not know the man I should avoid
　　　So soon as that spare Cassius. He reads much;
　　　He is a great observer and he looks
　　　Quite through the deeds of men; he loves no plays,
　　　As thou dost, Antony; he hears no music;
　　　Seldom he smiles, and smiles in such a sort
　　　As if he mock'd himself and scorn'd his spirit
　　　That could be moved to smile at any thing.
　　　Such men as he be never at heart's ease
　　　Whiles they behold a greater than themselves,
　　　And therefore are they very dangerous.

JULIUS CAESAR, I. ii. 191–209


16 *An Associate Fit and Unfit*

CASSIUS: But what of Cicero? shall we sound him?
　　　I think he will stand very strong with us.
CASCA: Let us not leave him out.

CINNA:                                No, by no means.
METELLUS: O let us have him, for his silver hairs
    Will purchase us a good opinion
    And buy men's voices to commend our deeds:
    It shall be said, his judgment ruled our hands:
    Our youths and wildness shall no whit appear,
    But all be buried in his gravity.
BRUTUS: O, name him not: let us not break with him:
    For he will never follow any thing
    That other men begin.
CASSIUS:                        Then leave him out.
CASCA: Indeed he is not fit.

                          JULIUS CAESAR, II. i. 141–153


## 17 *A Man in Suspense*

BRUTUS: Since Cassius first did whet me against Caesar,
    I have not slept.
    Between the acting of a dreadful thing
    And the first motion, all the interim is
    Like a phantasma, or a hideous dream:
    The Genius and the mortal instruments
    Are then in council; and the state of man,
    Like to a little kingdom, suffers then
    The nature of an insurrection.

                          JULIUS CAESAR, II. i. 61–69


## 18 *A Man Perturbed*

BRUTUS: Portia, what mean you? wherefore rise you now?
    It is not for your health thus to commit
    Your weak condition to the raw cold morning.
PORTIA: Not for yours neither. You've ungently, Brutus,
    Stole from my bed: and yesternight, at supper,
    You suddenly arose, and walk'd about,
    Musing and sighing, with your arms across,
    And when I ask'd you what the matter was,

You stared upon me with ungentle looks;
I urged you further; then you scratch'd your head,
And too impatiently stamp'd with your foot;
Yet I insisted, yet you answer'd not,
But, with an angry wafture of your hand,
Gave sign for me to leave you: so I did;
Fearing to strengthen that impatience
Which seem'd too much enkindled, and withal
Hoping it was but an effect of humour,
Which sometime hath his hour with every man.
It will not let you eat, nor talk, nor sleep,
And could it work so much upon your shape
As it hath much prevail'd on your condition,
I should not know you, Brutus. Dear my lord,
Make me acquainted with your cause of grief.

JULIUS CAESAR, II. i. 234–256


19 *A Plain Man, No Orator*

ANTONY: I come not, friends, to steal away your hearts:
I am no orator, as Brutus is;
But, as you know me all, a plain blunt man,
That love my friend; and that they know full well
That gave me public leave to speak of him:
For I have neither wit, nor words, nor worth,
Action, nor utterance, nor the power of speech,
To stir men's blood: I only speak right on;
I tell you that which you yourselves do know;
Show you sweet Caesar's wounds, poor poor dumb
      mouths,
And bid them speak for me: but were I Brutus,
And Brutus Antony, there were an Antony
Would ruffle up your spirits and put a tongue
In every wound of Caesar that should move
The stones of Rome to rise and mutiny.

JULIUS CAESAR, III. ii. 220–234

20 *A Friend Too Common*

CASSIUS: And be not jealous on me, gentle Brutus:
 Were I a common laugher, or did use
 To stale with ordinary oaths my love
 To every new protester; if you know
 That I do fawn on men and hug them hard
 And after scandal them; or if you know
 That I profess myself in banqueting
 To all the rout, then hold me dangerous.

       JULIUS CAESAR, I. ii. 71–78

21 *A Choice Friend*

BASSANIO: The dearest friend to me, the kindest man,
 The best-condition'd and unwearied spirit
 In doing courtesies, and one in whom
 The ancient Roman honour more appears
 Than any that draws breath in Italy.

    THE MERCHANT OF VENICE, III. ii. 293–297

22 *A Hot Friend Cooling*

BRUTUS:       A word, Lucilius,
 How he received you: let me be resolved.
LUCILIUS: With courtesy and with respect enough;
 But not with such familiar instances,
 Nor with such free and friendly conference,
 As he hath used of old.
BRUTUS:      Thou hast described
 A hot friend cooling: ever note, Lucilius,
 When love begins to sicken and decay,
 It useth an enforced ceremony.
 There are no tricks in plain and simple faith;
 But hollow men, like horses hot at hand,

Make gallant show and promise of their mettle;
But when they should endure the bloody spur
They fall their crests, and, like deceitful jades,
Sink in the trial.

JULIUS CAESAR, IV. ii. 13–27

## 23 *Two Characters in One—A Foolish Talented Knight*

MARIA: That quaffing and drinking will undo you: I heard my
lady talk of it yesterday; and of a foolish knight that you
brought in one night here to be her wooer.

SIR TOBY: Who, Sir Andrew Aguecheek?

MARIA: Ay, he.

SIR TOBY: He's as tall a man as any's in Illyria.

MARIA: What's that to the purpose?

SIR TOBY: Why, he has three thousand ducats a year.

MARIA: Ay, but he'll have but a year in all these ducats: he's a
very fool and a prodigal.

SIR TOBY: Fie, that you'll say so! he plays o' the viol-de-gam-
boys, and speaks three or four languages word for word
without book, and hath all the good gifts of nature.

MARIA: He hath, indeed, almost natural: for, besides that he's a
fool, he's a great quarreller; and, but that he hath the gift
of a coward to alley the gust he hath in quarrelling, 'tis
thought among the prudent he would quickly have the
gift of a grave.

SIR TOBY: By this hand, they are scoundrels and substractors that
say so of him. Who are they?

MARIA: They that add, moreover, he's drunk nightly in your
company.

SIR TOBY: With drinking healths to my niece: I'll drink to her
as long as there is a passage in my throat and drink in
Illyria: he's a coward and a coystril that will not drink to
my niece till his brains turn o' the toe like a parish-top.
What, wench! Castiliano vulgo; for her comes Sir Andrew
Agueface.

TWELFTH NIGHT, I. iii. 15–48

24 *A Changeable Man*

DUKE: Give me now leave to leave thee.

CLOWN: Now, the melancholy god protect thee: and the tailor make thy doublet of changeable taffeta, for thy mind is very opal! I would have men of such constancy put to sea, that their business might be every thing, and their intent every where; for that's it that always makes a good voyage of nothing. Farewell.

TWELFTH NIGHT, II. iv. 73–80

25 *An Aspirant to Greatness*

MALVOLIO: (*Reads*) "If this fall into thy hand, revolve. In my stars I am above thee; but be not afraid of greatness: some are born great, some achieve greatness, and some have greatness thrust upon 'em. Thy Fates open their hands; let thy blood and spirit embrace them: and, to inure thyself to what thou art like to be, cast thy humble slough and appear fresh. Be opposite with a kinsman, surly with servants; let thy tongue tang arguments of state; put thyself into the trick of singularity; she thus advises thee that sighs for thee. Remember who commended thy yellow stockings, and wished to see thee ever cross-gartered: I say, remember. Go to, thou art made, if thou desirest to be so; if not, let me see thee a steward still, the fellow of servants, and not worthy to touch Fortune's fingers. Farewell. She that would alter services with thee.

THE FORTUNATE-UNHAPPY."

Daylight and champain discovers not more: this is open. I will be proud, I will read politic authors, I will baffle Sir Toby, I will wash off gross acquaintance, I will be point-devise the very man. I do not now fool myself, to let imagination jade me; for every reason excites to this, that my lady loves me.

TWELFTH NIGHT, II. v. 157–180

26 *A Stout Fellow*

DUKE: That face of his I do remember well;
    Yet, when I saw it last, it was besmear'd
    As black as Vulcan in the smoke of war:
    A bawbling vessel was he captain of,
    For shallow draught and bulk unprizable;
    With which such scatheful grapple did he make
    With the most noble bottom of our fleet,
    That very envy and the tongue of loss
    Cried fame and honour on him.—What's the matter?

                    TWELFTH NIGHT, V. i. 55–63


27 *Prudence Personified*

POLONIUS: And these few precepts in thy memory
    Look thou character. Give thy thoughts no tongue,
    Nor any unproportioned thought his act.
    Be thou familiar, but by no means vulgar.
    Those friends thou hast, and their adoption tried,
    Grapple them to thy soul with hoops of steel;
    But do not dull thy palm with entertainment
    Of each new-hatched, unfledged comrade.
    Beware
    Of entrance to a quarrel; but being in,
    Bear't that the opposed may beware of thee.
    Give every man thy ear, but few thy voice;
    Take each man's censure, but reserve thy judgement.
    Costly thy habit as thy purse can buy,
    But not expressed in fancy; rich, not gaudy;
    For the apparel oft proclaims the man,
    And they in France of the best rank and station
    Are of a most select and generous chief in that.
    Neither a borrower nor a lender be;
    For loan oft loses both itself and friend,
    And borrowing dulls the edge of husbandry.
    This above all: to thine own self be true,

And it must follow, as the night the day,
Thou canst not then be false to any man.

HAMLET, I. iii. 58–80

## 28 Old Men

POLONIUS: I mean the matter that you read, my lord.

HAMLET: Slanders, sir; for the satirical rogue says here that old
men have grey beards, that their faces are wrinkled, their
eyes purging thick amber and plum-tree gum, and that
they have a plentiful lack of wit, together with most weak
hams; all which, sir, though I most powerfully and
potently believe, yet I hold it not honesty to have it thus
set down; for yourself, sir, shall grow old as I am, if, like
a crab, you could go backward.

HAMLET, II. ii. 200–210

## 29 A Complete Man

ANTONY: This was the noblest Roman of them all:
All the conspirators, save only he,
Did that they did in envy of great Caesar;
He only, in a general honest thought
And common good to all, made one of them.
His life was gentle, and the elements
So mix'd in him that Nature might stand up
And say to all the world 'This was a man!'

JULIUS CAESAR, V. v. 68–75

## 30 The Well-Balanced Man

HAMLET: Horatio, thou art e'en as just a man
As e'er my conversation coped withal.

HORATIO: O, my dear lord,—

HAMLET:                              Nay, do not think I flatter,
For what advancement may I hope from thee
That no revenue hast but thy good spirits

To feed and clothe thee? Why should the poor be flattered?
No, let the candied tongue lick absurd pomp,
And crook the pregnant hinges of the knee
Where thrift may follow fawning. Dost thou hear?
Since my dear soul was mistress of her choice
And could of men distinguish, her election
Hath sealed thee for herself; for thou hast been
As one, in suffering all, that suffers nothing,
A man that fortune's buffets and rewards
Hath ta'en with equal thanks; and blest are those
Whose blood and judgement are so well commingled,
That they are not a pipe for fortune's finger
To sound what stop she please. Give me that man
That is not passion's slave, and I will wear him
In my heart's core, ay, in my heart of heart,
As I do thee.

HAMLET, III. ii. 59–79

### 31 *A Composite Brute*

ALEXANDER: The noise goes, this: there is among the Greeks
    A lord of Trojan blood, nephew to Hector;
    They call him Ajax.

CRESSIDA:              Good; and what of him?

ALEXANDER: They say he is a very man *per se*,
    And stands alone.

CRESSIDA: So do all men; unless they are drunk, sick, or have
    no legs.

ALEXANDER: This man, lady, hath robbed many beasts of their
    particular additions: he is as valiant as the lion, churlish as
    the bear, slow as the elephant; a man into whom nature
    hath so crowded humours that his valour is crushed into
    folly, his folly sauced with discretion: there is no man hath
    a virtue that he hath not a glimpse of, nor any man an
    attaint but he carries some stain of it: he is melancholy
    without cause, and merry against the hair: he hath the
    joints of everything, but everything so out of joint that

he is a gouty Briareus, many hands and no use; or purblind
Argus, all eyes and no sight.

TROILUS AND CRESSIDA, I. ii. 12–31

## 32 *A Merry Sound Man*

DON PEDRO: I will only be bold with Benedick for his company;
for, from the crown of his head to the sole of his foot, he is
all mirth: he hath twice or thrice cut Cupid's bow-string,
and the little hangman dare not shoot at him. He hath a
heart as sound as a bell and his tongue is the clapper, for
what his heart thinks his tongue speaks.

MUCH ADO ABOUT NOTHING, III. ii. 7–14

## 33 *A Shrewd Sound Man*

PANDEVUS: That's Antenor: he has a shrewd wit, I can tell you;
and he's a man good enough: he's one o' the soundest judgments in Troy, whosoever, and a proper man of person.

TROILUS AND CRESSIDA, I. ii. 202–206

## 34 *The Spice and Salt of a Man*

PANDARUS: 'Well, well!' Why, have you any discretion? have
you any eyes? Do you know what a man is? Is not birth,
beauty, good shape, discourse, manhood, learning, gentle-
ness, virtue, youth, liberality, and such like, the spice and
salt that season a man?

TROILUS AND CRESSIDA, I. ii. 271–276

## 35 *A Plaguy Proud Man*

ULYSSES: Achilles will not to the field to-morrow.
AGAMEMNON: What's his excuse?
ULYSSES:                                          He doth rely on none,
But carries on the stream of his dispose
Without observance or respect of any,
In will peculiar and in self-admission.
AGAMEMNON: Why will he not upon our fair request
Untent his person and share the air with us?

ULYSSES: Things small as nothing, for request's sake only,
 He makes important: possess'd he is with greatness,
 And speaks not to himself but with a pride
 That quarrels at self-breath: imagin'd worth
 Holds in his blood such swoln and hot discourse,
 That 'twixt his mental and his active parts
 Kingdom'd Achilles in commotion rages
 And batters down himself: what should I say?
 He is so plaguy proud that the death-tokens of it
 Cry 'No recovery'.

      TROILUS AND CRESSIDA, II. iii. 174–190

## 36 *A Monstrous Fine Fellow*

NESTOR: What a vice were it in Ajax now,—
ULYSSES: If he were proud,—
DIOMEDES:        Or covetous of praise,—
ULYSSES: Ay, or surly borne,—
DIOMEDES:        Or strange, or self-affected!
ULYSSES: Thank the heavens, lord, thou art of sweet composure;
 Praise him that got thee, she that gave thee suck:
 Fam'd be thy tutor, and thy parts of nature
 Thrice-fam'd, beyond all erudition:
 But he that disciplin'd thine arms to fight,
 Let Mars divide eternity in twain,
 And give him half: and, for thy vigour,
 Bull-bearing Milo his addition yield
 To sinewy Ajax. I will not praise thy wisdom,
 Which, like a bourn, a pale, a shore, confines
 Thy spacious and dilated parts: here's Nestor,
 Instructed by the antiquary times,
 He must, he is, he cannot but be wise;
 But pardon, father Nestor, were your days
 As green as Ajax' and your brain so temper'd,
 You should not have the eminence of him,
 But be as Ajax.

      TROILUS AND CRESSIDA, II. iii. 249–270

Quid dabitis

Proditorum finis
funis

Lopez compounding to poyson the Queene.

THE COVERT TRAITOR — DR. LOPEZ

20

30

Sir John Russell was also taken there, who
faining himselfe to be out of his wittes, escaped A politike
their hands for a time. In this meane time, king madnesse.
Richard advertised, how the Duke of Lancaster
was landed in Englãd, & that the Lords, Gẽtle-
men & Cõmons, assembled thẽselues to take hys
40 part, he forthwith caused ý L. Henry, son to the

THE CATERPILLARS OF THE COMMONWEALTH

*Le narici aperte d'vn generoso Cauallo, & dell'huomo.*

Et in vn'altro luogo le narici aperte, schiacciate dimostrano iracondi, e si riferiscono a caualli generosi: e nella figura dell'iracondo gli da le narici concaue, & aperte. Adamantio le narici patenti son testimonio di ferocità, e d'ira. Suetonio scriue, Caio Cesare esser stato di bocca spumosa, e di narici humide, e sù dira assai feruente, e precipitosa.

#### Narici chiuse.

Al contrario le narici serrate, e strette dimostrano pazzi, dice Polemone: ma Adamantio dice altramente, & assai meglio: le narici strette, rotonde, e riserrate dimostrano pazzia. Alberto il medesimo; e dice quelle narici così serrate, e grosse, e chiuse, che appena odorino. Pianta, come scriue Filostrato nella sua imagine, haueua le narici ristrette, in modo, che faceuano baie al paso.

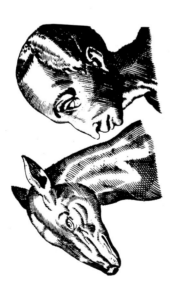

*L'orecchie del cane picciole, e distese con l'orecchie dell'huomo.*

*Orecchie picciole, e distese.*

L'orecchie picciole, e distese dimostrano stoltitia, perche tali si veggono ne' cani. Ma Ad mantio dice al rimen e da Polemone: Essendo l'orecchie mol e picciole, e come taglia-te d'intorno, dimostrano stoltitia: Mi il resto di Polemon: è corrotto, perche attribuisce la stoltitia a cani, a'quali muno de' restani Filosofi l'hà attribuito, ouero ci gl i ru i za de' cani custodi domestici. Alberd. Lossio: Le pu iol, e breui orecchie dicono notare stoltitia.

37 *A Promise-Breaker*

THERSITES: That same Diomed's a false-hearted rogue, a most
unjust knave; I will no more trust him when he leers than
I will a serpent when he hisses. He will spend his mouth,
and promise, like Brabbler the hound; but when he per-
forms, astronomers foretell it: it is prodigious, there will
come some change: the sun borrows of the moon when
Diomed keeps his word. I will rather leave to see Hector,
than not to dog him: they say he keeps a Trojan drab, and
uses the traitor Calchas' tent. I'll after. Nothing but lechery!
all incontinent varlets!

TROILUS AND CRESSIDA, V. i. 98–110

38 *Philosophical Persons*

LAFEU: They say miracles are past; and we have our philosophical persons, to make modern and familiar, things
supernatural and causeless. Hence it is that we make
trifles of terrors, ensconcing ourselves into seeming
knowledge, when we should submit ourselves to an unknown fear.

PAROLLES: Why, 'tis the rarest argument of wonder that hath
shot out in our latter times.

ALL'S WELL THAT ENDS WELL, II. iii. 1–8

39 *A Melancholy Man*

CLOWN: By my troth, I take my young lord to be a very
melancholy man.

COUNTESS: By what observance, I pray you?

CLOWN: Why, he will look upon his boot and sing; mend the
ruff and sing; ask questions and sing; pick his teeth and
sing. I know a man had this trick of melancholy sold a
goodly manor for a song.

ALL'S WELL THAT ENDS WELL, III. ii. 3–10

40 *Helpless Wretches*

LEAR: Poor naked wretches, wheresoe'er you are,
That bide the pelting of this pitiless storm,
How shall your houseless heads and unfed sides,
Your loop'd and window'd raggedness, defend you
From seasons such as these?

KING LEAR, III. iv. 28–32


41 *Underdogs*

CORIOLANUS: I muse my mother
Does not approve me further, who was wont
To call them woollen vassals, things created
To buy and sell with groats, to shew bare heads
In congregations, to yawn, be still, and wonder,
When one but of my ordinance stood up
To speak of peace or war.

CORIOLANUS, III. ii. 7–13


42 *A Cheese-Paring of a Man*

FALSTAFF: As I return, I will fetch off these justices: I do see the bottom of Justice Shallow. Lord, Lord, how subject we old men are to this vice of lying! This same starv'd justice hath done nothing but prate to me of the wildness of his youth, and the feats he hath done about Turnbull Street; and every third word a lie, duer paid to the hearer than the Turk's tribute. I do remember him at Clement's Inn like a man made after supper of a cheeseparing: when a was naked, he was, for all the world, like a forked radish, with a head fantastically carv'd upon it with a knife: a was so forlorn, that his dimensions to any thick sight were invincible: a was the very genius of famine; a came ever in the rearward of the fashion, and sung those tunes to the over-scutch'd huswives that he heard the carmen whistle, and sware they were his fancies or his good-nights. And

now is this Vice's dagger become a squire, and talks as
familiarly of John a Gaunt as if he had been sworn brother
to him; and I'll be sworn a ne'er saw him but once in the
Tilt-yard; and then he burst his head for crowding among
the marshal's men. I saw it, and told John a Gaunt he beat
his own name; for you might have thrust him and all his
apparel into an eel-skin; and case of a treble hautboy was a
mansion for him, a court: and now has he land and beefs.
Well, I'll be acquainted with him, if I return; and it shall
go hard but I will make him a philosopher's two stones to
me: if the young dace be a bait for the old pike, I see no
reason in the law of nature but I may snap at him. Let time
shape, and there an end.

HENRY IV, PT. II, III. ii. 326–361

## 43 *An Unmeritable Man*

ANTONY: This is a slight unmeritable man,
    Meet to be sent on errands: is it fit,
    The three-fold world divided, he should stand
    One of the three to share it?
OCTAVIUS:                    So you thought him,
    And took his voice who should be prick'd to die,
    In our black sentence and proscription.
ANTONY: Octavius, I have seen more days than you:
    And though we lay these honours on this man,
    To ease ourselves of divers slanderous loads,
    He shall but bear them as the ass bears gold,
    To groan and sweat under the business,
    Either led or driven, as we point the way;
    And having brought our treasure where we will,
    Then take we down his load and turn him off,
    Like to the empty ass, to shake his ears,
    And graze in commons.
OCTAVIUS:                You may do your will;
    But he's a tried and valiant soldier.

ANTONY: So is my horse, Octavius; and for that
    I do appoint him store of provender:
    It is a creature that I teach to fight,
    To wind, to stop, to run directly on,
    His corporal motion govern'd by my spirit.
    And, in some taste, is Lepidus but so;
    He must be taught, and train'd, and bid go forth;
    A barren-spirited fellow; one that feeds
    On abjects, orts and imitations,
    Which, out of use and staled by other men,
    Begin his fashion: do not talk of him,
    But as a property.

JULIUS CAESAR, IV. i. 12–40

## 44 *A Light Nut*

LAFEU: Fare you well, my lord; and believe this of me, there
can be no kernel in this light nut; the soul of this man is his
clothes. Trust him not in matter of heavy consequences;
I have kept of them tame, and know their natures. Farewell, monsieur: I have spoken better of you that you have
or will to deserve at my hand; but we must do good
against evil.

ALL'S WELL THAT ENDS WELL, II. V. 47–54

## 45 *A Bubble*

FIRST LORD: On my life, my lord, a bubble.
BERTRAM: Do you think I am so far deceived in him?
FIRST LORD: Believe it, my lord, in mine own direct knowledge,
without any malice, but to speak of him as my kinsman,
he's a most notable coward, an infinite and endless liar, an
hourly promise-breaker, the owner of no one good quality
worthy of your lordship's entertainment.

ALL'S WELL THAT ENDS WELL, III. vi. 5–12

46 *The Conscious Worm*

PAROLLES: Yet am I thankful: if my heart were great
  'Twould burst at this. Captain I'll be no more;
  But I will eat and drink, and sleep as soft
  As captain shall: simply the thing I am
  Shall make me live. Who knows himself a braggart,
  Let him fear this; for it will come to pass
  That every braggart shall be found an ass.
  Rust, sword! cool, blushes! and, Parolles, live
  Safest in shame! being fool'd, by foolery thrive!
  There's place and means for every man alive.
  I'll after them.

ALL'S WELL THAT ENDS WELL, IV. iii. 370-380

47 *A Hard Man*

ISABELLA: Can this be so? Did Angelo so leave her?
DUKE: Left her in her tears, and dried not one of them with his
  comfort; swallowed his vows whole, pretending in her
  discoveries of dishonour: in few, bestowed her on her own
  lamentation, which she yet wears for his sake, and he, a
  marble to her tears, is washed with them, but relents not.

MEASURE FOR MEASURE, III. i. 232-239

48 *A Cold Man*

LUCIO: They say this Angelo was not made by man and woman
  after this downright way of creation: is it true, think you?
DUKE: How should he be made, then?
LUCIO: Some report a sea-maid spawned him; some, that he
  was begot between two stock-fishes. But it is certain that
  when he makes water his urine is congealed ice; that I
  know to be true; and he is a motion generative; that's
  infallible.

MEASURE FOR MEASURE, III. ii. 113-121

49 *An Inveterate Foe*

SALANIO:                                    Not one, my lord.
Besides, it should appear, that if he had
The present money to discharge the Jew,
He would not take it. Never did I know
A creature, that did bear the shape of man,
So keen and greedy to confound a man:
He plies the duke at morning and at night,
And doth impeach the freedom of the state,
If they deny him justice: twenty merchants,
The duke himself, and the magnificoes
Of greatest port, have all persuaded with him;
But none can drive him from the envious plea
Of forfeiture, of justice and his bond.
JESSICA: When I was with him I have heard him swear
To Tubal and to Chus, his countrymen,
That he would rather have Antonio's flesh
Than twenty times the value of the sum
That he did owe him: and I know, my lord,
If law, authority and power deny not,
It will go hard with poor Antonio.

THE MERCHANT OF VENICE, III. ii. 272–291


50. *One Set on Revenge*

IAGO: Patience, I say; your mind perhaps may change.
OTHELLO: Never, Iago. Like to the Pontic sea,
Whose icy current and compulsive course
Ne'er feels retiring ebb, but keeps due on
To the Propontic and the Hellespont;
Even so my bloody thoughts, with violent pace,
Shall ne'er look back, ne'er ebb to humble love,
Till that a capable and wide revenge
Swallow them up. Now, by yond marble heaven,
In the due reverence of a sacred vow          (*Kneels*)
I here engage my words.

OTHELLO, III. iii. 453–463

51 *A Self-Feeder*

VOLUMNIA: Anger's my meat; I sup upon myself,
And so shall sterve with feeding. Come, let's go.
Leave this faint puling and lament as I do,
In anger, Juno-like. Come, come, come.

CORIOLANUS, IV. ii. 50–53

52 *One Not Ruthless*

LADY MACBETH:                    Art thou afeard
To be the same in thine own act and valour
As thou art in desire? Wouldst thou have that
Which thou esteem'st the ornament of life,
And live a coward in thine own esteem,
Letting 'I dare not' wait upon 'I would',
Like the poor cat i' the adage?

MACBETH, I. vii. 39–45

53 *One Insensible of Mortality*

DUKE: Hath he borne himself penitently in prison? how seems
he to be touched?

PROVOST: A man that apprehends death no more dreadfully but
as a drunken sleep; careless, reckless, and fearless of what's
past, present, or to come; insensible of mortality, and
desperately mortal.

DUKE: He wants advice.

PROVOST: He will hear none. He hath evermore had the liberty
of the prison: give him leave to escape hence, he would
not: drunk many times a day, if not many days entirely
drunk. We have very oft awaked him, as if to carry him to
execution, and showed him a seeming warrant for it: it
hath not moved him at all.

MEASURE FOR MEASURE, IV. ii. 146–160

### 54 *A Man Disillusioned*

MACBETH: Had I but died an hour before this chance,
 I had lived a blessed time; for, from this instant,
 There's nothing serious in mortality:
 All is but toys: renown and grace is dead;
 The wine of life is drawn, and the mere lees
 Is left this vault to brag of.

MACBETH, II. iii. 98–103

### 55 *A Man Born Lucky*

ANTONY:          Say to me,
 Whose fortunes shall rise higher, Caesar's or mine?
SOOTHSAYER: Caesar's.
 Therefore, O Antony, stay not by his side:
 Thy demon—that's thy spirit which keeps thee—is
 Noble, courageous, high, unmatchable,
 Where Caesar's is not; but, near him, thy angel
 Becomes a fear, as being o'erpower'd: therefore
 Make space enough between you.
ANTONY:          Speak this no more.
SOOTHSAYER: To none but thee; no more, but when to thee.
 If thou dost play with him at any game,
 Thou art sure to lose; and, of that natural luck,
 He beats thee 'gainst the odds: thy lustre thickens,
 When he shines by: I say again, thy spirit
 Is all afraid to govern thee near him;
 But, he away, 'tis noble.
ANTONY:        Get thee gone:
 Say to Ventidius I would speak with him:

(*Exit Soothsayer*)

 He shall to Parthia. Be it art or hap,
 He hath spoken true: the very dice obey him;
 And in our sports my better cunning faints
 Under his chance: if we draw lots, he speeds;
 His cocks do win the battle still of mine

When it is all to nought; and his quails ever
Beat mine, inhoop'd, at odds.

ANTONY AND CLEOPATRA, II. iii. 15–38


## 56 *Excessive Generosity*

FLAVIUS: (*Aside*) What will this come to?
He commands us to provide, and give great gifts,
And all out of an empty coffer:
Nor will he know his purse, or yield me this,
To show him what a beggar his heart is,
Being of no power to make his wishes good:
His promises fly so beyond his state
That what he speaks is all in debt; he owes
For every word: he is so kind that he now
Pays interest for 't; his land's put to their books.
Well, would I were gently put out of office
Before I were forc'd out!
Happier is he that has no friend to feed
Than such that do e'en enemies exceed.
I bleed inwardly for my lord.

TIMON OF ATHENS, I. ii. 200–214


## 57 *A Popular Hero* (*a*)

BRUTUS: All tongues speak of him, and the bleared sights
Are spectacled to see him: your prattling nurse
Into a rapture lets her baby cry
While she chats him: the kitchen malkin pins
Her richest lockram 'bout her reechy neck,
Clambering the walls to eye him: stalls, bulks, windows,
Are smother'd up, leads fill'd, and ridges hors'd
With variable complexions, all agreeing
In earnestness to see him: seld-shown flamens
Do press among the popular throngs, and puff
To win a vulgar station: our veil'd dames
Commit the war of white and damask in

Their nicely-gawded cheeks, to the wanton spoil
Of Phoebus' burning kisses: such a pother,
As if that whatsoever god who leads him
Were slily crept into his human powers,
And gave him graceful posture.

*CORIOLANUS*, II. i. 200–218

### 57 *A Popular Hero* (*b*)

BRUTUS:                          What's the matter?
MESSENGER; You are sent for to the Capitol. 'Tis thought
    That Marcius shall be consul.
    I have seen the dumb men throng to see him, and
    The blind to hear him speak: matrons flung gloves,
    Ladies and maids their scarfs and handkerchers,
    Upon him as he pass'd; the nobles bended,
    As to Jove's statue, and the commons made
    A shower and thunder with their caps and shouts:
    I never saw the like.

*CORIOLANUS*, II. i. 278–286

### 58 *A Shrewd Blunt Fellow*

BRUTUS: What a blunt fellow is this grown to be!
    He was quick mettle when he went to school.
CASSIUS: So is he now in execution
    Of any bold or noble enterprise,
    However he puts on this tardy form.
    This rudeness is a sauce to his good wit,
    Which gives men stomach to digest his words
    With better appetite.

*JULIUS CAESAR*, I. ii. 300–307

### 59. *A Humorous Blunt Politician*

MENENIUS: I am known to be a humorous patrician, and one
    that loves a cup of hot wine with not a drop of allaying
    Tiber in't; said to be something imperfect in favouring

the first complaint; hasty and tinder-like upon too trivial
motion; one that converses more with the buttock of the
night than with the forehead of the morning. What I
think I utter, and spend my malice in my breath. Meeting
two such weals-men as you are,—I cannot call you
Lycurguses—if the drink you give me touch my palate
adversely, I make a crooked face at it. I cannot say your
worships have delivered the matter well when I find the
ass in compound with the major part of your syllables; and
though I must be content to bear with those that say you
are reverend grave man, yet they lie deadly that tell you
have good faces. If you see this in the map of my micro-
cosm, follows it that I am known well enough too? What
harm can your bisson conspectuities glean out of this
character, if I be known well enough too?

BRUTUS: Come, sir, come, we know you well enough.

CORIOLANUS, II. i. 42–74

## 60 *Fearless Bluntness*

FIRST PATRICIAN: This man has marr'd his fortune.
MENENIUS: His nature is too noble for the world:
He would not flatter Neptune for his trident,
Or Jove for's power to thunder. His heart's his mouth:
What his breast forges, that his tongue must vent;
And, being angry, does forget that ever
He heard the name of death.        (*A noise within*)
Here's goodly work!

CORIOLANUS III. ii. 253–260

## 61 *Bold Swimmer*

FRANCISCO:            Sir, he may live.
I saw him beat the surges under him
And ride upon their backs. He trod the water,
Whose enmity he flung aside, and breasted
The surge most swol'n that met him. His bold head

'Bove the contentious waves he kept, and oar'd
Himself with his good arms in lusty stroke
To th' shore, that o'er his wave-worn basis bow'd,
As stooping to relieve him. I not doubt
He came alive to land.

THE TEMPEST, II. i. 120–129

### 1 *A Character of One Long-Imprisoned*

MORTIMER: Kind keepers of my weak decaying age,
 Let dying Mortimer here rest himself.
 Even like a man new haled from the rack,
 So fare my limbs with long imprisonment;
 And these grey locks, the pursuivants of death,
 Nestor-like aged in an age of care,
 Argue the end of Edmund Mortimer.
 These eyes, like lamps whose wasting oil is spent,
 Wax dim, as drawing to their exigent;
 Weak shoulders, overborne with burdening grief,
 And pithless arms, like to a wither'd vine
 That droops his sapless branches to the ground:
 Yet are these feet, whose strengthless stay is numb,
 Unable to support this lump of clay,
 Swift-winged with desire to get a grave,
 As witting I no other comfort have.

KING HENRY VI, PT. I, II. V. 1–16

### 2 *A Drugged Person*

FRIAR: Hold, then; go home, be merry, give consent
 To marry Paris: Wednesday is to-morrow:
 To-morrow night look that thou lie alone,
 Let not thy nurse lie with thee in thy chamber:
 Take thou this vial, being then in bed,
 And this distilled liquor drink thou off;
 When presently through all thy veins shall run
 A cold and drowsy humour; for no pulse
 Shall keep his native progress, but surcease;
 No warmth, no breath, shall testify thou livest;
 The roses in thy lips and cheeks shall fade
 To paly ashes; thy eyes' windows fall,

Like death, when he shuts up the day of life;
Each part, deprived of supple government,
Shall, stiff and stark and cold, appear like death;
And in this borrow'd likeness of shrunk death
Thou shalt continue two and forty hours,
And then awake as from a pleasant sleep.

ROMEO AND JULIET, IV. i. 89–106

## 3 *The Exile*

MOWBRAY: A dearer merit, not so deep a maim
As to be cast forth in the common air,
Have I deserved at your highness' hands
The language I have learn'd these forty years,
My native English, now I must forgo:
And now my tongue's use is to me no more
Than an unstringed viol or a harp,
Or like a cunning instrument cased up,
Or, being open, put into his hands
That knows no touch to tune the harmony:
Within my mouth you have engaol'd my tongue,
Doubly portcullis'd with my teeth and lips;
And dull unfeeling barren ignorance
Is made my gaoler to attend on me.
I am too old to fawn upon a nurse,
Too far in years to be a pupil now:
What is thy sentence then but speechless death,
Which robs my tongue from breathing native breath?

KING RICHARD II, I. iii. 156–173

## 4 *Just Judge Cruel Father*

KING RICHARD: Thy son is banish'd upon good advice,
Whereto thy tongue a party-verdict gave:
Why at our justice seem'st thou then to lour?
GAUNT: Things sweet to taste prove in digestion sour.
Your urged me as a judge; but I had rather

You would have bid me argue like a father.
O, had it been a stranger, not my child,
To smooth his fault I should have been more mild:
A partial slander sought I to avoid,
And in the sentence my own life destroy'd.
Alas, I look'd when some of you should say,
I was too strict to make mine own away;
But you gave leave to my unwilling tongue
Against my will to do myself this wrong.

KING RICHARD II, I. iii. 233–246

### 5 Despair unto Death

KING PHILIP: Patience, good lady! comfort, gentle Constance!
CONSTANCE: No, I defy all counsel, all redress,
But that which ends all counsel, true redress,
Death, death; O amiable lovely death!
Thou odoriferous stench! sound rottenness!
Arise forth from the couch of lasting night,
Thou hate and terror to prosperity,
And I will kiss thy detestable bones
And put my eyeballs in thy vaulty brows
And ring these fingers with thy household worms
And stop this gap of breath with fulsome dust
And be a carrion monster like thyself:
Come, grin on me, and I will think thou smilest
And buss thee as thy wife. Misery's love,
O, come to me!

KING JOHN, III. iv. 22–36

### 6 Grief a Companion

PANDULPH: You hold too heinous a respect of grief.
CONSTANCE: He talks to me that never had a son.
KING PHILIP: You are as fond of grief as of your child.
CONSTANCE: Grief fills the room up of my absent child,
Lies in his bed, walks up and down with me,

Puts on his pretty looks, repeats his words,
Remembers me of all his gracious parts,
Stuffs out his vacant garments with his form;
Then, have I reason to be fond of grief?

KING JOHN, III. iv. 90–98


### 7 Strange Melancholy

ANTONIO: In sooth, I know not why I am so sad:
It wearies me; you say it wearies you;
But how I caught it, found it, or came by it,
What stuff 't is made of, whereof it is born,
I am to learn;
And such a want-wit sadness makes of me,
That I have much ado to know myself.

THE MERCHANT OF VENICE, I. i. 1–7


### 8 One Misled by Hope

ARCHBISHOP: It was young Hotspur's case at Shrewsbury.
LORD BARDOLPH: It was, my lord: who lin'd himself with hope,
Eating the air on promise of supply,
Flattering himself in project of a power
Much smaller than the smallest of his thoughts:
And so, with great imagination
Proper to madmen, led his powers to death,
And winking leap'd into destruction.

HENRY IV, PT. II, I. iii. 26–33


### 9 Men Set for War

KING HENRY: In peace there's nothing so becomes a man
As modest stillness and humility:
But when the blast of war blows in our ears,
Then imitate the action of the tiger;
Stiffen the sinews, summon up the blood,
Disguise fair nature with hard-favour'd rage;

Then lend the eye a terrible aspect;
Let it pry through the portage of the head
Like the brass cannon; let the brow o'erwhelm it
As fearfully as doth a galled rock
O'erhang and jutty his counfounded base,
Swill'd with the wild and wasteful ocean.
Now set the teeth and stretch the nostril wide,
Hold hard the breath, and bend up every spirit
To his full height.

HENRY V, III. i. 3–17


## 10 *All the Melancholies—and then One*

JAQUES: I have neither the scholar's melancholy, which is
emulation, nor the musician's, which is fantastical, not the
courtier's, which is proud, nor the soldier's, which is
ambitious, nor the lawyer's, which is politic, nor the lady's,
which is nice, nor the lover's, which is all these: but it is
a melancholy of mine own, compounded of many simples,
extracted from many objects, and indeed the sundry
contemplation of my travels, in which my often rumina-
tion wraps me in a most humorous sadness.

AS YOU LIKE IT, IV. i. 11–21


## 11 *A Man Horrified*

GHOST:                                  But that I am forbid
To tell the secrets of my prison-house,
I could a tale unfold whose lightest word
Would harrow up thy soul, freeze thy young blood,
Make thy two eyes, like stars, start from their spheres,
Thy knotted and combined locks to part,
And each particular hair to stand on end,
Like quills upon the fretful porpentine.
But this eternal blazon must not be
To ears of flesh and blood.

HAMLET, I. V. 13–22

12 *Stubborn Sorrow*

KING:                                  but to persever
   In obstinate condolement is a course
   Of impious stubborness; 'tis unmanly grief;
   It shows a will most incorrect to heaven,
   A heart unfortified, a mind impatient,
   An understanding simple and unschooled;
   For what we know must be and is as common
   As any the most vulgar thing to sense,
   Why should we in our peevish opposition
   Take it to heart? Fie! 'tis a fault to heaven,
   A fault against the dead, a fault to nature,
   To reason most absurd, whose common theme
   Is death of fathers, and who still hath cried,
   From the first corse till he that died to-day,
   'This must be so.'
                       HAMLET, I. ii. 92–106

13 *One Unprepared for Death*

GHOST: Thus was I, sleeping, by a brother's hand
   Of life, of crown, of queen, at once dispatched;
   Cut off even in the blossoms of my sin,
   Unhouseled, disappointed, unaneled,
   No reckoning made, but sent to my account
   With all my imperfections on my head.
   O, horrible! O, horrible! most horrible!
                      HAMLET, I. v. 74–80

14 *One without Love or Hope*

MACBETH: I have lived long enough: my way of life
   Is fall'n into the sear, the yellow leaf;
   And that which should accompany old age,
   As honour, love, obedience, troops of friends,
   I must not look to have; but, in their stead,
   Curses, not loud but deep, mouth-honour, breath,
   Which the poor heart would fain deny, and dare not.
                 MACBETH, V. iii. 22–28

15 *Desperate Courage*

ENOBARBUS: Now he'll outstare the lightning. To be furious,
Is to be frighted out of fear; and in that mood
The dove will peck the estridge; and I see still
A diminution in our captain's brain
Restores his heart: when valour preys on reason,
It eats the sword it fights with. I will seek
Some way to leave him.

ANTONY AND CLEOPATRA, III. xi. 194–200

16 *Rash Choler*

BRUTUS: Go; about it.
Put him to choler straight. He hath been us'd
Ever to conquer, and to have his worth
Of contradiction: being once chaf'd, he cannot
Be rein'd again to temperance; then he speaks
What's in his heart; and that is there which looks
With us to break his neck.

CORIOLANUS, III. iii. 24–30

17 *Guilt*

ALONSO: O, it is monstrous, monstrous!
Methought the billows spoke and told me of it;
The winds did sing it to me; and the thunder,
That deep and dreadful organ pipe, pronounc'd
The name of Prosper. It did bass my trespass.
Therefore my son i' th' ooze is bedded; and
I'll seek him deeper than e'er plummet sounded
And with him there lie mudded.

THE TEMPEST, III. iii. 95–102

18 *A Man Distraught*

KING: Now, my lords,
Saw you the cardinal?

NORFOLK:                    My lord, we have
Stood here observing him: some strange commotion
Is in his brain: he bites his lip, and starts;
Stops on a sudden, looks upon the ground,
Then lays his finger on his temple; straight
Springs out into fast gait; then stops again,
Strikes his breast hard, and anon he casts
His eye against the moon: in most strange postures
We have seen him set himself.

KING HENRY VIII, III. ii. 111–120

1 *The Traveller*

ROSALIND: A traveller! By my faith, you have great reason to
be sad: I fear you have sold your own lands to see other
men's; then, to have seen much and to have nothing, is to
have rich eyes and poor hands.

JAQUES: Yes, I have gained my experience.

ROSALIND: And your experience makes you sad: I had rather
have a fool to make me merry than experience to make me
sad; and to travel for it too.                    *Enter Orlando*

ORLANDO: Good day and happiness, dear Rosalind!

JAQUES: Nay, then, God be wi' you, an you talk in blank verse.

ROSALIND: Farewell, Monsieur Traveller: look you lisp and
wear strange suits, disable all the benefits of your own
country, be out of love with your nativity, and almost
chide God for making you that countenance you are, or I
will scarce think you have swam in a gondola.

AS YOU LIKE IT, IV. i. 22–40

2. *The Refined Traveller*

KING: Ay, that there is. Our Court, you know, is haunted
With a refined traveller of Spain;
A man in all the world's new fashion planted,
That hath a mint of phrases in his brain;
One whom the music of his own vain tongue
Doth ravish like enchanting harmony;
A man of complements, whom right and wrong
Have chose as umpire of their mutiny:
This child of fancy that Armado hight
For interim to our studies shall relate
In high-born words the worth of many a knight
From tawny Spain lost in the world's debate.

LOVE'S LABOUR'S LOST, I. i. 161–172

### 3 *An Illiterate*

DULL: I said the deer was not a *haud credo*; 't was a pricket.

HOLOFERNES: Twice-sod simplicity, bis coctus!

O thou monster Ignorance, how deformed dost thou look!

NATHANIEL: Sir, he hath never fed of the dainties that are bred
in a book; he hath not eat paper, as it were; he hath not
drunk ink: his intellect is not replenished; he is only an
animal, only sensible in the duller parts:

And such barren plants are set before us, that we thankful
should be,

Which we of taste and feeling are, for those parts that do
fructify in us more than he.

For as it would ill become me to be vain, indiscreet, or
a fool,

So were there a patch set on learning, to see him in a
school:

But *omne bene*, say I; being of an old father's mind,

Many can brook the weather that love not the wind.

LOVE'S LABOUR'S LOST, IV. ii. 21–34

### 4 *Conceited Pedant*

HOLOFERNES: This is a gift that I have, simple, simple; a foolish
extravagant spirit, full of forms, figures, shapes, objects,
ideas, apprehensions, motions, revolutions: these are begot
in the ventricle of memory, nourished in the womb of pia
mater, and delivered upon the mellowing of occasion. But
the gift is good in those in whom it is acute, and I am
thankful for it.

LOVE'S LABOUR'S LOST, IV. ii. 67–74

### 5 *Peregrinate Pedant*

HOLOFERNES: *Novi hominem tanquam te*: his humour is lofty, his
discourse peremptory, his tongue filed, his eye ambitious,
his gait majestical, and his general behaviour vain, ridiculous, and thrasonical. He is too picked, too spruce, too
affected, too old, as it were, too peregrinate, as I may call it.

NATHANIEL: A most singular and choice epithet.

*(Draws out his table-book)*

HOLOFERNES: He draweth out the thread of his verbosity finer than the staple of his argument. I abhor such fanatical phantasimes, such insociable and point-devise companions; such rackers of orthography, as to speak dout, fine, when he should say doubt; det, when he should pronounce debt,—d,e,b,t, not d,e,t: he clepeth a calf, cauf; half, hauf; neighbour vocatur nebour; neigh abbreviated ne. This is abhominable,—which he would call abbominable: it insinuateth me of insanie: *anne intelligis, domine?* to make frantic, lunatic.

LOVE'S LABOUR'S LOST, V. i. 10–29

## 6 *The Ape of Form*

BIRON: This fellow picks up wit as pigeons pease,
And utters it again when God doth please:
He is wit's pedlar, and retails his wares
At wakes and wassails, meetings, markets, fairs;
And we that sell by gross, the Lord doth know,
Have not the grace to grace it with such show.
This gallant pins the wenches on his sleeve;
Had he been Adam, he had tempted Eve,
A' can carve too, and lisp: why, this is he
That kiss'd his hand away in courtesy;
This is the ape of form, monsieur the nice,
That, when he plays at tables, chides the dice
In honourable terms: nay, he can sing
A mean most meanly; and in ushering
Mend him who can: the ladies call him sweet;
The stairs, as he treads on them, kiss his feet:
This is the flower that smiles on every one,
To show his teeth as white as whales-bone;
And consciences, that will not die in debt,
Pay him the due of honey-tongu'd Boyet.

LOVE'S LABOUR'S LOST, V. ii. 316–335

### 7. A 'Clam'

MONTAGUE: But he, his own affections' counsellor,
Is to himself—I will not say how true—
But to himself so secret and so close,
So far from sounding and discovery,
As is the bud bit with an envious worm,
Ere he can spread his sweet leaves to the air,
Or dedicate his beauty to the sun.

ROMEO AND JULIET, I. i. 152–158

### 8 A Fashionable Duellist

BENVOLIO: Why, what is Tybalt?
MERCUTIO: More than prince of cats, I can tell you. O, he is the courageous captain of compliments. He fights as you sing prick-song, keeps time, distance, and proportion; rests, me his minim rest one, two, and the third in your bosom; the very butcher of a silk button, a duellist, a duellist; a gentleman of the very first house, of the first and second cause. Ah, the immortal passado! the punto reverso! the hay!
BENVOLIO: The what?
MERCUTIO: The pox of such antic, lisping, affecting fantasticoes, these new tuners of accents! 'By Jesu, a very good blade! a very tall man! a very good whore!' Why, is not this a lamentable thing, grandsire, that we should be thus afflicted with these strange flies, these fashionmongers, these *pardonnez-mois*, who stand so much on the new form that they cannot sit at ease on the old bench? O, their *bons*, their *bons*!

ROMEO AND JULIET, II. iv. 19–38

### 9 Character of a Quarreller

MERCUTIO: Thou art like one of those fellows that when he enters the confines of a tavern claps me his sword upon the table and says, 'God send me no need of thee!' and by the operation of the second cup draws it on the drawer, when indeed there is no need.

BENVOLIO: Am I like such a fellow?

MERCUTIO: Come, come, thou art as hot a Jack in thy mood as any in Italy, and as soon moved to be moody, and as soon moody to be moved.

BENVOLIO: And what to?

MERCUTIO: Nay, an there were two such, we should have none shortly, for one would kill the other. Thou! why, thou wilt quarrel with a man that hath a hair more or a hair less in his beard than thou hast. Thou wilt quarrel with a man for cracking nuts, having no other reason but because thou hast hazel eyes; what eye, but such an eye, would spy out such a quarrel? Thy head is as full of quarrels as an egg is full of meat, and yet thy head hath been beaten as addle as an egg for quarrelling. Thou hast quarrelled with a man for coughing in the street, because he hath wakened thy dog that hath lain asleep in the sun. Didst thou not fall out with a tailor for wearing his new doublet before Easter? with another, for tying his new shoes with old riband? and yet thou wilt tutor me from quarrelling!

ROMEO AND JULIET, III. i. 5–33

### 10 *The Needy Outcast*

APOTHECARY: Such mortal drugs I have; but Mantua's law
    Is death to any he that utters them.

ROMEO: Art thou so bare, and full of wretchedness,
    And fear'st to die? famine is in thy cheeks,
    Need and oppression starveth in thy eyes,
    Contempt and beggary hangs upon thy back;
    The world is not thy friend nor the world's law:
    The world affords no law to make thee rich;
    Then be not poor, but break it, and take this.

ROMEO AND JULIET, V. i. 66–74

11 *Worshipful Society—New-Hatched Knight and the Traveller*

BASTARD: Well, now can I make any Joan a lady.
    'Good den, Sir Richard!'—'God-a-mercy, fellow!—
    And if his name be George, I'll call him Peter;
    For new-made honour doth forget men's names;
    'Tis too respective and too sociable
    For your conversion. Now your traveller,
    He and his toothpick at my worship's mess,
    And when my knightly stomach is sufficed,
    Why then I suck my teeth and catechize
    My picked man of countries: 'My dear sir',
    Thus, leaning on mine elbow, I begin,
    'I shall beseech you'—that is question now;
    And then comes answer like an Absey book:
    'O sir', says answer, 'at your best command;
    At your employment; at your service, sir':
    'No, sir', says question, 'I, sweet sir, at your':
    And so, ere answer knows what question would,
    Saving in dialogue of compliment,
    And talking of the Alps and Appennines,
    The Pyrenean and the river Po,
    It draws towards supper in conclusion so.
    But this is worshipful society
    And fits the mounting spirit like myself,
    For he is but a bastard to the time
    That doth not smack of observation;
    And so am I, whether I smack or no;
    And not alone in habit and device,
    Exterior form, outward accoutrement,
    But from the inward motion to deliver
    Sweet, sweet, sweet poison for the age's tooth:
    Which, though I will not practise to deceive,
    Yet, to avoid deceit, I mean to learn;
    For it shall strew the footsteps of my rising.

                        KING JOHN, I. i. 184–216

12 *Gargantuan Thunderer*

BASTARD:                               Here's a stay
   That shakes the rotten carcass of old Death
   Out of his rags! Here's a large mouth, indeed,
   That spits forth death and mountains, rocks and seas,
   Talks as familiarly of roaring lions
   As maids of thirteen do of puppy-dogs!
   What cannoneer begot this lusty blood?
   He speaks plain cannon fire, and smoke and bounce;
   He gives the bastinado with his tongue:
   Our ears are cudgell'd; not a word of his
   But buffets better than a fist of France:
   Zounds! I was never so bethump'd with words
   Since I first call'd my brother's father dad.

                                   KING JOHN, II. i. 455–467


13 *The Affectation of Gravity*

ANTONIO: I hold the world but as the world, Gratiano;
   A stage where very man must play a part,
   And mine a sad one.
GRATIANO:                        Let me play the fool:
   With mirth and laughter let old wrinkles come,
   And let my liver rather heat with wine
   Than my heart cool with mortifying groans.
   Why should a man, whose blood is warm within,
   Sit like his grandsire cut in alabaster?
   Sleep when he wakes and creep into the jaundice
   By being peevish? I tell thee what, Antonio—
   I love thee, and it is my love that speaks—
   There are a sort of men whose visages
   Do cream and mantle like a standing pond,
   And do a wilful stillness entertain,
   With purpose to be dress'd in an opinion
   Of wisdom, gravity, profound conceit,
   As who should say 'I am Sir Oracle,

And when I ope my lips let no dog bark!'
O my Antonio, I do know of these
That therefore only are reputed wise
For saying nothing, when, I am very sure,
If they should speak would almost damn those ears
Which, hearing them, would call their brothers fools.

THE MERCHANT OF VENICE, I. i. 77–99

### 14 A Sober-Seeming Man.

GRATIANO:        Signior Bassanio, hear me:
If I do not put on a sober habit,
Talk with respect and swear but now and then,
Wear prayer-books in my pocket, look demurely,
Nay more, while grace is saying, hood mine eyes
Thus with my hat, and sigh and say 'amen',
Use all the observance of civility,
Like one well studied in a sad ostent
To please his grandam, never trust me more.

THE MERCHANT OF VENICE, II. ii. 204–212

### 15 A Bragging Jack

PORTIA:        I'll hold thee any wager,
When we are both accoutred like young men,
I'll prove the prettier fellow of the two,
And wear my dagger with the braver grace,
And speak between the change of man and boy
With a reed voice, and turn two mincing steps
Into a manly stride, and speak of frays
Like a fine bragging youth, and tell quaint lies,
How honourable ladies sought my love,
Which I denying, they fell sick and died;
I could not do withal; then I'll repent,
And wish, for all that, that I had not kill'd them;
And twenty of these puny lies I'll tell,

That men shall swear I have discountinued school
Above a twelvemonth. I have within my mind
A thousand raw tricks of these bragging Jacks,
Which I will practise.

THE MERCHANT OF VENICE, III. iv. 62–78

## 16 *Antic Youth*

ANTONIO: Hold you content. What, man! I know them, yea,
   And what they weigh, even to the utmost scruple,
   Scambling, out-facing, fashion-monging boys,
   That lie and cog and flout, deprave and slander,
   Go antickly, and show outward hideousness,
   And speak off half a dozen dangerous words,
   How they might hurt their enemies, if they durst;
   And this is all.

MUCH ADO ABOUT NOTHING, V. i. 92–99

## 17 *Three Filching Swashers*

BOY: As young as I am, I have observed these three swashers.
   I am boy to them all three: but all they three, though they
   would serve me, could not be man to me; for indeed three
   such antics do not amount to a man. For Bardolph, he is
   white-livered and red-faced; by the means whereof a'
   faces it out, but fights not. For Pistol, he hath a killing
   tongue and a quiet sword; by the means whereof a' breaks
   words, and keeps whole weapons. For Nym, he hath
   heard that men of few words are the best men; and therefore he scorns to say his prayers, lest a' should be thought
   a coward: but his few bad words are matched with as few
   good deeds; for a' never broke any man's head but his
   own, and that was against a post when he was drunk. They
   will steal any thing, and call it purchase. Bardolph stole a
   lute-case, bore it twelve leagues, and sold it for three
   half-pence. Nym and Bardolph are sworn brothers in
   filching, and in Callice they stole a fire-shovel: I knew by

that piece of service the men would carry coals. They would have me as familiar with men's pockets as their gloves or their handkerchers: which makes much against my manhood, if I should take from another's pocket to put into mine; for it is plain pocketing up of wrongs. I must leave them, and seek some better service: their villainy goes against my weak stomach, and therefore I must cast it up.

KING HENRY V, III. ii. 30–59

### 18 *An Affectioned Ass*

MARIA: Marry, Sir, sometimes he is a kind of puritan.

SIR ANDREW: O, if I thought that, I'd beat him like a dog!

SIR TOBY: What, for being a puritan? thy exquisite reason, dear knight?

SIR ANDREW: I have no exquisite reason for't, but I have reason good enough.

MARIA: The devil a puritan that he is, or any thing constantly, but a time-pleaser; an affectioned ass, that cons state without book, and utters it by great swarths: the best persuaded of himself, so crammed, as he thinks, with excellences, that it is his grounds of faith that all that look on him love him; and on that vice in him will my revenge find notable cause to work.

TWELFTH NIGHT, II. iii. 153–169

### 19 *The Swaggering Swearer*

SIR TOBY: Go, Sir Andrew; scout me for him at the corner of the orchard, like a bum-baily: so soon as ever thou seest him, draw; and, as thou drawest, swear horrible; for it comes to pass oft that a terrible oath, with a swaggering accent sharply twanged off, gives manhood more approbation than ever proof itself would have earned him. Away!

TWELFTH NIGHT, III, iv. 196–203

### 20 *A Devil of a Fellow*

SIR TOBY: You'll find it otherwise, I assure you: therefore, if you hold your life at any price, betake you to your guard; for your opposite hath in him what youth, strength, skill, and wrath can furnish man withal.

VIOLA: I pray you, sir, what is he?

SIR TOBY: He is knight, dubbed with unhatched rapier and on carpet consideration; but he is a devil in private brawl: souls and bodies hath he divorced three; and his incensement at this moment is so implacable, that satisfaction can be none but by pangs of death and sepulchre: hob, nob, is word; giv't or take't.

TWELFTH NIGHT, III. iv. 254–266

### 21 *Another Devil*

SIR TOBY: Why, man he's a very devil; I have not seen such a firago. I had a pass with him, rapier, scabbard, and all, and he gives me the stuck in which such a mortal motion, that it is inevitable; and on the answer, he pays you as surely as your feet hit the ground they step on: they say he has been fencer to the Sophy.

SIR ANDREW: I'll not meddle with him.

SIR TOBY: Ay, but he will not now be pacified: Fabian can scarce hold him yonder.

TWELFTH NIGHT, III. iv. 304–313

### 22 *The Pseudo-Mourner*

HAMLET: Seems, madam! Nay, it is; I know not 'seems'.
'Tis not alone my inky cloak, good mother,
Nor customary suits of solemn black,
Nor windy suspiration of forced breath,
No, nor the fruitful river in the eye,
Nor the dejected haviour of the visage,
Together with all forms, moods, shapes of grief,
That can denote me truly. These indeed seem,

> For they are actions that a man might play;
> But I have that within which passeth show;
> These but the trappings and the suits of woe.

HAMLET, I. ii. 76–86


### 23 *Pretenders to Inside Knowledge*

HAMLET: Here, as before, never, so help you mercy,
>    How strange or odd soe'r I bear myself,
>    As I perchance hereafter shall think meet
>    To put an antic disposition on,
>    That you, at such times seeing me, never shall,
>    With arms encumbered thus, or this headshake,
>    Or by pronouncing of some doubtful phrase,
>    As 'Well, well, we know', or 'We could, an if we would',
>    Or 'If we list to speak', or 'There be, an if they might',
>    Or such ambiguous giving out, to note
>    That you know aught of me,—this not to do,
>    So grace and mercy at your most need help you,
>    Swear.

HAMLET, I. v. 169–180


### 24 *The Scurrilous Mimic*

ULYSSES: The great Achilles, whom opinion crowns
>    The sinew and the forehand of our host,
>    Having his ear full of his airy fame,
>    Grows dainty of his worth, and in his tent
>    Lies mocking our designs: with him Patroclus
>    Upon a lazy bed the livelong day
>    Breaks scurril jests;
>    And with ridiculous and awkward action,
>    Which, slanderer, he imitation calls,
>    He pageants us. Sometime, great Agamemnon,
>    Thy topless deputation he puts on,
>    And, like a strutting player, whose conceit
>    Lies in his hamstring, and doth think it rich
>    To hear the wooden dialogue and sound

# Greenes Tu quoque,

## OR,
## The Cittie Gallant.

*As it hath beene diuers times acted by the Queenes*
*Maiesties Seruants.*

Written by Io. COOKE Gent.

Printed at London for *Iohn Trundle*. 1614.

Nobilis Anglus    Nobilis matrona in Anglia

Fœmina Londinensis ornatus    Ciuis Londinensis honesto vestitu

TWO STYLES OF AUDIENCE — COURTIERS AND CITIZENS

'Twixt his stretch'd footing and the scaffoldage,—
Such to-be-pitied and o'er-wrested seeming
He acts thy greatness in: and when he speaks,
'Tis like a chime a-mending; with terms unsquared,
Which, from the tongue of roaring Typhon dropp'd
Would seem hyperboles. At this fusty stuff
The large Achilles, on his press'd bed lolling,
From his deep chest laughs out a loud applause;
Cries 'Excellent! 'tis Agamemnon just.
Now play me Nestor; hem, and stroke thy beard,
As he being dress'd to some oration.'
That's done; as near as the extremest ends
Of parallels, as like as Vulcan and his wife:
Yet god Achilles still cries 'Excellent!
'Tis Nestor right. Now play him me, Patroclus,
Arming to answer in a night alarm.'
And then, forsooth, the faint defects of age
Must be the scene of mirth; to cough and spit,
And with a palsy-fumbling on his gorget,
Shake in and out the rivet; and at this port
Sir Valour dies; cries 'O, enough, Patroclus,
Or give me ribs of steel! I shall split all
In pleasure of my spleen.' And in this fashion
All our abilities, gifts, natures, shapes,
Severals and generals of grace exact,
Achievements, plots, orders, preventions,
Excitements to the field, or speech for truce,
Success or loss, what is or is not, serves
As stuff for these two to make paradoxes.

TROILUS AND CRESSIDA, I. iii. 142–184

### 25 *The Bastard*

EDMUND: Thou, Nature, art my goddess; to thy law
My services are bound. Wherefore should I
Stand in the plague of custom, and permit
The curiosity of nations to deprive me,

13

For that I am some twelve or fourteen moonshines
Lag of a brother? Why bastard? wherefore base?
When my dimensions are as well compact,
My mind as generous, and my shape as true,
As honest madam's issue? Why brand they us
With base? With baseness? bastardy? base, base?
Who, in the lusty stealth of nature, take
More composition and fierce quality
Than doth, within a dull, stale, tired bed,
Go to th' creating a whole tribe of fops
Got 'tween asleep and wake? Well then,
Legitimate Edgar, I must have your land.
Our father's love is to the bastard Edmund
As to th' legitimate. Fine word—'legitimate'!
Well, my legitimate, if this letter speed,
And my invention thrive, Edmund the base
Shall top th' legitimate. I grow; I prosper.
Now, gods, stand up for bastards!

KING LEAR, I. ii. I–22

26 *A Bedlamite* (a)

EDGAR: I heard myself proclaim'd,
And by the happy hollow of a tree
Escap'd the hunt. No port is free, no place
That guard and most unusual vigilance
Does not attend my taking. Whiles I may scape,
I will preserve myself; and am bethought
To take the basest and most poorest shape
That ever penury, in contempt of man,
Brought near to beast. My face I'll grime with filth,
Blanket my loins, elf all my hair in knots,
And with presented nakedness outface
The winds and persecutions of the sky.
The country gives me proof and precedent
Of Bedlam beggars, who, with roaring voices,
Strike in their numb'd and mortified bare arms
Pins, wooden pricks, nails, springs of rosemary;

And with this horrible object, from low farms,
Poor pelting villages, sheepcotes, and mills,
Sometime with lunatic bans, sometime with prayers,
Enforce their charity. 'Poor Turlygod! poor Tom!'
That's something yet! Edgar I nothing am.

KING LEAR, II. iii. 1–21

## 26 *A Bedlamite* (*b*)

EDGAR: Who gives anything to poor Tom? whom the foul
fiend hath led through fire and through flame, through
ford and whirlpool, o'er bog and quagmire; that hath laid
knives under his pillow and halters in his pew, set ratsbane
by his porridge, made him proud of heart, to ride on a
bay trotting horse over four-inch'd bridges, to course his
own shadow for a traitor. Bless thy five wits! Tom's
a-cold. O, do de, do de, do de. Bless thee from whirlwinds,
star-blasting, and taking! Do poor Tom some charity,
whom the foul fiend vexes. There could I have him now—
and there—and there again—and there!

KING LEAR, III. iv. 49–62

## 26 *A Bedlamite* (*c*)

GLOUCESTER: What are you there? Your names?

EDGAR: Poor Tom, that eats the swimming frog, the toad, the
tadpole, the wall-newt and the water; that in the fury of
his heart, when the foul fiend rages, eats cow-dung for
sallets, swallows the old rat and the ditch-dog, drinks the
green mantle of the standing pool; who is whipp'd from
tithing to tithing, and stock-punish'd and imprison'd; who
hath had three suits to his back, six shirts to his body, horse
to ride, and weapon to wear;
> 'But mice and rats, and such small deer,
> Have been Tom's food for seven long year.'
Beware my follower. Peace, Smulkin! peace, thou fiend!

KING LEAR, III. iv. 131–145

### 27 *A Failure Analysed*

AUFIDIUS:                              First he was
   A noble servant to them, but he could not
   Carry his honours even; whether 'twas pride,
   Which out of daily fortune ever taints
   The happy man; whether defect of judgment,
   To fail in the disposing of those chances
   Which he was lord of; or whether nature,
   Not to be other than one thing, not moving
   From the casque to the cushion, but commanding peace
   Even with the same austerity and garb
   As he controll'd the war; but one of these,
   As he hath spices of them all, not all,
   For I dare so far free him, made him fear'd,
   So hated, and so banish'd: but he has a merit
   To choke it in the utterance. So our virtues
   Lie in the interpretation of the time;
   And power, unto itself most commendable,
   Hath not a tomb so evident as a chair
   To extol what it hath done.
   One fire drives out one fire; one nail, one nail;
   Rights by rights founder, strengths by strengths do fail.
   Come, let's away. When, Caius, Rome is thine,
   Thou art poor'st of all; then shortly art thou mine.

                         CORIOLANUS, IV. vii. 35–57

### 28 *Parasites*

APEMANTUS: I scorn thy meat; 'twould choke me, for I should
   Ne'er flatter thee. O you gods! what a number
   Of men eat Timon, and he sees 'em not.
   It grieves me to see so many dip their meat
   In one man's blood; and all the madness is,
   He cheers them up too.
   I wonder men dare trust themselves with men:
   Methinks they should invite them without knives;

Good for their meat, and safer for their lives.
There's much example for't; the fellow that
Sits next him now, parts bread with him, and pledges
The breadth of him in a divided draught,
Is the readiest man to kill him: it has been proved.
If I were a huge man, I should fear to drink at meals,
Lest they should spy my windpipe's dangerous notes:
Great men should drink with harness on their throats.

TIMON OF ATHENS, I. ii. 39–54

## 29 Flatterers

APEMANTUS: Like madness is the glory of this life,
As this pomp shows to a little oil and root.
We make ourselves fools to disport ourselves;
And spend our flatteries to drink those men
Upon whose age we void it up again,
With poisonous spite and envy.
Who lives that's not depraved or depraves?
Who dies that bears not one spurn to their graves
Of their friends' gift?
I should fear those that dance before me now
Would one day stamp upon me: 't has been done;
Men shut their doors against a setting sun.

TIMON OF ATHENS, I. ii. 141–152

## 30 Whores

PHRYNIAD AND TIMANDRA: Give us some gold, good Timon:
        hast thou more?
TIMON: Enough to make a whore forswear her trade,
And to make whores, a bawd. Hold up, you sluts,
Your aprons mountant: you are not oathable,
Although, I know, you'll swear, terribly swear
Into strong shudders and to heavenly agues
The immortal gods that hear you; spare your oaths,
I'll trust to your conditions: be whores still;

And he whose pious breath seeks to convert you,
Be strong in whore, allure him, burn him up;
Let your close fire predominate his smoke,
And be no turncoats: yet may your pains, six months,
Be quite contrary: and thatch your poor thin roofs
With burdens of the dead; some that were hang'd,
No matter; wear them, betray with them: whore still;
Paint till a horse may mire upon your face:
A pox of wrinkles!

PHRYNIA AND TIMANDRA: Well, more gold. What then?
Believe't that we'll do any thing for gold.

TIMON: Consumptions sow
In hollow bones of man; strike their sharp shins,
And mar men's spurring. Crack the lawyer's voice,
That he may never more false title plead,
Nor sound his quillets shrilly: hoar the flamen,
That scolds against the quality of flesh,
And not believes himself: down with the nose,
Down with it flat; take the bridge quite away
Of him that, his particular to foresee,
Smells from the general weal: make curl'd-pate ruffians
      bald;
And let the unscarr'd braggarts of the war
Derive some pain from you: plague all,
That your activity may defeat and quell
The source of all erection. There's more gold;
Do you damn others, and let this damn you,
And ditches grave you all!

                    TIMON OF ATHENS, IV. iii. 133–167


31 *Two Kinds of Misanthrope*

TIMON: Thou art a slave, whom Fortune's tender arm
With favour never clasp'd, but bred a dog.
Hadst thou, like us, from our first swath, proceeded
The sweet degrees that this brief world affords

To such as may the passive drugs of it
Freely command, thou would'st have plung'd thyself
In general riot; melted down thy youth
In different beds of lust; and never learn'd
The icy precepts of respect, but follow'd
The sugar'd game before thee. But myself,
Who had the world as my confectionary,
The mouths, the tongues, the eyes and hearts of men
At duty, more than I could frame employment,
That numberless upon me stuck as leaves
Do on the oak, have with one winter's brush
Fell from their boughs and left me open, bare
For every storm that blows; I, to bear this,
That never knew but better, is some burden:
Thy nature did commence in sufferance, time
Hath made thee hard in 't. Why should'st thou hate
        men?
They never flatter'd thee: what has thou given?
If thou wilt curse, thy father, that poor rag,
Must be thy subject, who in spite put stuff
To some she beggar and compounded thee
Poor rogue hereditary. Hence! be gone!
If thou hadst not been born the worst of men,
Thou hadst been a knave and flatterer.

                    TIMON OF ATHENS, IV. iii. 251–277


## 32 *Voracious Miser*

FIRST FISHERMAN: Why, as men do a-land; the great ones eat up
    the little ones. I can compare our rich misers to nothing so
    fitly as to a whale; a' plays and tumbles, driving the poor
    fry before him, and at last devours them all at a mouthful.
    Such whales have I heard on o' the land, who never leave
    gaping till they've swallowed the whole parish, church, steeple,
    steeple, bells, and all.

                        PERICLES, II. i. 31–38

**33** *A Man-Monster*

TRINCULO: What have we here? a man or a fish? dead or alive?
A fish: he smells like a fish; a very ancient and fishlike
smell; a kind of, not of the newest, poor-John. A strange
fish! Were I in England now, as once I was, and had but
this fish painted, not a holiday fool there but would give a
piece of silver. There would this monster make a man.
Any strange beast there makes a man. When they will not
give a doit to relieve a lame beggar, they will lay out ten
to see a dead Indian. Legg'd like a man! and his fins like
arms! Warm, o' my troth! I do now let loose my opinion,
hold it no longer: this is no fish, but an islander, that hath
lately suffered by a thunderbolt. (*Thunder*) Alas, the
storm is come again! My best way is to creep under his
gaberdine. There is no other shelter hereabout. Misery
acquaints a man with strange bedfellows. I will shroud till
the dregs of the storm be past

THE TEMPEST, II. ii. 25–44

### 1 *The Principle of Subordination*

LUCIANA: A man is master of his liberty:
    Time is their master; and, when they see time,
    They'll go or come: if so, be patient, sister.
ADRIANA: Why should their liberty than ours be more?
LUCIANA: Because their business still lies out o' door.
ADRIANA: Look, when I serve him so he takes it ill.
LUCIANA: O, know he is the bridle of your will.
ADRIANA: There's none but asses will be bridled so.
LUCIANA: Why, headstrong liberty is lash'd with woe.
    There's nothing situate under heaven's eye
    But hath his bound, in earth, in sea, in sky:
    The beasts, the fishes, and the winged fowls,
    Are their males' subjects and at their controls:
    Men, more divine, the masters of all these,
    Lords of the wide world, and wild watery seas,
    Indued with intellectual sense and souls,
    Of more pre-eminence than fish and fowls,
    Are masters to their females, and their lords:
    Then, let your will attend on their accords.
ADRIANA: This servitude makes you to keep unwed.
LUCIANA: Not this, but troubles of the marriage-bed.
ADRIANA: But, were you wedded, you would bear some sway.
LUCIANA: Ere I learn love I'll practise to obey.

COMEDY OF ERRORS, II. i. 7–29

### 2 *The Order and Balance of Nature*

FRIAR: The grey-eyed morn smiles on the frowning night,
    Chequering the eastern clouds with streaks of light;
    And flecked darkness like a drunkard reels
    From forth day's path and Titan's fiery wheels:
    Now, ere the sun advance his burning eye

The day to cheer and night's dank dew to dry,
I must up-fill this osier cage of ours
With baleful weeds and precious-juiced flowers.
The earth that's nature's mother is her tomb,
What is her burying grave, that is her womb,
And from her womb children of divers kind
We sucking on her natural bosom find,
Many for many virtues excellent,
None but for some, and yet all different.
O, mickle is the powerful grace that lies
In herbs, plants, stones, and their true qualities:
For nought so vile that on the earth doth live
But to the earth some special good doth give;
Nor aught so good but, strain'd from that fair use,
Revolts from true birth, stumbling on abuse:
Virtue itself turns vice, being misapplied,
And vice sometime's by action dignified.
Within the infant rind of this weak flower
Poison hath residence and medicine power:
For this, being smelt, with that part cheers each part;
Being tasted, slays all senses with the heart.
Two such opposed kings encamp them still
In man as well as herbs, grace and rude will;
And where the worser is predominant,
Full soon the canker death eats up that plant.

ROMEO AND JULIET, II. iii. 1–30

### 3 The Nature of Degree

ULYSSES: Troy, yet upon his bases, had been down,
And the great Hector's sword had lack'd a master,
But for these instances.
The speciality of rule hath been neglected:
And, look, how many Grecian tents do stand
Hollow upon this plain, so many hollow factions.
When that the general is not like the hive
To whom the foragers shall all repair,

What honey is expected? Degree being vizarded,
The unworthiest shows as fairly in the mask.
The heavens themselves, the planets, and this centre,
Observe degree, priority, and place,
Insisture, course, proportion, season, form,
Office, and custom, in all line of order:
And therefore is the glorious planet Sol
In noble eminence enthron'd and spher'd
Amidst the other; whose med'cinable eye
Corrects the ill aspects of planets evil,
And posts, like the commandment of a king,
Sans check to good and bad: but when the planets
In evil mixture to disorder wander,
What plagues, and what portents, what mutiny,
What raging of the sea, shaking of earth,
Commotion in the winds, frights, changes, horrors,
Divert and crack, rend and deracinate
The unity and married calm of states
Quite from their fixture! O, when degree is shak'd,
Which is the ladder to all high designs,
The enterprise is sick! How could communities,
Degrees in schools, and brotherhoods in cities,
Peaceful commerce from dividable shores,
The primogenity and due of birth,
Prerogative of age, crowns, sceptres, laurels,
But by degree, stand in authentic place?
Take but degree away, untune that string,
And hark! what discord follows; each thing meets
In mere oppugnancy: the bounded waters
Should lift their bosoms higher than the shores,
And make a sop of all this solid globe:
Strength should be lord of imbecility,
And the rude son should strike his father dead:
Force should be right; or rather, right and wrong,
Between whose endless jar justice resides,
Should lose their names, and so should justice too.
Then every thing includes itself in power,

Power into will, will into appetite;
And appetitite, an universal wolf,
So double seconded with will and power,
Must make perforce an universal prey,
And last eat up himself. Great Agamemnon,
This chaos, when degree is suffocate,
Follows the choking.
And this neglection of degree it is
That by a pace goes backward, with a purpose
It hath to climb. The general's disdain'd
By him one step below, he by the next,
That next by him beneath; so every step,
Exampled by the first pace that is sick
Of his superior, grows to an envious fever
Of pale and bloodless emulation:
And 'tis this fever that keeps Troy on foot,
Not her own sinews. To end a tale of length,
Troy in our weakness stands, not in her strength.

TROILUS AND CRESSIDA, I. iii. 75–137

*4 Man in Authority*

LUCIO: (*Aside to Isabella*) That's well said.
ISABELLA: Could great men thunder
 As Jove himself does, Jove would ne'er be quiet,
 For every pelting, petty officer
 Would use his heaven for thunder; nothing but thunder!
 Merciful heaven,
 Thou rather with thy sharp and sulphurous bolt
 Splitt'st the unwedgeable and gnarled oak
 Than the soft myrtle; but man, proud man,
 Drest in a little brief authority,
 Most ignorant of what he's most assur'd,
 His glassy essence, like an angry ape,
 Plays such fantastic tricks before high heaven
 As make the angels weep; who, with our spleens,
 Would all themselves laugh mortal.

MEASURE FOR MEASURE. II. ii. 109–123

*5 Character of the Shepherd's Life*

KING HENRY: O God! methinks it were a happy life,
    To be no better than a homely swain;
    To sit upon a hill, as I do now,
    To carve out dials quaintly, point by point,
    Thereby to see the minutes how they run,
    How many make the hour full complete;
    How many hours bring about the day;
    How many days will finish up the year;
    How many years a mortal man may live.
    When this is known, then to divide the times:
    So many hours must I tend my flock;
    So many hours must I take my rest;
    So many hours must I contemplate;
    So many hours must I sport myself;
    So many days my ewes have been with young;
    So many weeks ere the poor fools will ean;
    So many years ere I shall shear the fleece:
    So minutes, hours, days, months, and years,
    Pass'd over to the end they were created,
    Would bring white hairs unto a quiet grave.
    Ah! what a life were this; how sweet! how lovely!
    Gives not the hawthorn-bush a sweeter shade
    To shepherds looking on their silly sheep,
    Than doth a rich embroider'd canopy
    To kings that fear their subjects' treachery?
    O yes! it doth; a thousand-fold it doth.
    And to conclude, the shepherd's homely curds,
    His cold thin drink out of his leather bottle,
    His wonted sleep under a fresh tree's shade,
    All which secure and sweetly he enjoys,
    Is far beyond a prince's delicates,
    His viands sparkling in a golden cup,
    His body couched in a curious bed,
    When care, mistrust, and treason waits on him.

KING HENRY VI, PT. III, II. V. 21–54

*6 Conflict of Pity and Profit*

KING HENRY: My queen and son are gone to France for aid;
　　　　And, as I hear, the great commanding Warwick
　　　　Is thither gone, to crave the French king's sister
　　　　To wife for Edward. If this news be true,
　　　　Poor queen and son, your labour is but lost;
　　　　For Warwick is a subtle orator,
　　　　And Lewis a prince soon won with moving words.
　　　　By this account then Margaret may win him,
　　　　For she's a woman to be pitied much:
　　　　Her sighs will make a battery in his breast;
　　　　Her tears will pierce into a marble heart;
　　　　The tiger will be mild whiles she doth mourn;
　　　　And Nero will be be tainted with remorse,
　　　　To hear and see her plaints, her brinish tears.
　　　　Ay, but she's come to beg; Warwick, to give;
　　　　She on his left side craving aid for Henry,
　　　　He on his right asking a wife for Edward.
　　　　She weeps, and says her Henry is deposed;
　　　　He smiles, and says his Edward is install'd;
　　　　That she, poor wretch, for grief can speak no more:
　　　　Whiles Warwick tells his title, smooths the wrong,
　　　　Inferreth arguments of mighty strength,
　　　　And in conclusion wins the king from her,
　　　　With promise of his sister, and what else,
　　　　To strengthen and support King Edward's place.
　　　　O Margaret! thus 'twill be; and thou, poor soul,
　　　　Art then forsaken, as thou went'st forlorn.

　　　　　　　　KING HENRY VI, PT. III, III. i. 28–54

*7 Character of Conscience*

FIRST MURDERER: Where is thy conscience now?
SECOND MURDERER: In the Duke of Gloucester's purse.
FIRST MURDERER: So when he opens his purse to give us our
　　reward, thy conscience flies out.

SECOND MURDERER: Let it go; there's a few or none will entertain it.

FIRST MURDERER: How if it came to thee again?

SECOND MURDERER: I'll not meddle with it: it is a dangerous thing: it makes a man a coward: a man cannot steal, but it accuseth him; he cannot swear, but it checks him; 'tis a blushing shamefast spirit that mutinies in a man's bosom; it fills one full of obstacles: it made me once restore a purse of gold that I found; it beggars any man that keeps it: it is turned out of all towns and cities for a dangerous thing; and every man that means to live well endeavours to trust to himself and to live without it.

KING RICHARD III, I. iv. 130–149

### 8 *The Universal Principle of Trouncing*

ANTIPHOLUS OF EPHESUS: Thou art sensible in nothing but blows, and so is an ass.

DROMIO OF EPHESUS: I am an ass, indeed; you may prove it by my long ears. I have served him from the hour of my nativity to this instant, and have nothing at his hands for my service but blows. When I am cold, he heats me with beating; when I am warm, he cools me with beating; I am waked with it, when I sleep; raised with it, when I sit; driven out of doors with it, when I go from home; welcomed home with it, when I return; nay, I bear it on my shoulders, as a beggar wont her brat, and, I think, when he hath lamed me, I shall beg with it from door to door.

ANTIPHOLUS OF EPHESUS: Come, go along;

COMEDY OF ERRORS, IV. iv. 26–41

### 9 *Good Talk Characterized*

NATHANIEL: I praise God for you, sir: your reasons at dinner have been sharp and sententious; pleasant without scurrility, witty without affection, audacious without impudency, learned without opinion, and strange without heresy.

LOVE'S LABOUR'S LOST, V.i. 2–6

10 *The Character of Excess*

GAUNT: His rash fierce blaze of riot cannot last,
 For violent fires soon burn out themselves;
 Small showers last long, but sudden storms are short;
 He tires betimes that spurs too fast betimes;
 With eager feeding food doth choke the feeder:
 Light vanity, insatiate cormorant,
 Consuming means, soon preys upon itself.

KING RICHARD II, II. i. 33–39

11 *Nature's Opposites*

SALARINO:     Now, by two-headed Janus,
 Nature hath framed strange fellows in her time:
 Some that will evermore peep through their eyes
 And laugh like parrots at a bag-piper,
 And other of such vinegar aspect
 That they'll not show their teeth in way of smile,
 Though Nestor swear the jest be laughable.

THE MERCHANT OF VENICE, I. i. 50–56

12 *A Character of Common Humanity*

SALARINO: Why, I am sure, if he forfeit, thou wilt not take his flesh: what's that good for?

SHYLOCK: To bait fish withal: if it will feed nothing else, it will feed my revenge. He hath disgraced me, and hindered me half a million; laughed at my losses, mocked at my gains, scorned my nation, thwarted my bargains, cooled my friends, heated mine enemies; and what's his reason? I am a Jew. Hath not a Jew eyes? hath not a Jew hands, organs, dimensions, senses, affections, passions? fed with the same food, hurt with the same weapons, subject to the same diseases, healed by the same means, warmed and cooled by the same winter and summer, as a Christian is? If you prick us, do we not bleed? If you tickle us, do we not laugh? if you poison us, do we not die? and if you wrong us, shall

# *THE*
# Melancholie Knight.

*By* S. R.

¶ Imprinted at *London* by R. B. and are to be fold by
*George Loftus*, in Biſhops-gate ſtreete, neere the
Angell. 1 6 1 5.

Sono li cieli organi divi
ni
Per la potentia di natura
eterna
Che in lor splendendo son
de gloria plini
Informa del desio inamo
rati
Mouendo cosi el mondo
si gouerna
Per questi excelsi lumi immaculati

Fortuna

O Bel paese con gli
dolci colli
Perche nol cognoscete
o gente acerba
Cogliacti auari inuidio
sie folli
Io pur te piango dolce
mio paese
Chio non so chi nel mo
do ti conserba
Facendo contra dio cotante offese
Verra el tempo de gli tristi giorni

Inuidia

VINCIT LAEVA PERIMIT DEXTRA
AS INISTRA CAVETOs
OPINIO

we not revenge? If we are like you in the rest, we will resemble you in that. If a Jew wrong a Christian, what is his humility? Revenge. If a Christian wrong a Jew, what should his sufferance be by Christian example? Why, revenge. The villany you teach me, I will execute, and it shall go hard but I will better the instruction.

THE MERCHANT OF VENICE, III. i. 55–78

13 *The Character of Poetry*

HIPPOLYTA: 'Tis strange, my Theseus, that these lovers speak of.
THESEUS: More strange than true: I never may believe
    Those antique fables, nor these fairy toys.
    Lovers and madmen have such seething brains,
    Such shaping fantasies, that apprehend
    More than cool reason ever comprehends,
    The lunatic, the lover and the poet,
    Are of imagination all compact:
    One sees more devils than vast hell can hold;
    That is the madman: the lover, all as frantic,
    Sees Helen's beauty in a brow of Egypt:
    The poet's eye, in a fine frenzy rolling,
    Doth glance from heaven to earth, from earth to heaven;
    And, as imagination bodies forth
    The forms of things unknown, the poet's pen
    Turns them to shapes, and gives to airy nothing
    A local habitation and a name.
    Such tricks hath strong imagination,
    That, if it would but apprehend some joy,
    It comprehends some bringer of that joy;
    Or, in the night, imagining some fear,
    How easy is a bush supposed a bear!

A MIDSUMMER-NIGHT'S DREAM, V. i. 1–22

14 *Friend and Foe of Poetry*

GLENDOWER: I can speak English, lord, as well as you;
    For I was train'd up in the English court;
    14

Where, being but young, I framed to the harp
Many an English ditty lovely well,
And gave the tongue a helpful ornament,
A virtue that was never seen in you.
HOTSPUR: Marry,
And I am glad of it with all my heart:
I had rather be a kitten and cry mew
Than one of these same metre ballad-mongers;
I had rather hear a brazen canstick turn'd,
Or a dry wheel grate on the axle-tree;
And that would set my teeth nothing on edge,
Nothing so much as mincing poetry:
'Tis like the forc'd gait of a shuffling nag.

HENRY IV, PT. I, III. i. 121–134

15 *The Nature of Value*

HECTOR: Brother, she is not worth what she doth cost
The holding.
TROILUS:        What is aught but as 'tis valued?
HECTOR: But value dwells not in particular will;
It holds his estimate and dignity
As well wherein 'tis precious of itself
As in the prizer. 'Tis mad idolatry
To make the service greater than the god;
And the will dotes that is inclinable
To what infectiously itself affects,
Without some image of the affected merit.

TROILUS AND CRESSIDA, II. ii. 51–60

16 *Character of True Honour*

KING: 'Tis only title thou disdain'st in her, the which
I can build up. Strange is it that our bloods,
Of colour, weight, and heat, pour'd all together,
Would quite confound distinction, yet stands off
In differences so mighty. If she be

All that is virtuous, save what thou dislik'st,
A poor physician's daughter, thou dislik'st
Of virtue for the name; but do not so:
From lowest place when virtuous things proceed,
The place is dignified by the doer's deed:
Where great additions swell's, and virtue none,
It is a dropsied honour. Good alone
Is good without a name? Vileness is so:
The property by what it is should go,
Not by the title. She is young, wise, fair;
In these to nature she's immediate heir,
And these breed honour: that is honour's scorn
Which challenges itself as honour's born,
And is not like the sire: honours thrive
When rather from our acts we them derive
Than our foregoers: the mere word's a slave,
Debosh'd on every tomb, on every grave
A lying trophy, and as oft is dumb
Where dust and damn'd oblivion is the tomb
Of honour'd bones indeed. What should be said:?
If thou canst like this creature as a maid,
I can create the rest: virtue and she
Is her own dower; honour and wealth from me.

ALL'S WELL THAT ENDS WELL, II. iii. 124–151

17 *Popularity*

CASCA: O, he sits high in all the people's hearts:
   And that which would appear offence in us,
   His countenance, like richest alchemy,
   Will change to virtue and to worthiness.

JULIUS CAESAR, I. iii. 157–160

18 *Character of the Mob*

FIRST CITIZEN: We have ever your good word.
MARCIUS: He that will give good words to thee will flatter

Beneath abhorring. What would you have, you curs,
That like nor peace nor war? the one affrights you,
The other makes you proud. He that trusts to you,
Where he should find you lions, finds you hares;
Where foxes, geese: you are no surer, no,
Than is the coal of fire upon the ice,
Or hailstone in the sun. Your virtue is
To make him worthy whose offence subdues him,
And curse that Justice did it. Who deserves greatness
Deserves your hate; and your affections are
A sick man's appetite, who desires most that
Which would increase his evil. He that depends
Upon your favours swims with fins of lead,
And hews down oaks with rushes. Hang ye! Trust ye?
With every minute you do change a mind,
And call him noble that was now your hate,
Him vilde that was your garland.

CORIOLANUS, I. i. 172–190

### 19 *The Many-Headed Multitude*

FIRST CITIZEN: And to make us no better thought of, a little
help will serve; for once when we stood up about the
corn, he himself stuck not to call us the many-headed
multitude.

THIRD CITIZEN: We have been called so of many; not that our
heads are some brown, some black, some abram, some
bald, but that our wits are so diversely coloured: and truly
I think if all our wits were to issue out of one skull, they
would fly east, west, north, south; and their consent of one
direct way should be at once to all the points o' the
compass.

CORIOLANUS, II. iii. 15–26

### 20 *Whoremaster Man*

VARRO'S SERVANT: What is a whoremaster, fool?

FOOL: A fool in good clothes, and something like thee. 'Tis a spirit: sometime 't appears like a lord; sometime like a lawyer; sometime like a philosopher, with two stones moe than's artificial one. He is very often like a knight; and generally in all shapes that man goes up and down in from fourscore to thirteen, this spirit walks in.

TIMON OF ATHENS, II. ii. 113–121

## 21 *Life a Mingled Yarn*

SECOND LORD: I am heartily sorry that he'll be glad of this.

FIRST LORD: How mightily sometimes we make us comforts of our losses!

SECOND LORD: And how mightily some other times we drown our gain in tears! The great dignity that his valour hath here acquired for him shall at home be encountered with a shame as ample.

FIRST LORD: The web of our life is of a mingled yarn, good and ill together: our virtues would be proud, if our faults whipped them not; and our crimes would despair, if they were not cherished by our virtues.

ALL'S WELL THAT ENDS WELL, IV. iii. 74–87

## 22 *A Character of Man's Ages*

JAQUES:                                       All the world's a stage,
And all the men and women merely players:
They have their exits and their entrances;
And one man in his time plays many parts,
His acts being seven ages. At first the infant,
Mewling and puking in the nurse's arms.
And then the whining school-boy, with his satchel
And shining morning face, creeping like snail
Unwillingly to school. And then the lover,
Sighing like furnace, with a woeful ballad
Made to his mistress's eyebrow. Then a soldier,
Full of strange oaths and bearded like the pard,

Jealous in honour, sudden and quick in quarrel,
Seeking the bubble reputation
Even in the cannon's mouth. And then the justice,
In fair round belly and beard of formal cut,
Full of wise saws and modern instances;
And so he plays his part. The sixth age shifts
Into the lean and slipper'd pantaloon,
With spectacles on nose and pouch on side,
His youthful hose, well saved, aworld too wide
For his shrunk shank; and his big manly voice,
Turning again toward childish treble, pipes
And whistles in his sound. Last scene of all,
That ends this strange eventful history,
Is second childishness and mere oblivion,
Sans teeth, sans eyes, sans taste, sans everything.

AS YOU LIKE IT, II. vii. 139–166


23 *A Character of the Life of Man*

CLAUDIO: I've hope to live, and am prepar'd to die.
DUKE: Be absolute for death; either death or life
    Shall thereby be the sweeter. Reason thus with life:
    If I do lose thee, I do lose a thing
    That none but fools would keep: a breath thou art,
    Servile to all the skyey influences,
    That do this habitation, where thou keep'st,
    Hourly afflict. Merely, thou art death's fool;
    For him thou labour'st by thy flight to shun,
    And yet runn'st toward him still. Thou art not noble;
    For all the accommodations that thou bear'st
    Are nurs'd by baseness. Thou art by no means valiant;
    For thou dost fear the soft and tender fork
    Of a poor worm. Thy best of rest is sleep,
    And that thou oft provok'st; yet grossly fear'st
    Thy death, which is no more. Thou art not thyself;
    For thou exist'st on many a thousand grains

That issue out of dust. Happy thou art not;
For what thou hast not, still thou striv'st to get,
And what thou hast, forget'st. Thou art not certain;
For thy complexion shifts to strange effects,
After the moon. If thou art rich, thou'rt poor;
For, like an ass whose back with ingots bows,
Thou bear'st thy heavy riches but a journey,
And death unloads thee. Friend hast thou none;
For thine own bowels, which do call thee sire,
The mere effusion of thy proper loins,
Do curse the gout, serpigo, and the rheum,
For ending thee no sooner. Thou hast nor youth nor age,
But, as it were, an after-dinner's sleep,
Dreaming on both; for all thy blessed youth
Becomes as aged, and doth beg the alms
Of palsied eld: and when thou art old and rich,
Thou hast neither heat, affection, limb, nor beauty,
To make thy riches pleasant. What's yet in this
That bears the name of life? Yet in this life
Lie hid more thousand deaths; yet death we fear,
That makes these odds all even.

MEASURE FOR MEASURE, III. i. 4–41

## 24 *The Nature of Life*

MACBETH: To-morrow, and to-morrow, and to-morrow
Creeps in this petty pace from day to day,
To the last syllable of recorded time;
And all our yesterdays have lighted fools
The way to dusty death. Out, out, brief candle!
Life's but a walking shadow, a poor player
That struts and frets his hour upon the stage,
And then is heard no more: it is a tale
Told by an idiot, full of sound and fury,
Signifying nothing.

MACBETH, V. v. 19–28

### 25 *Teeming Mother-Earth*

TIMON: That nature, being sick of man's unkindness,
    Should yet be hungry! Common mother, thou

(Digging)

    Whose womb unmeasurable, and infinite breast,
    Teems, and feeds all; whose self-same mettle,
    Whereof thy proud child, arrogant man, is puff'd,
    Engenders the black toad and adder blue,
    The gilded newt and eyeless venom'd worm,
    With all the abhorred births below crisp heaven
    Whereon Hyperion's quickening fire doth shine;
    Yield him, who all thy human sons doth hate,
    From forth thy plenteous bosom, one poor root!
    Ensear thy fertile and conceptious womb,
    Let it no more bring our ingrateful man!
    Go great with tigers, dragons, wolves, and bears;
    Teem with new monsters, whom thy upward face
    Hath to the marbled mansion all above
    Never presented! O, a root; dear thanks!
    Dry up thy marrows, vines, and plough-torn leas;
    Whereof ingrateful man, with liquorish draughts
    And morsels unctuous, greases his pure mind,
    That from it all consideration slips!

TIMON OF ATHENS, IV. iii. 177–197

### 26 *Indifferent Nature*

APEMANTUS: Thou has cast away thyself, being like thyself;
    A madman so long, now a fool. What, think'st
    That the bleak air, thy boisterous chamberlain,
    Will put thy shirt on warm? will these moss'd trees,
    That have outliv'd the eagle, page thy heels
    And skip when thou point'st out? will the cold brook,
    Candied with ice, caudle thy morning taste
    To cure thy o'er-night's surfeit? Call the creatures
    Whose naked natures live in all the spite
    Of wreakful heaven, whose bare unhoused trunks,

To the conflicting elements exposed,
Answer mere nature; bid them flatter thee.

TIMON OF ATHENS, IV. iii. 221–232

## 27 Beastly Life

TIMON: What would'st thou do with the world, Apemantus, if it lay in thy power?

APEMANTUS: Give it to the beasts, to be rid of the men.

TIMON: Would'st thou have thyself fall in the confusion of men, and remain a beast with the beasts?

APEMANTUS: Ay, Timon.

TIMON: A beastly ambition, which the gods grant thee t' attain to. If thou wert the lion, the fox would beguile thee; if thou wert the lamb, the fox would eat thee; if thou wert the fox, the lion would suspect thee, when peradventure thou wert accused by the ass; if thou wert the ass, thy dulness would torment thee, and still thou livedst but as a breakfast to the wolf; if thou wert the wolf, thy greediness would afflict thee, and oft thou should'st hazard thy life for thy dinner; wert thou the unicorn, pride and wrath would confound thee and make thine own self the conquest of thy fury; wert thou a bear, thou would'st be killed by the horse; wert thou a horse, thou would'st be seized by the leopard; wert thou a leopard, then wert german to the lion, and the spots of thy kindred were jurors on thy life; all thy safety were remotion, and thy defence absence. What beast could'st thou be that were not subject to a beast? and what a beast art thou already, that seest not thy loss in transformation!

TIMON OF ATHENS, IV. iii. 321–351

## 28 The Fashion of Promising

PAINTER: Promising is the very air o' the time; it opens the eyes of expectation; performance is ever the duller for his act; and, but in the plainer and simpler kind of people, the deed of saying is quite out of use. To promise is most courtly

and fashionable; performance is a kind of will or testament
which argues a great sickness in his judgment that makes it.

                              TIMON OF ATHENS, V. i. 25–33


## 29 *Thievery*

ALL: We are not thieves, but men that much do want.
TIMON: Your greatest want is, you want much of meat.
   Why should you want? Behold, the earth hath roots;
   Within this mile break forth a hundred springs;
   The oaks bear mast, the briers scarlet hips;
   The bounteous houswife, nature, on each bush
   Lays her full mess before you. Want! why want?
FIRST THIEF: We cannot live on grass, on berries, water,
   As beasts and birds and fishes.
TIMON: Nor on the beasts themselves, the birds, and fishes;
   You must eat men. Yet thanks I must you con
   That you are thieves profess'd, that work not
   In holier shapes; for there is boundless theft
   In limited professions. Rascal thieves,
   Here's gold. Go, suck the subtle blood o' the grape,
   Till the high fever seethe your blood to froth.
   And so 'scape hanging: trust not the physician;
   His antidotes are poison, and he slays
   More than you rob: take wealth and lives together;
   Do villany do, since you protest to do 't,
   Like workmen. I'll example you with thievery:
   The sun's a thief, and with his great attraction
   Robs the vast sea; the moon's an arrant thief,
   And her pale fire she snatches from the sun;
   The sea's a thief, whose liquid surge resolves
   The moon into salt tears; the earth's a thief,
   That feeds and breeds by a composure stolen
   From general excrement; each thing's a thief;
   The laws, your curb and whip, in their rough power
   Have uncheck'd theft. Love not yourselves; away!
   Rob one another. There's more gold. Cut throats;

All that you meet are thieves: to Athens go,
Break open shops; nothing can you steal
But thieves do lose it: steal no less for this
I give you; and gold confound you howsoe'er!
Amen.

TIMON OF ATHENS, IV. iii. 421–456

## 30 *Adolescence*

SHEPHERD: I would there were no age between ten and three-
and-twenty, or that youth would sleep out the rest; for
there is nothing in the between but getting wenches with
child, wronging the ancientry, stealing, fighting—Hark
you now! Would any but these boiled-brains of nineteen
and two-and-twenty hunt this weather? They have scared
away two of my best sheep which I fear the wolf will
sooner find than the master: if any where I have them, 'tis
by the seaside, browzing of ivy. Good luck, an 't be thy
will!

THE WINTER'S TALE, III. iii. 58–68

## 31 *The Corruption of the Best*

KING: The gentleman is learn'd and a most rare speaker;
To nature none more bound; his training such
That he may furnish and instruct great teachers,
And never seek for aid out of himself. Yet see,
When these so noble benefits shall prove
Not well disposed, the mind growing once corrupt,
They turn to vicious forms, ten times more ugly
Than ever they were fair. This man so complete,
Who was enroll'd 'mongst wonders, and when we,
Almost with ravish'd listening, could not find
His hour of speech a minute; he, my lady,
Hath into monstrous habits put the graces
That once were his, and is become as black
As if besmear'd in hell.

KING HENRY VIII, I. ii. 111–124

## 32 *The Nature of Art and of Life*

PROSPERO: You do look, my son, in a mov'd sort,
As if you were dismay'd. Be cheerful, sir.
Our revels now are ended. These our actors,
As I foretold you, were all spirits and
Are melted into air, into thin air;
And, like the baseless fabric of this vision,
The cloud-clapp'd towers, the gorgeous palaces,
The solemn temples, the great globe itself,
Yea, all which it inherit, shall dissolve,
And, like this insubstantial pageant faded,
Leave not a rack behind. We are such stuff
As dreams are made on, and our little life
Is rounded with a sleep.

THE TEMPEST, IV. i. 146–158

## 1 *The Nature of Death*

TITUS: In peace and honour rest you here, my sons;
    Rome's readiest champions, repose you here in rest,
    Secure from wordly chances and mishaps!
    Here lurks no treason, here no envy swells,
    Here grow no damned drugs, here are no storms,
    No noise, but silence and eternal sleep.
    In peace and honour rest you here, my sons!

                TITUS ANDRONICUS, I. i. 150–156

## 2 *Death the Debt-Payer*

FIRST GAOLER: Come, sir, are you ready for death?

POSTHUMUS: Over-roasted rather; ready long ago.

FIRST GAOLER: Hanging is the word, sir: if you be ready for that, you are well cooked.

POSTHUMUS: So, if I prove a good repast to the spectators, the dish pays the shot.

FIRST GAOLER: A heavy reckoning for you sir. But the comfort is, you shall be called to no more payments, fear no more tavern-bills; which are often the sadness of parting, as the procuring of mirth: you come in faint for want of meat, depart reeling with too much drink; sorry that you have paid too much, and sorry that you are paid too much; purse and brain both empty, the brain the heavier for being too light, the purse too light, being drawn of heaviness: O, of this contradiction you shall now be quit. O, the charity of a penny cord! it sums up thousands in a trice: you have no true debitor and creditor but it; of what's past, is, and to come, the discharge: your neck, sir, is pen, book, and counters; so the acquittance follows.

                CYMBELINE, V. iv. 153–174

### 3 *The Nature of Homicide*

ALCIBIADES: I am an humble suitor to your virtues;
    For pity is the virtue of the law,
    And none but tyrants use it cruelly.
    It pleases time and fortune to lie heavy
    Upon a friend of mine, who, in hot blood,
    Hath stepp'd into the law, which is past depth
    To those that without heed do plunge into 't.
    He is a man, setting his fault aside,
    Of comely virtues;
    Nor did he soil the fact with cowardice—
    An honour in him which buys out his fault—
    But with a noble fury and fair spirit,
    Seeing his reputation touched to death,
    He did oppose his foe;
    And with such sober and unnoted passion
    He did behave his anger, ere 'twas spent,
    As if he had but prov'd an argument.

FIRST SENATOR: You undergo too strict a paradox,
    Striving to make an ugly deed look fair:
    Your words have took such pains as if they labour'd
    To bring manslaughter into form, and set quarrelling
    Upon the head of valour; which indeed
    Is valour misbegot, and came into the world
    When sects and factions were newly born.
    He's truly valiant that can wisely suffer
    The worst that man can breathe, and make his wrongs
    His outsides, to wear them like his raiment, carelessly,
    And ne'er prefer his injuries to his heart,
    To bring it into danger.
    If wrongs be evils and enforce us kill,
    What folly 'tis to hazard life for ill!

TIMON OF ATHENS, III. V. 7–37

### 4 *Paradox of Love and Hate*

ROMEO: Here's much to do with hate, but more with love:
 Why then, O brawling love! O loving hate!
 O any thing, of nothing first created!
 O heavy lightness! serious vanity!
 Misshapen chaos of well-seeming forms!
 Feather of lead, bright smoke, cold fire, sick health!
 Still-waking sleep, that is not what it is!
 This love feel I, that feel no love in this.

ROMEO AND JULIET, I. i. 180–187

### 5 *Paradox of Appearance and Reality*

JULIET: O God!—did Romeo's hand shed Tybalt's blood?
NURSE: It did, it did; alas the day, it did!
JULIET: O serpent heart, hid with a flowering face!
 Did ever dragon keep so fair a cave?
 Beautiful tyrant! fiend angelical!
 Dove-feather'd raven! wolvish-ravening lamb!
 Despised substance of divinest show!
 Just opposite to what thou justly seem'st;
 A damned saint, an honourable villain!
 O nature, what hadst thou to do in hell
 When thou didst bower the spirit of a fiend
 In mortal paradise of such sweet flesh?
 Was ever book containing such vile matter
 So fairly bound? O, that deceit should dwell
 In such a gorgeous palace!

ROMEO AND JULIET, III. ii. 71–85

### 6 *Character of Commodity*

BASTARD: Mad world! mad kings! mad composition!
 John, to stop Arthur's title in the whole,
 Hath willingly departed with a part,
 And France, whose armour conscience buckled on,
 Whom zeal and charity brought to the field

As God's own soldier, rounded in the ear
With that same purpose-changer, that sly devil,
That broker, that still breaks the pate of faith,
That daily break-vow, he that wins of all,
Of kings, of beggars, old men, young men, maids,
Who, having no external thing to lose
But the word 'maid', cheats the poor maid of that,
That smooth-faced gentleman, tickling Commodity,
Commodity, the bias of the world,
The world, who of itself is peised well,
Made to run even upon even ground,
Till this advantage, this vile-drawing bias,
This sway of motion, this Commodity,
Makes it take head from all indifferency,
From all direction, purpose, course, intent:
And this same bias, this Commodity,
This bawd, this broker, this all-changing word,
Clapp'd on the outward eye of fickle France,
Hath drawn him from his own determined aid,
From a resolved and honourable war,
To a most base and vile-concluded peace.

KING JOHN, II. i. 561–586

## 7 Rumour

*Rumour*: Open your ears; for which of you will stop
    The vent of hearing when loud Rumour speaks?
    I, from the orient to the drooping west,
    Making the wind my post-horse, still unfold
    The acts commenced on this ball of earth:
    Upon my tongues continual slanders ride,
    The which in every language I pronounce,
    Stuffing the ears of men with false reports.
    I speak of peace, while covert enmity
    Under the smile of safety wounds the world:
    And who but Rumour, who but only I,
    Make fearful musters and prepar'd defence,

DISSIMULATION

FEAR

DISDAIN

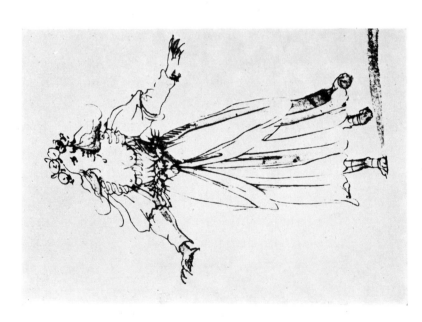

JEALOUSY

Whiles the big year, swoln with some other grief,
Is thought with child by the stern tyrant war,
And no such matter? Rumour is a pipe
Blown by surmises, jealousies, conjectures,
And of so easy and so plain a stop
That the blunt monster with uncounted heads,
The still-discordant wavering multitude,
Can play upon it.

HENRY IV, PT. II, INDUCTION. I–20

## 8 *Fashion*

BORACHIO: But seest thou not what a deformed thief this fashion is?

WATCH: (*Aside*) I know that Deformed; a' has been a vile thief this seven year; a' goes up and down like a gentleman: I remember his name.

BORACHIO: Didst thou not hear somebody?

CONRADE: No; 'twas the vane on the house.

BORACHIO: Seest thou not, I say, what a deformed thief this fashion is? how giddily a' turns about all the hot bloods between fourteen and five-and-thirty? sometimes fashioning them like Pharaoh's soldiers in the reechy painting, sometime like god Bel's priests in the old church-window, sometime like the shaven Hercules in the smirched worm-eaten tapestry, where his codpiece seems as massy as his club?

CONRADE: All this I see, and I see that the fashion wears out more apparel than the man.

MUCH ADO ABOUT NOTHING, III. iii. 130–148

## 9 *Fortune*

PISTOL: Bardolph, a soldier, firm and sound of heart,
And of the buxom valour, hath, by cruel fate,
And giddy Fortune's furious fickle wheel,
That goddess blind,
That stands upon the rolling restless stone—

15

FLUELLEN: By your patience, Aunchient Pistol. Fortune is painted blind, with a muffler afore her eyes, to signify to you that Fortune is blind; and she is painted also with a wheel, to signify to you, which is the moral of it, that she is turning, and inconstant, and mutability, and variation: and her foot, look you, is fixed upon a spherical stone, which rolls, and rolls, and rolls: in good truth, the poet makes a most excellent description of it: Fortune is an excellent moral.

KING HENRY V, III. vi. 26–40

10 *Character of Ceremony*

KING HENRY: And what art thou, thou idol ceremony?
What kind of god art thou, that suffer'st more
Of mortal griefs than do thy worshippers?
What are thy rents? what are thy comings in?
O ceremony, show me but thy worth!
What is thy soul of adoration?
Art thou aught else but place, degree and form,
Creating awe and fear in other men?
Wherein thou art less happy being fear'd
Than they in fearing.
What drink'st thou oft, instead of homage sweet,
But poison'd flattery? O, be sick, great greatness,
And bid thy ceremony give thee cure!
Think'st thou the fiery fever will go out
With titles blown from adulation?
Will it give place to flexure and low bending?
Canst thou, when thou command'st the beggar's knee,
Command the health of it? No, thou proud dream,
That play'st so subtly with a king's repose;
I am a king find that thee, and I know
'Tis not the balm, the sceptre and the ball,
The sword, the mace, the crown imperial,
The intertissued robe of gold and pearl,
The farced title running 'fore the king,

The throne he sits on, nor the tide of pomp
That beats upon the high shore of this world,
No, not all these, thrice-gorgeous ceremony,
Not all these, laid in bed majestical,
Can sleep so soundly as the wretched slave,
Who with a body fill'd and vacant mind
Gets him to rest, cramm'd with distressful bread;
Never sees horrid night, the child of hell,
But, like a lackey, from the rise to set
Sweats in the eye of Phoebus and all night
Sleeps in Elysium; next day after dawn,
Doth rise and help Hyperion to his horse,
And follows so the ever-running year,
With profitable labour, to his grave:
And, but for ceremony, such a wretch,
Winding up days with toil and nights with sleep,
Had the fore-hand and vantage of a king.
The slave, a member of the country's peace,
Enjoys it; but in gross brain little wots
What watch the king keeps to maintain the peace,
Whose hours the peasant best advantages.

KING HENRY V, IV. i. 260–304

## 11 The Nature of Reputation

IAGO: Good name in man and woman, dear my lord,
    Is the immediate jewel of their souls:
    Who steals my purse steals trash; 'tis something, nothing;
    'Twas mine, 'tis his, and has been slave to thousands;
    But he that filches from me my good name
    Robs me of that which not enriches him
    And makes me poor indeed.

OTHELLO, III. iii. 155–161

## 12 Jealousy

IAGO:                    O, beware, my lord, of jealousy;
    It is the green-eyed monster, which doth mock

The meat it feeds on: that cuckold lives in bliss
Who, certain of his fate, loves not his wronger;
But, O, what damned minutes tells he o'er
Who dotes, yet doubts, suspects, yet strongly loves!
OTHELLO; O misery!
IAGO: Poor and content is rich, and rich enough;
    But riches fineless is as poor as winter
    To him that ever fears he shall be poor:
    Good heaven, the souls of all my tribe defend
    From jealousy!

                        OTHELLO, III. iii. 166–176

## 13 *Sleep*

MACBETH:            the innocent sleep,
    Sleep that knits up the ravell'd sleave of care,
    The death of each day's life, sore labour's bath,
    Balm of hurt minds, great nature's second course,
    Chief nourisher in life's feast,—

                        MACBETH, II. ii. 37–51

## 14 *The Character of Gold (a)*

TIMON: Who seeks for better of thee, sauce his palate
    With thy most operant poison! What is here?
    Gold! yellow, glittering, precious gold! No, gods,
    I am no idle votarist. Roots, you clear heavens!
    Thus much of this will make black white, foul fair,
    Wrong right, base noble, old young, coward valiant.
    Ha! you gods, why this? What this, you gods? Why this,
    Will lug your priests and servants from your sides,
    Pluck stout men's pillows from below their heads:
    This yellow slave
    Will knit and break religions; bless the accurs'd;
    Make the hoar leprosy ador'd; place thieves,
    And give them title, knee, and approbation,
    With senators on the bench; this is it

That makes the wappen'd widow wed again;
She, whom the spital-house and ulcerous sores
Would cast the gorge at, this embalms and spices
To the April day again. Come, damned earth,
Thou common whore of mankind, that putt'st odds
Among the rout of nations, I will make thee
Do thy right nature.

TIMON OF ATHENS, IV. iii. 24–43

14 *The Character of Gold (b)*

TIMON: (*Looking on the gold*) O thou sweet king-killer, and dear
        divorce
'Twixt natural son and sire! thou bright defiler
Of Hymen's purest bed! thou valiant Mars!
Thou ever young, fresh, lov'd, and delicate wooer,
Whose blush doth thaw the consecrated snow
That lies on Dian's lap! thou visible god,
That solder'st close impossibilities,
And mak'st them kiss! that speak'st with every tongue,
To every purpose! O thou touch of hearts!
Think thy slave man rebels; and by thy virtue
Set them into confounding odds, that beasts
May have the world in empire!

TIMON OF ATHENS, IV. iii. 384–395

### 1 *A Monstrous Birth*

KING HENRY: Hadst thou been kill'd when first thou didst
    presume,
    Thou hadst not liv'd to kill a son of mine.
    And thus I prophesy: that many a thousand,
    Which now mistrust no parcel of my fear,
    And many an old man's sigh, and many a widow's,
    And many an orphan's water-standing eye,
    Men for their sons's, wives for their husbands',
    And orphans for their parents' timeless death,
    Shall rue the hour that ever thou wast born.
    The owl shriek'd at thy birth, an evil sign;
    The night-crow cried, aboding luckless time;
    Dogs howl'd, and hideous tempest shook down trees;
    The raven rook'd her on the chimney's top,
    And chattering pies in dismal discords sung.
    Thy mother felt more than a mother's pain,
    And yet brought forth less than a mother's hope;
    To wit, an indigested and deformed lump,
    Not like the fruit of such a goodly tree.
    Teeth hadst thou in thy head when thou wast born,
    To signify thou camest to bite the world.

KING HENRY VI, PT. III, V. vi. 35–54

### 2 *Birth of a Wizard*

GLENDOWER: Give me leave
    To tell you once again that at my birth
    The front of heaven was full of fiery shapes,
    The goats ran from the mountains, and the herds
    Were strangely clamorous to the frighted fields.
    These signs have mark'd me extraordinary;
    And all the courses of my life do show

I am not in the roll of common men.
Where is he living, clipp'd in with the sea
That chides the banks of England, Scotland, Wales,
Which calls me pupil, or hath read to me?
And bring him out that is but woman's son
Can trace me in the tedious ways of art
And hold me pace in deep experiments.
HOTSPUR: I think there's no man speaks better Welsh.
I'll to dinner.

HENRY IV, PT. I, III. i. 36–51

3 *Queen Mab*

MERCUTIO: O, then I see Queen Mab hath been with you.
She is the fairies' midwife, and she comes
In shape no bigger than an agate-stone
On the forefinger of an alderman,
Drawn with a team of little atomies
Athwart men's noses as they lie asleep:
Her waggon-spokes made of long spinners' legs;
The cover, of the wings of grasshoppers;
Her traces, of the smallest spider's web;
Her collars, of the moonshine's watery beams;
Her whip, of cricket's bone; the lash, of film;
Her waggoner, a small grey-coated gnat,
Not half so big as a round little worm
Prick'd from the lazy finger of a maid:
Her chariot is an empty hazel-nut,
Made by the joiner squirrel or old grub,
Time out o'mind the fairies' coach-makers.
And in this state she gallops night by night
Through lovers' brains, and then they dream of love;
O'er courtiers' knees, that dream on court'sies straight;
O'er lawyers' fingers, who straight dream on fees;
O'er ladies' lips, who straight on kisses dream,
Which oft the angry Mab with blisters plagues,
Because their breaths with sweetmeats tainted are:
Sometime she gallops o'er a courtier's nose,

And then dreams he of smelling out a suit;
And sometime comes she with a tithe-pig's tail
Tickling a parson's nose as a' lies asleep,
Then dreams he of another benefice;
Sometimes she driveth o'er a soldier's neck,
Then dreams he of cutting foreign throats,
Of breaches, ambuscadoes, Spanish blades,
Of healths five fathom deep; and then anon
Drums in his ear, at which he starts and wakes,
And, being thus frighted, swears a prayer or two,
And sleeps again. This is that very Mab
That plats the manes of horses in the night,
And bakes the elf-locks in foul sluttish hairs,
Which once untangled much misfortune bodes;
This is the hag, when maids lie on their backs,
That presses them and learns them first to bear,
Making them women of good carriage.

ROMEO AND JULIET, I. iv. 53–95

## 4 *Rogue Goodfellow*

FAIRY: Either I mistake your shape and making quite,
Or else you are that shrewd and knavish sprite
Call'd Robin Good-fellow: are not you he
That frights the maidens of the villagery;
Skim milk, and sometimes labour in the quern,
And bootless make the breathless housewife churn;
And sometime make the drink to bear no barm;
Mislead night-wanderers, laughing at their harm?
Those that Hobgoblin call you, and sweet Puck,
You do their work, and they shall have good luck:
Are not you he?
PUCK:                    Fairy, thou speak'st aright;
I am that merry wanderer of the night,
I jest to Oberon, and make him smile,
When I a fat and bean-fed horse beguile,
Neighing in likeness of a filly foal:
And sometime lurk I in a gossip's bowl,

In very likeness of a roasted crab;
And, when she drinks, against her Hips I bob,
And on her wither'd dew-lap pour the ale.
The wisest aunt, telling the saddest tale,
Sometime for three-foot stool mistaketh me;
Then slip I from her bum, down topples she,
And 'tailor' cries, and falls into a cough;
And then the whole quire hold their hips, and laugh;
And waxen in their mirth, and neeze, and swear
A merrier hour was never wasted there.

A MIDSUMMER-NIGHT'S DREAM, II. i. 32–57

## 5 Fairy Companion

TITANIA: The fairy land buys not the child of me.
His mother was a votaress of my order:
And, in the spiced Indian air, by night,
Full often hath she gossip'd by my side;
And sat with me on Neptune's yellow sands,
Marking the embarked traders on the flood;
When we have laugh'd to see the sails conceive,
And grow big-bellied with the wanton wind;
Which she, with pretty and with swimming gait,
Following,—her womb then rich with my young squire,—
Would imitate, and sail upon the land,
To fetch me trifles, and return again,
As from a voyage, rich with merchandise.

A MIDSUMMER-NIGHT'S DREAM, II. i. 122–134

## 6 Ghosts and Fairies

PUCK: My fairy lord, this must be done with haste;
For night's swift dragons cut the clouds full fast,
And yonder shines Aurora's harbinger;
At whose approach, ghosts, wandering here and there,
Troop home to churchyards: damned spirits all,
That in cross-ways and floods have burial,
Already to their wormy beds are gone;

For fear lest day should look their shames upon,
They wilfully themselves exile from light,
And must for aye consort with black-brow'd night.

OBERON: But we are spirits of another sort:
I with the morning's love have oft made sport:
And, like a forester, the groves may tread,
Even till the eastern gate, all fiery-red,
Opening on Neptune with fair blessed beams,
Turns into yellow gold his salt-green streams.

A MIDSUMMER-NIGHT'S DREAM, III. ii. 378–393


## 7 A Tedious Necromancer

MORTIMER: Fie, cousin Percy! how you cross my father!

HOTSPUR: I cannot choose: sometime he angers me
With telling me of the moldwarp and the ant,
Of the dreamer Merlin and his prophecies,
And of a dragon and a finless fish,
A clip-wing'd griffin and and a moulten raven,
A couching lion and a ramping cat,
And such a deal of skimble-skamble stuff
As puts me from my faith. I tell you what;
He held me last night at least nine hours
In reckoning up the several devils' names
That were his lackeys: I cried 'hum' and 'well, go to',
But mark'd him not a word. O, he is as tedious
As a tired horse, a railing wife;
Worse than a smoky house: I had rather live
With cheese and garlic in a windmill, far,
Than feed on cates and have him talk to me
In any summer-house in Christendom.

MORTIMER: In faith, he is a worthy gentleman,
Exceedingly well read, and profited
In strange concealments, valiant as a lion
And wondrous affable, and as bountiful
As mines of India.

HENRY IV, PT. I, III. i. 146–168

## 8 *Witches*

BANQUO: What are these
So wither'd, and so wild in their attire,
That look not like the inhabitants o' the earth,
And yet are on't? Live you? or are you aught
That man may question? You seem to understand me,
By each at once her choppy finger laying
Upon her skinny lips: you should be women,
And yet your beards forbid me to interpret
That you are so.

MACBETH, I. iii. 39–47

## 9 *The Fiend Flibbertigibbet*

EDGAR: This is the foul fiend Flibbertigibbet. He begins at
curfew, and walks till the first cock. He gives the web and
the pin, squints the eye, and makes the harelip; mildews
the white wheat, and hurts the poor creature of earth.

KING LEAR, III. iv. 118–122

## 10 *A Hunter's Ghost*

MRS. PAGE: There is an old tale goes that Herne the hunter,
Sometime a keeper here in Windsor forest,
Doth all the winter-time, at still midnight,
Walk round about an oak, with great ragg'd horns;
And there he blasts the tree, and takes the cattle,
And makes milch-kine yield blood, and shakes a chain
In a most hideous and dreadful manner:
You have heard of such a spirit; and well you know
The superstitious idle-headed eld
Received, and did deliver to our age,
This tale of Herne the hunter for a truth.

THE MERRY WIVES OF WINDSOR, IV. iv. 29–39

### 1 *A Flaunting Dame*

QUEEN: Not all these lords to vex me half so much
    As that proud dame, the lord protector's wife:
    She sweeps it through the court with troops of ladies,
    More like an empress than Duke Humphrey's wife.
    Strangers in court do take her for the queen:
    She bears a duke's revenues on her back,
    And in her heart she scorns our poverty.
    Shall I not live to be avenged on her?
    Contemptuous base-born callat as she is,
    She vaunted 'mongst her minions t'other day,
    The very train of her worst wearing gown
    Was better worth than all my father's lands,
    Till Suffolk gave two dukedoms for his daughter.

               KING HENRY VI, PT. II, I. iii. 78–90

### 2 *Tigerish Woman*

YORK: She-wolf of France, but worse than wolves of France,
    Whose tongue more poisons than the adder's tooth!
    How ill-beseeming is it in thy sex
    To triumph like an Amazonian trull,
    Upon their woes whom fortune captivates!
    But that thy face is, vizard-like, unchanging,
    Made impudent with use of evil deeds,
    I would assay, proud queen, to make thee blush:
    To tell thee whence thou cam'st, of whom derived,
    Were shame enough to shame thee, wert thou not shame-
        less.
    Thy father bears the type of King of Naples,
    Of both the Sicils and Jerusalem,
    Yet not so wealthy as an English yeoman.

Hath that poor monarch taught thee to insult?
It needs not, nor it boots thee not, proud queen,
Unless the adage must be verified,
That beggars mounted run their horse to death.
'Tis beauty that doth oft make women proud;
But, God he knows, thy share thereof is small:
'Tis virtue that doth make them most admired;
The contrary doth make thee wonder'd at:
'Tis government that makes them seem divine;
The want thereof makes thee abominable.
Thou art as opposite to every good
As the Antipodes are unto us,
Or as the south to the Septentrion.
O tiger's heart wrapp'd in a woman's hide!
How could'st thou drain the life-blood of the child,
To bid the father wipe his eyes withal,
And yet be seen to bear a woman's face?
Women are soft, mild, pitiful, and flexible.

KING HENRY VI, PT. III, I. iv. 111–142


## 3 *A Woman Fearful*

CONSTANCE: It cannot be; thou dost but say 'tis so:
I trust I may not trust thee; for thy word
Is but the vain breath of a common man:
Believe me, I do not believe thee, man;
I have a king's oath to the contrary.
Thou shalt be punish'd for thus frighting me,
For I am sick and capable of fears,
Oppress'd with wrongs and therefore full of fears,
A widow, husbandless, subject to fears,
A woman, naturally born to fears,
And though thou now confess thou didst but jest,
With my vex'd spirits I cannot take a truce,
But they will quake and tremble all this day.

KING JOHN, III. i. 6–18

### 4 *An Absolute Court Lady*

MRS. FORD: I your lady, Sir John! alas, I should be a pitiful lady!

FALSTAFF: Let the court of France show me such another. I see
how thine eye would emulate the diamond: thou hast the
right arched beauty of the brow that becomes the ship-tire,
the tire-valiant, or any tire of Venetian admittance.

MRS. FORD: A plain kerchief, Sir John: my brows become nothing else; nor that well neither.

FALSTAFF: By the Lord thou art a traitor to say so: thou wouldst
make an absolute courtier; and the firm fixture of thy foot
would give an excellent motion to thy gait in a semicircled
farthingale. I see what thou wert, if Fortune thy foe were
not, Nature thy friend. Come, thou canst not hide it.

THE MERRY WIVES OF WINDSOR, III. iii. 55–71

### 5 *Variable Woman*

IAGO: Come on, come on; you are pictures out of doors,
Bells in your parlours, wild-cats in your kitchens,
Saints in your injuries, devils being offended,
Players in your housewifery, and housewives in your beds.

OTHELLO, II. i. 109–112

### 6 *A Virtuous Simple Woman*

IAGO: She that was ever fair and never proud,
Had tongue at will and yet was never loud,
Never lack'd gold and yet went never gay,
Fled from her wish and yet said 'Now I may';
She that, being anger'd, her revenge being nigh,
Bade her wrong stay and her displeasure fly;
She that in wisdom never was so frail
To change the cod's head for the salmon's tail;
She that could think and ne'er disclose her mind,
See suitors following and not look behind;
She was a wight, if ever such wight were,—

DESDEMONA: To do what?

IAGO: To suckle fools and chronicle small beer.

OTHELLO, II. i. 148–160

### 7 *A Woman Infinite* (*a*)

ANTONY: She is cunning past man's thought.

ENOBARBUS: Alack, sir, no; her passions are made of nothing but the finest part of pure love: we cannot call her winds and waters sighs and tears; they are greater storms and tempests than almanacs can report: this cannot be cunning in her; if it be, she makes a shower of rain as well as Jove.

ANTONY: Would I had never seen her!

ENOBARBUS: O, sir, you had then left unseen a wonderful piece of work; which not to have been blest withal would have discredited your travel.

ANTONY AND CLEOPATRA, I. ii. 155–166

### 7 *A Woman Infinite* (*b*)

MAECENAS: No Antony must leave her utterly.

ENOBARBUS: Never: he will not:
Age cannot wither her, nor custom stale
Her infinite variety: other women cloy
The appetites they feed: but she makes hungry
Where most she satisfies; for vilest things
Become themselves in her, that the holy priests
Bless her when she is riggish.

ANTONY AND CLEOPATRA, II. ii. 241–248

### 8 *A Country Hostess*

SHEPHERD: Fie, daughter! when my old wife lived, upon
This day she was both pantler, butler, cook,
Both dame and servant; welcomed all, served all;
Would sing her song and dance her turn; now here,
At upper end o' the table, now i' the middle;
On his shoulder, and his; her face o'fire
With labour, and the thing she took to quench it
She would to each one sip. You are retired,
As if you were a feasted one and not

The hostess of the meeting: pray you, bid
These unknown friends to 's welcome; for it is
A way to make us better friends, more known.
Come, quench your blushes and present yourself
That which you are, mistress o' the feast: come on
And bid us welcome to your sheep-shearing,
As your good flock shall prosper.

THE WINTER'S TALE, IV. iii. 55–70

### 9 *The Nature of Woman*

ANNE: By my troth and maidenhead,
    I would not be a queen.
OLD LADY:                  Beshrew me, I would,
    And venture maidenhead for't; and so would you,
    For all this spice of your hypocrisy:
    You, that have so fair parts of woman on you,
    Have too a woman's heart; which ever yet
    Affected eminence, wealth, sovereignty;
    Which, to say sooth, are blessings; and which gifts,
    Saving your mincing, the capacity
    Of your soft cheveril conscience would receive,
    If you might please to stretch it.

KING HENRY VII, III. iii. 23–33

SENTIMENTAL DANDY

# Well met Goſsip:

### OR,

## Tis merrie when

#### Goſsips meete

## NEWLY ENLARGED WITH

#### diuers merrie Songs.

*Widdow* · *Wif.* · *Mayde.*

*LONDON,*
Printed by *I. W.* for *Iohn Deane* and are to be ſold at his
Shop iuſt vnder *Temple-barre* 1619.

SOCIAL TYPES — WIDOW, WIFE, AND MAID

## 1 *A Gentle Lady Slandered*

PETRUCHIO: No, not a whit: I find you passing gentle.
    'Twas told me you were rough and coy and sullen,
    And now I find report a very liar;
    For thou art pleasant, gamesome, passing courteous,
    But slow in speech, yet sweet as spring-time flowers:
    Thou canst not frown, thou canst not look askance,
    Nor bite the lip, as angry wenches will,
    Nor hast thou pleasure to be cross in talk,
    But thou with mildness entertain'st thy wooers,
    With gentle conference, soft and affable.
    Why does the world report that Kate doth limp?
    O slanderous world! Kate like the hazel-twig
    Is straight and slender, and as brown in hue
    As hazel-nuts and sweeter than the kernels.
    O, let me see thee walk: thou dost not halt.
KATHERINA: Go, fool, and whom thou keep'st command.
PETRUCHIO: Did ever Dian so become a grove
    As Kate this chamber with her princely gait?
    O, be thou Dian, and let her be Kate;
    And then let Kate be chaste and Dian sportful!

                  THE TAMING OF THE SHREW, II. i. 237–256

## 2 *Virtues Misconstrued*

PETRUCHIO: Father, 'tis thus: yourself and all the world,
    That talk'd of her, have talk'd amiss of her:
    If she be curst, it is for policy,
    For she's not froward, but modest as the dove;
    She is not hot, but temperate as the morn;
    For patience she will prove a second Grissel,
    And Roman Lucrece for her chastity:

And to conclude, we have 'greed so well together,
That upon Sunday is the wedding-day.

THE TAMING OF THE SHREW, II. i. 284–292

### 3 Handsome Lady Unhandsomely Praised

BENEDICT: Why, i' faith, methinks she's too low for a high
praise, too brown for a fair praise, and too little for a great
praise: only this commendation I can afford her, that were
she other than she is, she were unhandsome, and being no
other but as she is, I do not like her.

MUCH ADO ABOUT NOTHING, I. i. 178–184

### 4 An Infernal Ate of a Woman

DON PEDRO: The Lady Beatrice hath a quarrel to you: the
gentleman that danced with her told her she is much
wronged by you.

BENEDICT: O, she misused me past the endurance of a block!
an oak but with one green leaf on it, would have answered
her: my very visor began to assume life and scold with her.
She told me, not thinking I had been myself, that I was the
prince's jester; that I was duller than a great thaw; hud-
dling jest upon jest with such impossible conveyance upon
me, that I stood like a man at a mark, with a whole army
shooting at me. She speaks poniards, and every word
stabs: if her breath were as terrible as her terminations,
there would be no living near her; she would infect to the
north star. I would not marry her, though she were
endowed with all that Adam had left him before he
transgressed: she would have made Hercules have turned
spit, yea, and have cleft his club to make the fire too.
Come, talk not of her: you shall find her the infernal Ate
in good apparel. I would to God some scholar would
conjure her, for certainly, while she is here, a man may
live as quiet in hell as in a sanctuary; and people sin upon

purpose, because they would go thither; so, indeed, all
disquiet, horror and perturbation follows her.

MUCH ADO ABOUT NOTHING, II. i. 245–271

### 5 A Merry Lady

DON PEDRO: By my troth, a pleasant-spirited lady.
LEONATO: There's little of the melancholy element in her, my
lord: she is never sad but when she sleeps, and not ever sad
then; for I have heard my daughter say, she hath often
dreamed of unhappiness and waked herself with laughing.

MUCH ADO ABOUT NOTHING, II. i. 358–364

### 6 A Pround Self-Endeared Woman

HERO: But nature never framed a woman's heart
Of prouder stuff than that of Beatrice:
Disdain and scorn ride sparkling in her eyes,
Misprising what they look on, and her wit
Values itself so highly that to her
All matter else seems weak: she cannot love,
Nor take no shape nor project of affection,
She is so self-endeared.

MUCH ADO ABOUT NOTHING, III. i. 49–56

### 7 An Innocent Lady

FRIAR: By noting of the lady I have mark'd
A thousand blushing apparitions
To start into her face; a thousand innocent shames
In angel whiteness beat away those blushes;
And in her eye there hath appear'd a fire
To burn the errors that these princes hold
Against her maiden truth.

MUCH ADO ABOUT NOTHING, IV. i. 160–166

8 *Inseparables*

CELIA: If she be a traitor,
  Why so am I; we still have slept together,
  Rose at an instant, learn'd, play'd, eat together,
  And wheresoe'er we went, like Juno's swans,
  Still went coupled and inseparable.

AS YOU LIKE IT, I. iii. 75–79

9 *A Wanton*

NESTOR: A woman of quick sense.
ULYSSES:        Fie, fie upon her!
  There's language in her eye, her cheek, her lip,
  Nay, her foot speaks; her wanton spirits look out
  At every joint and motive of her body.
  O! these encounterers, so glib of tongue,
  That give accosting welcome ere it comes,
  And wide unclasp the tables of their thoughts
  To every ticklish reader, set them down
  For sluttish spoils of opportunity
  And daughters of the game.

TROILUS AND CRESSIDA, IV. V. 54–63

10 *A Lady of Birth and Breeding*

COUNTESS: His sole child, my lord: and bequeathed to my
overlooking. I have those hopes of her good that her
education promises; her dispositions she inherits, which
makes fair gifts fairer; for where an unclean mind carries
virtuous qualities, there commendations go with pity;
they are virtues and traitors too: in her they are the better
for their simpleness; she derives her honesty and achieves
her goodness.

ALL'S WELL THAT ENDS WELL, I. i. 45–53

## 11 *A Woman Compounded of Excellences*

CLOTEN: I love and hate her: for she's fair and royal,
  And that she hath all courtly parts more exquisite
  Than lady, ladies, woman; from every one
  The best she hath, and she, of all compounded,
  Outsells them all; I love her therefore: but
  Disdaining me and throwing favours on
  The low Posthumus slanders so her judgement
  That what's else rare is choked; and in that point
  I will conclude to hate her, nay, indeed,
  To be revenged upon her.
          CYMBELINE, III. V. 70–79

## 12 *Woman into Wag*

PISANIO: You must forget to be a woman; change
  Command into obedience; fear and niceness—
  The handmaids of all women, or, more truly,
  Woman it pretty self—into a waggish courage;
  Ready in gibes, quick-answer'd, saucy and
  As quarrelous as the weasel; nay, you must
  Forget that rarest treasure of your cheek,
  Exposing it—but, O, the harder heart!
  Alack, no remedy!—to the greedy touch
  Of common-kissing Titan, and forget
  Your laboursome and dainty trims, wherein
  You made great Juno angry.
         CYMBELINE, III. iv. 157–168

## 13 *A Woman Perfect in All Things*

FLORIZEL:       What you do
  Still betters what is done. When you speak, sweet,
  I'ld have you do it ever: when you sing,
  I'ld have you buy and sell so, so give alms,
  Pray so; and, for the ordering your affairs,
  To sing them too: when you do dance, I wish you

A wave o' the sea, that you might ever do
Nothing but that; move still, still so,
And own no other function: each your doing,
So singular in each particular,
Crowns what you are doing in the present deeds,
That all your acts are queens.

THE WINTER'S TALE, IV. iii. 135–146

### 14 *The Sum of Excellences*

FERDINAND:                    Admir'd Miranda!
Indeed the top of admiration, worth
What's dearest to the world! Full many a lady
I have ey'd with best regard, and many a time
Th' harmony of their tongues hath into bondage
Brought my too diligent ear: for several virtues
Have I lik'd several women; never any
With so full soul but some defect in her
Did quarrel with the noblest grace she ow'd,
And put it to the foil; but you, O you,
So perfect and so peerless, are created
Of every creature's best!

THE TEMPEST, III. i. 37–48

## (a)   The Nature of Love

### 1 *A Character of Love*

BIRON: Other slow arts entirely keep the brain;
　　　And therefore, finding barren practisers,
　　　Scarce show a harvest of their heavy toil:
　　　But love, first learned in a lady's eyes,
　　　Lives not alone immured in the brain;
　　　But, with the motion of all elements,
　　　Courses as swift as thought in every power,
　　　And gives to every power a double power,
　　　Above their functions and their offices.
　　　It adds a precious seeing to the eye;
　　　A lover's eyes will gaze an eagle blind;
　　　A lover's ear will hear the lowest sound,
　　　When the suspicious head of theft is stopp'd:
　　　Love's feeling is more soft and sensible
　　　Than are the tender horns of cockled snails;
　　　Love's tongue proves dainty Bacchus gross in taste:
　　　For valour, is not Love a Hercules,
　　　Still climbing trees in the Hesperides?
　　　Subtle as Sphinx; as sweet and musical
　　　As bright Apollo's lute, strung with his hair;
　　　And when Love speaks, the voice of all the gods
　　　Make heaven drowsy with the harmony.
　　　Never durst poet touch a pen to write
　　　Until his ink were temper'd with Love's sighs;
　　　O, then his lines would ravish savage ears
　　　And plant in tyrants' mild humility.

LOVE'S LABOUR'S LOST, IV. iii. 324–346

2 *Essential Love*

VALENTINE: What light is light, if Silvia be not seen?
What joy is joy, if Silvia be not by?
Unless it be to think that she is by,
And feed upon the shadow of perfection.
Except I be by Silvia in the night,
There is no music in the nightingale;
Unless I look on Silvia in the day,
There is no day for me to look upon:
She is my essence; and I leave to be,
If I be not by her fair influence
Foster'd, illumined, cherish'd, kept alive.
I fly not death, to fly his deadly doom:
Tarry I here, I but attend on death;
But, fly I hence, I fly away from life.

THE TWO GENTLEMEN OF VERONA, III. i. 174–187


3 *The Character of Love*

ROMEO: Love is a smoke raised with the fume of sighs;
Being purged, a fire sparkling in lovers' eyes;
Being vex'd, a sea nourish'd with lovers' tears;
What is it else? a madness most discreet,
A choking gall, and a preserving sweet.

ROMEO AND JULIET, I. i. 196–200


4 *The Nature of Love*

HELENA: Things base and vile, holding no quantity,
Love can transpose to form and dignity.
Love looks not with the eyes, but with the mind;
And therefore is winged Cupid painted blind:
Nor hath Love's mind of any judgement taste;
Wings, and no eyes, figure unheedy haste:
And therefore is Love said to be a child,
Because in choice he is so oft beguiled.

As waggish boys in game themselves forswear,
So the boy Love is perjured everywhere:

A MIDSUMMER-NIGHT'S DREAM, I. i. 232–241


### 5 True Love, Indeed

LUCETTA: All these are servants to deceitful men.
JULIA: Base men, that use them to so base effect!
    But truer stars did govern Proteus' birth:
    His words are bonds, his oaths are oracles;
    His love sincere, his thoughts immaculate;
    His tears pure messengers sent from his heart;
    His heart as far from fraud as heaven from earth.
LUCETTA: Pray heaven he prove so, when you come to him!

THE TWO GENTLEMEN OF VERONA, II. vii. 72–79


### 6 Love Subject to Time and Crosses

LYSANDER: How, now, my love? Why is your cheek so pale?
    How chance the roses there do fade so fast?
HERMIA: Belike, for want of rain; which I could well
    Beteem them from the tempest of my eyes.
LYSANDER: Ay me! for aught that I could ever read,
    Could ever hear by tale or history,
    The course of true love never did run smooth:
    But, either it was different in blood;—
HERMIA: O cross! too high to be enthrall'd to low!
LYSANDER: Or else misgraffed in respect of years;—
HERMIA: O spite! too old to be engaged to young!
LYSANDER: Or else it stood upon the choice of friends;—
HERMIA: O hell! to choose love by another's eyes!
LYSANDER: Or, if there were a sympathy in choice,
    War, death, or sickness did lay siege to it;
    Making it momentary as a sound,
    Swift as a shadow, short as any dream;
    Brief as the lightning in the collied night,

That, in a spleen, unfolds both heaven and earth,
And ere a man hath power to say,—Behold!
The jaws of darkness do devour it up:
So quick bright things come to confusion.

A MIDSUMMER-NIGHT'S DREAM, I. i. 128–149

### 7 The Common Course of Love

BEATRICE: For, hear me, Hero: wooing, wedding, and repent-
ing, is as a Scotch jig, a measure, and a cinque-pace: the
first suit is hot and hasty, like a Scotch jig, and full as
fantastical; the wedding, mannerly-modest, as a measure,
full of state and ancientry; and then comes repentance,
and, with his bad legs, falls into the cinque-pace faster and
faster, till he sink into his grave.

MUCH ADO ABOUT NOTHING, II. i. 76–84

### 8 Character of Love's Metamorphosis

VALENTINE: Why, how know you that I am in love?
SPEED: Marry, by these special marks: first, you have learn'd,
like Sir Proteus, to wreathe your arms, like a male-content;
to relish a love-song, like a robin-redbreast; to walk alone,
like one that had the pestilence; to sigh, like a school-boy
that had lost his A B C; to weep, like a young wench that
had buried her grandam; to fast, like one that takes diet;
to watch, like one that fears robbing; to speak puling, like
a beggar at Hallowmas. You were wont, when you
laugh'd, to crow like a cock; when you walk'd, to walk
like one of the lions; when you fasted, it was presently after
dinner; when you look'd sadly, it was for want of money:
and now you are metamorphosed with a mistress, that,
when I look on you, I can hardly think you my master.

THE TWO GENTLEMEN OF VERONA, II. i. 18–35

9 *Ill Effects of Love*

PROTEUS: He after honour hunts, I after love:
He leaves his friends to dignify them more;
I leave myself, my friends, and all, for love.
Thou, Julia, thou hast metamorphosed me,
Make me neglect my studies, lose my time,
War with good counsel, set the world at nought;
Made wit with musing weak, heart sick with thought.

THE TWO GENTLEMEN OF VERONA, I, i. 63–69

10 *The Marks of a Man in Love*

ORLANDO: I am he that is love-shaked: I pray you, tell me your
remedy.
ROSALIND: There is none of my uncle's marks upon you: he
taught me how to know a man in love; in which cage of
rushes I am sure you are not prisoner.
ORLANDO: What were his marks?
ROSALIND: A lean cheek, which you have not, a blue eye and
sunken, which you have not, an unquestionable spirit,
which you have not, a beard neglected, which you have
not; but I pardon you for that, for simply your having in
beard is a younger brother's revenue: then your hose
should be ungartered, your bonnet unbanded, your sleeve
unbuttoned, your shoe untied and every thing about you
demonstrating a careless desolation; but you are no such
man; you are rather point-device in your accoutrements
as loving yourself than seeming the lover of any other.

AS YOU LIKE IT, III. ii. 390–409

## (b)  The Lovers

### 1 The Contrary Character of Wooing

DUKE: There is a lady in Verona here
  Whom I affect; but she is nice and coy,
  And nought esteems my aged eloquence:
  Now, therefore, would I have thee to my tutor,—
  For long agone I have forgot to court;
  Besides, the fashion of the time is changed,—
  How and which way I may bestow myself,
  To be regarded in her sun-bright eye.
VALENTINE: Win her with gifts, if she respect not words:
  Dumb jewels often in their silent kind
  More than quick words do move a woman's mind.
DUKE: But she did scorn a present that I sent her.
VALENTINE: A woman sometimes scorns what best contents her.
  Send her another; never give her o'er;
  For scorn at first makes after-love the more.
  If she do frown, 'tis not in hate of you,
  But rather to beget more love in you:
  If she do chide, 'tis not to have you gone;
  For why, the fools are mad, if left alone.
  Take no repulse, whatever she doth say;
  For 'get you gone', she doth not mean 'away!'
  Flatter and praise, commend, extol their graces;
  Though ne'er so black, say they have angels' faces.
  That man that hath a tongue, I say, is no man,
  If with his tongue he cannot win a woman.

THE TWO GENTLEMEN OF VERONA, III. i. 81–105

### 2 The Ardent Wooer

EGEUS: Stand forth, Lysander; and, my gracious duke,
  This man hath witch'd the bosom of my child:
  Thou, thou, Lysander, thou hast given her rhymes,

And interchanged love-tokens with my child:
Thou hast by moonlight at her window sung,
With feigning voice, verses of feigning love;
And stolen the impression of her fantasy
With bracelets of thy hair, rings, gawds, conceits,
Knacks, trifles, nosegays, sweetmeats; messengers
Of strong prevailment in unharden'd youth:
With cunning hast thou filch'd my daughter's heart;
Turn'd her obedience, which is due to me,
To stubborn harshness.

A MIDSUMMER-NIGHT'S DREAM, I. i. 26–38

## 3 An Incomparable Lover

DUKE: There is no woman's sides
Can bide the beating of so strong a passion
As love doth give my heart; no woman's heart
So big, to hold so much; they lack retention.
Alas, their love may be call'd appetite,—
No motion of the liver, but the palate,—
That suffer surfeit, cloyment, and revolt;
But mine is all as hungry as the sea,
And can digest as much: make no compare
Between that love a woman can bear me
And that I owe Olivia.

TWELFTH NIGHT, II. iv. 95–105

## 4 A Likely Ambassador of Love

SERVANT: Madam, there is alighted at your gate
A young Venetian, one that comes before
To signify the approaching of his lord;
From whom he bringeth sensible regrets,
To wit, besides commends and courteous breath,
Gifts of rich value. Yet I have not seen
So likely an ambassador of love:
A day in April never came so sweet,

To show how costly summer was at hand,
As this fore-spurrer comes before his lord.
PORTIA: No more, I pray thee: I am half afeard
Thou wilt say anon he is some kin to thee,
Thou spend'st such high-day wit in praising him.
Come, come, Nerissa; for I long to see
Quick Cupid's post that comes so mannerly.

THE MERCHANT OF VENICE, II. ix. 86–100

5 *A Singing Suitor*

OLIVIA: Why, what would you?
VIOLA: Make me a willow cabin at your gate,
And call upon my soul within the house;
Write loyal cantons of contemned love,
And sing them loud even in the dead of night;
Holla your name to the reverberate hills,
And make the babbling gossip of the air
Cry out, 'Olivia!' O, you should not rest
Between the elements of air and earth,
But you should pity me!

TWELFTH NIGHT, I. v. 288–297

6 *A Likely Young Wooer*

HOSTESS: What say you to young Master Fenton? he capers, he
dances, he has eyes of youth, he writes verses, he speaks
holiday, he smells April and May; he will carry't, he will
carry't; 'tis in his buttons; he will carry't.

THE MERRY WIVES OF WINDSOR, III. ii. 70–74

7 *Persevering Pursuer*

FORD: There is a gentlewoman in this town; her husband's
name is Ford.
FALSTAFF: Well, sir.
FORD: I have long loved her, and, I protest to you, bestowed

much on her; followed her with a doting observance; engrossed opportunities to meet her; fee'd every slight occasion that could but niggardly give me sight of her; not only bought many presents to give her, but have given largely to many to know what she would have given; briefly, I have pursued her as love hath pursued me; which hath been on the wing of all occasions. But whatsoever I have merited, either in my mind or in my means, meed, I am sure, I have received none; unless experience be a jewel that I have purchased at an infinite rate, and that hath taught me to say this:

'Love like a shadow flies when substance love pursues; Pursuing that that flies, and flying what pursues.'

THE MERRY WIVES OF WINDSOR, II. ii. 202–221

## 8 *A Contrary Wooer*

PETRUCHIO: I pray you do; I will attend her here,

(*Exeunt Baptista, Gremio, Tranio, and Hortensio*)

And woo her with some spirit when she comes.
Say that she rail; why then I'll tell her plain
She sings as sweetly as a nightingale:
Say that she frown; I'll say she looks as clear
As morning roses newly wash'd with dew:
Say she be mute and will not speak a word;
Then I'll commend her volubility,
And say she uttereth piercing eloquence:
If she do bid me pack, I'll give her thanks,
As though she bid me stay by her a week:
If she deny to wed, I'll crave the day
When I shall ask the banns, and when be married.

THE TAMING OF THE SHREW, II. i. 169–181

## 9 *Jesting Wooer*

BAPTISTA: Signior Lucentio (*To Tra.*), this is the 'pointed day
That Katherine and Petruchio should be married,
And yet we hear not of our son-in-law.

What will be said? what mockery will it be,
To want the bridegroom when the priest attends
To speak the ceremonial rites of marriage!
What says Lucentio to this shame of ours?
KATHERINE: No shame but mine: I must, forsooth, be forced
To give my hand, opposed against my heart,
Unto a mad-brain rudesby, full of spleen;
Who woo'd in haste, and means to wed at leisure.
I told you, I, he was a frantic fool,
Hiding his bitter jests in blunt behaviour:
And, to be noted for a merry man,
He'll woo a thousand, 'point the day of marriage,
Make friends, invite, and proclaim the banns;
Yet never means to wed where he hath woo'd.
Now must the world point at poor Katherine,
And say, 'Lo, there is mad Petruchio's wife,
If it would please him come and marry her!'

THE TAMING OF THE SHREW, III. ii. 1–20


10 *A Wild-Cat Tamer*

PETRUCHIO: Born in Verona, old Antonio's son:
My father dead, my fortune lives for me;
And I do hope good days and long to see.
GREMIO: O sir, such a life, with such a wife, were strange!
But if you have a stomach, to 't a God's name:
You shall have me assisting you in all.
But will you woo this wild-cat?
PETRUCIO                              Will I live?
GRUMIO: Will he woo her? ay, or I'll hang her.
PETRUCHIO: Why came I hither but to that intent?
Think you a little din can daunt mine ears?
Have I not in my time heard lions roar?
Have I not heard the sea, puff'd up with winds,
Rage like an angry boar chafed with sweat?
Have I not heard great ordnance in the field,
And heaven's artillery thunder in the skies?

# Love's Lunacie;

### Or,

### Mad Bessie's Fegary.

Declaring her sorrow, care, and mone,
Which may cause many a sigh and grone :
A young man did this maid some wrong,
Wherefore she writ this mournfull song.

To the tune of *The mad man's morris.*

Poore Besse, mad Besse, so they call me,
   I'm metamorposéd ;
Strange sights and visions I doe see,
   By Furies I am led :         4
Tom was the cause of all my woe,
   To him I loudly cry,
My love to him there's none doth know,
   Yet heere he lets me lie.       **8**

Le Comedien Serieux
Il parle en elegent discours
Contre l'Amour et ses detours

LOVE-HIT — THE INNAMORATO

Have I not in a pitched battle heard
Loud 'larums, neighing steeds, and trumpets' clang?
And do you tell me of a woman's tongue,
That gives not half so great a blow to hear
As will a chestnut in a farmer's fire?
Tush, tush! fear boys with bugs.

THE TAMING OF THE SHREW, I. ii. 193–214

## 11 *Uncouth Bridegroom, Horse and Lackey*

BIONDELLO: Why, Petruchio is coming in a new hat and an old
jerkin, a pair of old breeches thrice turn'd, a pair of boots
that have been candlecases, one buckled, another laced, an
old rusty sword ta'en out of the town-armoury, with a
broken hilt, and chapeless; with two broken points: his
horse hipp'd, with an old mothy saddle and stirrups of no
kindred; besides, possess'd with the glanders and like to
mose in the chine; troubled with the lampass, infected with
the fashions, full of windgalls, sped with spavins, 'wray'd
with the yellows, past cure of the fives, stark spoil'd with
the staggers, begnawn with the bots, sway'd in the back
and shoulder-shotten; near-legg'd before and with a half-
check'd bit and a head-stall of sheep's leather which, being
restrain'd to keep him from stumbling, hath been often
burst and now repair'd with knots; one girth six times
pieced and a woman's crupper of velure, which hath two
letters for her name fairly set down in studs, and here and
there pieced with pack-thread.

BAPTISTA: Who comes with him?

BIONDELLO: O, sir, his lackey, for all the world caparison'd like
the horse; with a linen stock on one leg, and a kersey boot-
hose on the other, garter'd with a red and blue list; an old
hat, and 'the humour of forty fancies' prick'd in't for a
feather: a monster, a very monster in apparel, and not like
a Christian footboy or a gentleman's lackey.

THE TAMING OF THE SHREW, III. ii. 44–74

12 *A Blunt Wooer*

KING HENRY: Marry, if you would put me to verses or to dance for your sake, Kate, why you undid me: for the one, I have neither words nor measure, and for the other, I have no strength in measure, yet a reasonable measure in strength. If I could win a lady at leap-frog, or by vaulting into my saddle with my armour on my back, under the correction of bragging be it spoken, I should quickly leap into a wife. Or if I might buffet for my love, or bound my horse for her favours, I could lay on like a butcher and sit like a jack-an-apes, never off. But, before God, Kate, I cannot look greenly nor gasp out my eloquence, nor I have no cunning in protestation; only downright oaths, which I never use till urged, nor never break for urging. If thou canst love a fellow of this temper, Kate, whose face is not worth sun-burning, that never looks in his glass for love of any thing he sees there, let thine eye be thy cook. I speak to thee plain soldier: if thou canst love me for this, take me; if not, to say to thee that I shall die, is true; but for thy love, by the Lord, no; yet I love thee too. And while thou livest, dear Kate, take a fellow of plain and uncoined constancy; for he perforce must do thee right, because he hath not the gift to woo in other places: for these fellows of infinite tongue, that can rhyme themselves into ladies' favours, they do always reason themselves out again. What! a speaker is but a prater; a rhyme is but a ballad. A good leg will fall; a straight back will stoop; a black beard will turn white; a curled pate will grow bald; a fair face will wither; a full eye will wax follow; but a good heart, Kate, is the sun and the moon; or rather the sun and not the moon; for it shines bright and never changes, but keeps his course truly. If thou would have such a one, take me; and take me, take a soldier; take a soldier, take a king. And what sayest thou then to my love? speak, my fair, and fairly, I pray thee.

KING HENRY V, V. ii. 136–176

13 *A Mere Soldier in Love*

OTHELLO: Most potent, grave, and reverend signiors,
    My very noble and approved good masters,
    That I have ta'en away this old man's daughter,
    It is most true; true, I have married her:
    The very head and front of my offending
    Hath this extent, no more. Rude am I in my speech,
    And little blest with the soft phrase of peace;
    For since these arms of mine had seven years' pith,
    Till now some nine moons wasted, they have used
    Their dearest action in the tented field;
    And little of this great world can I speak,
    More than pertains to feats of broil and battle;
    And therefore little shall I grace my cause
    In speaking for myself. Yet, by your gracious patience,
    I will a round unvarnish'd tale deliver
    Of my whole course of love; what drugs, what charms,
    What conjuration and what mighty magic—
    For such proceeding I am charged withal—
    I won his daughter.
                              OTHELLO, I. iii. 76–94


14 *A Captain Transformed*

PHILO: Nay, but this dotage of our general's
    O'erflows the measure: those his goodly eyes,
    That o'er the files and musters of the war
    Have glow'd like plated Mars, now bend, now turn
    The office and devotion of their view
    Upon a tawny front: his captain's heart,
    Which in the scuffles of great fights hath burst
    The buckles of his breast, reneges all temper,
    And is become the bellows and the fan
    To cool a gipsy's lust.
    *Flourish. Enter Antony, Cleopatra, her Ladies, the Train,*
            *with Eunuchs fanning her.*
                    Look, where they come:

Take but good note, and you shall see in him
The triple pillar of the world transform'd
Into a strumpet's fool: behold and see.

ANTONY AND CLEOPATRA, I. i. 1–13

### 15 *One Conquered by Love*

PROTEUS: My tales of love were wont to weary you;
 I know you joy not in a love-discourse.
VALENTINE: Ay, Proteus, but that life is alter'd now:
 I have done penance for contemning Love,
 Whose high imperious thoughts have punish'd me
 With bitter fasts, with penitential groans,
 With nightly tears, and daily heart-sore sighs;
 For, in revenge of my contempt of love,
 Love hath chased sleep from my enthralled eyes,
 And made them watchers of mine own heart's sorrow.
 O gentle Proteus, Love's a mighty lord,
 And hath so humbled me, as I confess
 There is no woe to his correction,
 Nor to his service no such joy on earth.
 Now, no discourse, except it be of love;
 Now can I break my fast, dine, sup and sleep,
 Upon the very naked name of love.

THE TWO GENTLEMEN OF VERONA, II. iv. 127–143

### 16 *A Lover Enchanted with Gazing*

BOYET: If my observation, which very seldom lies
 By the heart's still rhetoric disclosed with eyes,
 Deceive me not now, Navarre is infected.
PRINCESS: With what?
BOYET: With that which we lovers entitle affected.
PRINCESS: Your reason?
BOYET: Why, all his behaviours did make their retire
 To the court of his eye, with your print impress'd,
 Proud with his form, in his eye pride express'd:

His tongue, all impatient to speak and not see,
Did stumble with haste in his eyesight to be;
All senses to that sense did make their repair,
To feel only looking on fairest of fair:
Methought all his senses were lock'd in his eye,
As jewels in crystal for some prince to buy;
Who, tend'ring their own worth from where they were
    glass'd,
Did point you to buy them, along as you pass'd:
His face's own margent did quote such amazes
That all eyes saw his eyes enchanted with gazes.
I'll give you Aquitaine and all that is his,
An you give him for my sake but one loving kiss.

LOVE'S LABOUR'S LOST, II. i. 226–247

### 17 Love-Hit

MERCUTIO: Alas, poor Romeo, he is already dead! stabbed with
a white wench's black eye; shot thorough the ear with a
love-song; the very pin of his heart cleft with the blind
bow-boy's butt-shaft; and is he a man to encounter
Tybalt?

ROMEO AND JULIET, II. iv. 13–18

### 18 Love Fantastic

SILVIUS: How many actions most ridiculous
    Hast thou been drawn to by thy fantasy?
CORIN: Into a thousand that I have forgotten.
SILVIUS: O, thou didst then ne'er love so heartily!
    If thou remember'st not the slightest folly
    That ever love did make thee run into,
    Thou hast not loved:
    Or if thou has not sat as I do now,
    Wearing thy hearer in thy mistress' praise,
    Thou hast not loved:
    Or if thou hast not broke from company

    Abruptly, as my passion now makes me,
Thou hast not loved.
O Phebe, Phebe, Phebe!

ROSALIND: Alas, poor shepherd! searching of thy wound,
    I have by hard adventure found mine own.

TOUCHSTONE: And I mine. I remember, when I was in love I
    broke my sword upon a stone and bid him take that for
    coming a-night to Jane Smile; and I remember the kissing
    of her batlet and the cow's dugs that her pretty chopt
    hands had milked; and I remember the wooing of a
    peascod instead of her, from whom I took two cods, and,
    giving her them again, said with weeping tears 'Wear
    these for my sake'. We that are true lovers run into strange
    capers; but as all is mortal in nature, so is all nature in love
    mortal in folly.

AS YOU LIKE IT, II. iv. 30–56

### 19 *Humoresque Love*

MOTH: Master, will you win your love with a French brawl?

ARMADO: How meanest thou? brawling in French?

MOTH: No, my complete master: but to jig off a tune at the
    tongue's end, canary to it with your feet, humour it with
    turning up your eye, sigh a note and sing a note, sometime
    through the throat, as if you swallowed love with singing
    love, sometime through the nose, as if you snuffed up love
    by smelling love; with your hat penthouse-like o'er the
    shop of your eyes; with your arms crossed on your thin-
    belly doublet like a rabbit on a spit; or your hands in your
    pocket like a man after the old painting; and keep not too
    long in one tune, but a snip and away. These are comple-
    ments, these are humours; these betray nice wenches, that
    would be betrayed without these; and make them men
    of note—do you note, men?—that most are affected to
    these.

LOVE'S LABOUR'S LOST, III. i. 8–27

## 20 *Love's Critic Caught*

BIRON: And I, forsooth, in love! I, that have been love's whip;
    A very beadle to a humorous sigh;
    A critic, nay, a night-watch constable;
    A domineering pedant o'er the boy;
    Than whom no mortal so magnificent!
    This wimpled, whining, purblind, wayward boy;
    This senior-junior, giant-dwarf, Dan Cupid;
    Regent of love-rhymes, lord of folded arms,
    The anointed sovereign of sighs and groans,
    Liege of all loiterers and malcontents,
    Dread prince of plackets, king of codpieces,
    Sole imperator and great general
    Of trotting paritors:—O my little heart!
    And I to be a corporal of his field,
    And wear his colours like a tumbler's hoop!

LOVE'S LABOUR'S LOST, III. i. 183–198

## 21 *Love's Scorner Scorned*

ROSALIND: That same Biron I'll torture ere I go:
    O that I knew he were but in by the week!
    How I would make him fawn and beg and seek
    And wait the season and observe the times
    And spend his prodigal wits in bootless rhymes
    And shape his service wholly to my hests
    And make him proud to make me proud that jests!
    So pertaunt-like would I o'ersway his state
    That he should be my fool and I his fate.
PRINCESS: None are so surely caught, when they are catch'd,
    As wit turn'd fool.

LOVE'S LABOUR'S LOST, V. ii. 60–70

## 22 *Fair She that Will not Love*

ROMEO: In sadness, cousin, I do love a woman.
BENVOLIO: I aim'd so near when I supposed you loved.
ROMEO: A right good mark-man! And she's fair I love.

BENVOLIO: A right fair mark, fair coz, is soonest hit.

ROMEO: Well, in that hit you miss: she'll not be hit
　　With Cupid's arrow; she hath Dian's wit;
　　And, in strong proof of chastity well arm'd,
　　From love's weak childish bow she lives unharm'd.
　　She will not stay the siege of loving terms,
　　Nor bide the encounter of assailing eyes,
　　Nor ope her lap to saint-seducing gold:
　　O, she is rich in beauty; only poor
　　That, when she dies, with beauty dies her store.

ROMEO AND JULIET, I. i. 210–222

### 23 *Bootless Love*

VALENTINE: No, I will not, for it boots thee not.

PROTEUS: 　　　　　　　　　　　　　　　　What?

VALENTINE: To be in love, where scorn is bought with groans;
　　Coy looks with heart-sore sighs; one fading moment's
　　　　mirth
　　With twenty watchful, weary, tedious nights:
　　If haply won, perhaps a hapless gain;
　　If lost, why then a grievous labour won;
　　However, but a folly bought with wit,
　　Or else a wit by folly vanquished.

THE TWO GENTLEMAN OF VERONA, I. i. 28–35

### 24 *Spaniel Love*

HELENA: And even for that do I love you the more.
　　I am your spaniel; and, Demetrius,
　　The more you beat me, I will fawn on you:
　　Use me but as your spaniel, spurn me, strike me,
　　Neglect me, lose me; only give me leave,
　　Unworthy as I am, to follow you.
　　What worser place can I beg in your love
　　(And yet a place of high respect with me)
　　Than to be used as you use your dog?

A MIDSUMMER-NIGHT'S DREAM, II. i. 202–210

25 *Girlhood Love*

HELENA: Is all the counsel that we two have shared,
   The sisters' vows, the hours that we have spent,
   When we have chid the hasty-footed time
   For parting us,—O me! is all forgot?
   All school-days' friendship, childhood innocence?
   We, Hermia, like two artificial gods,
   Have with our neelds created both one flower,
   Both on one sampler, sitting on one cushion,
   Both warbling of one song, both in one key;
   As if our hands, our sides, voices, and minds,
   Had been incorporate. So we grew together,
   Like to a double cherry, seeming parted,
   But yet a union in partition;
   Two lovely berries moulded on one stem:
   So, with two seeming bodies, but one heart;
   Two of the first, like coats in heraldry,
   Due but to one, and crowned with one crest.
   And will you rend our ancient love asunder,
   To join with men in scorning your poor friend?
   It is not friendly, 'tis not maidenly:
   Our sex, as well as I, may chide you for it;
   Though I alone do feel the injury.

A MIDSUMMER-NIGHT'S DREAM, III. ii. 198–219


26 *Conceited Love*

KING PHILIP: What say'st thou, boy? look in the lady's face.
LEWIS: I do, my lord: and in her eye I find
   A wonder, or a wondrous miracle,
   The shadow of myself form'd in her eye;
   Which, being but the shadow of your son
   Becomes a sun and makes your son a shadow:
   I do protest I never loved myself
   Till now infixed I beheld myself
   Drawn in the flattering table of her eye.
BASTARD: Drawn in the flattering table of her eye!

Hang'd in the frowning wrinkle of her brow!
And quarter'd in her heart he doth espy
Himself love's traitor: this is pity now,
That, hang'd and drawn and quarter'd there should be
In such a love so vile a lout as he.

KING JOHN, II. i. 495–509


### 27 Capricious Love

ROSALIND: Now tell me how long you would have her after
you have possessed her.

ORLANDO: For ever and a day.

ROSALIND: Say 'a day', without the 'ever'. No, no, Orlando;
men are April when they woo, December when they wed:
maids are May when they are maids, but the sky changes
when they are wives. I will be more jealous of thee than a
Barbary cock-pigeon over his hen, more clamorous than a
parrot against rain, more new-fangled than an ape, more
giddy in my desires than a monkey; I will weep for
nothing, like Diana in the fountain, and I will do that
when you are disposed to be merry; I will laugh like a
hyen, and that when thou art inclined to sleep.

ORLANDO: But will my Rosalind do so?

ROSALIND: By my life, she will do as I do.

AS YOU LIKE IT, IV. i. 149–165


### 28 One Who Could Cure Love

ORLANDO: Did you ever cure any so?

ROSALIND: Yes, one, and in this manner. He was to imagine me
his love, his mistress; and I set him every day to woo me.
At which time would I, being but a moonish youth, grieve,
be effeminate, changeable, longing and liking, proud,
fantastical, apish, shallow, inconstant, full of tears, full of
smiles, for every passion something and for no passion
truly any thing, as boys and women are for the most part
cattle of this colour: would now like him now loathe him;

then entertain him, then forswear him; now weep for
him, then spit at him; that I drave my suitor from his mad
humour of love to a living humour of madness; which
was, to forswear the full stream of the world and to live
in a nook merely monastic. And thus I cured him: and in
this way will I take upon me to wash your liver as clean as
a sound sheep's heart, that there shall not be one spot of
love in't.

AS YOU LIKE IT, III. iii. 432–451

## 29 *Lover Distracted*

OPHELIA; My Lord, as I was sewing in my closet,
    Lord Hamlet, with his doublet all unbraced,
    No hat upon his head, his stockings fouled,
    Ungartered, and down-gyved to his ancle,
    Pale as his shirt, his knees knocking each other,
    And with a look so piteous in purport
    As if he had been loosed out of hell
    To speak of horrors,—he comes before me.

HAMLET, II. i. 77–84

## 30 *An Untold Love*

VIOLA: My father had a daughter lov'd a man,
    As it might be, perhaps, were I a woman,
    I should your lordship.
DUKE: And what's her history?
VIOLA: A blank, my lord. She never told her love,
    But let concealment, like a worm i' the bud,
    Feed on her damask cheek: she pin'd in thought;
    And with a green and yellow melancholy
    She sat like Patience on a monument,
    Smiling at grief. Was not this love indeed?
    We men may say more, swear more: but, indeed,
    Our shows are more than will; for still we prove
    Much in our vows, but little in our love.

DUKE: But died thy sister of her love, my boy?
VIOLA: I am all the daughters of my father's house,
And all the brothers too;—and yet I know not.

TWELFTH NIGHT, II. iv. 109–123


31 *Secret Ambitious Love* (*a*)

HELENA: O! were that all. I think not on my father;
And these great tears grace his remembrance more
Than those I shed for him. What was he like?
I have forgot him: my imagination
Carries no favour in 't but Bertram's.
I am undone: there is no living, none,
If Bertram be away. 'Twere all one
That I should love a bright particular star
And think to wed it, he is so above me:
In his bright radiance and collateral light
Must I be comforted, not in his sphere.
Th' ambition in my love thus plagues itself:
The hind that would be mated by the lion
Must die for love. 'Twas pretty, though a plague,
To see him every hour; to sit and draw
His arched brows, his hawking eye, his curls,
In our heart's table; heart too capable
Of every line and trick of his sweet favour:
But now he's gone, and my idolatrous fancy
Must sanctify his relics.

ALL'S WELL THAT ENDS WELL, I. i. 91–110


31 *Secret Ambitious Love* (*b*)

HELENA:                                    Then, I confess
Here on my knee, before high heaven and you,
That before you, and next unto high heaven,
I love your son.
My friends were poor, but honest; so's my love:
Be not offended, for it hurts not him

That he is lov'd of me: I follow him not
By any token of presumptuous suit;
Nor would I have him till I do deserve him;
Yet never know how that desert should be.
I know I love in vain, strive against hope;
Yet in this captious and intenible sieve
I still pour in the waters of my love,
And lack not to lose still. Thus, Indian-like,
Religious in mine error, I adore
The sun, that looks upon his worshipper,
But knows of him no more. My dearest madam,
Let not your hate encounter with my love
For loving where you do: but if yourself,
Whose aged honour cites a virtuous youth,
Did ever in so true a flame of liking
Wish chastely and love dearly, that your Dian
Was both herself and Love: O! then, give pity
To her, whose state is such, that cannot choose
But lend and give where she is sure to lose;
That seeks not to find that her search implies,
But riddle-like, lives sweetly where she dies.

ALL'S WELL THAT ENDS WELL, I. iii. 199–225


32 *Guilty Love*

LEONTES:                           Is whispering nothing?
   In leaning cheek to cheek? is meeting noses?
   Kissing with inside lip? stopping the career
   Of laughter with a sigh?—a note infallible
   Of breaking honesty;—horsing foot on foot?
   Skulking in corners? wishing clocks more swift?
   Hours, minutes? noon, midnight? and all eyes
   Blind with the pin and web but theirs, theirs only,
   That would unseen be wicked? is this nothing?
   Why, then the world and all that's in 't is nothing;
   The covering sky is nothing; Bohemia nothing;

My wife is nothing; nor nothing have these nothings,
If this be nothing.

THE WINTER'S TALE, I. ii. 284–296


## 33 *Love Desolate*

DESDEMONA: My mother had a maid call'd Barbara:
   She was in love; and he she loved proved mad
   And did forsake her: she had a song of 'willow';
   An old thing 'twas, but it express'd her fortune,
   And she died singing it: that song to-night
   Will not go from my mind; I have much to do
   But to go hang my head all at one side
   And sing it like poor Barbara.

OTHELLO, IV. iii. 26–33


## 34 *Love Awry*

OTHELLO: Soft you; a word or two before you go.
   I have done the state some service, and they know't.
   No more of that. I pray you, in your letters,
   When you shall these unlucky deeds relate,
   Speak of me as I am; nothing extenuate,
   Nor set down aught in malice: then must you speak
   Of one that loved not wisely but too well;
   Of one not easily jealous, but, being wrought,
   Perplex'd in the extreme; of one whose hand,
   Like the base Indian, threw a pearl away
   Richer than all his tribe; of one whose subdued eyes,
   Albeit unusued to the melting mood,
   Drop tears as fast as the Arabian trees
   Their medicinal gum. Set you down this;
   And say besides, that in Aleppo once,
   Where a malignant and a turban'd Turk
   Beat a Venetian and traduced the state,
   I took by the throat the circumcised dog
   And smote him, thus.                    (*Stabs himself*)

1 *The Nature of Sherris-Sack*

FALSTAFF: Good faith, this same young sober-blooded boy doth not love me; nor a man cannot make him laugh; but that's no marvel, he drinks no wine. There's never none of these demure boys come to any proof; for thin drink doth so over-cool their blood, and making many fish-meals, that they fall into a kind of male green-sickness; they are generally fools and cowards; which some of us should be too, but for inflammation. A good sherris-sack hath a two-fold operation in it. It ascends me into the brain; dries me there all the foolish and dull and crudy vapours which environ it; makes it apprehensive, quick, forgetive, full of nimble, fiery and delectable shapes; which, deliver'd o'er to the voice, the tongue, which is the birth, becomes excellent wit. The second property of your excellent sherris is, the warming of the blood; which, before cold and settled, left the liver white and pale, which is the badge of pusillanimity and cowardice; but the sherris warms it and makes it course from the inwards to the parts extreme: it illumineth the face, which as a beacon gives warning to all the rest of this little kingdom, man, to arm; and then the vital commoners and inland petty spirits muster me all to their captain, the heart, who, great and puff'd up with this retinue, doth any deed of courage; and this valour comes of sherris. So that skill in the weapon is nothing without sack, for that sets it a-work; and learning a mere hoard of gold kept by a devil, till sack commences it and sets it in act and use. Hereof comes it that Prince Harry is valiant; for the cold blood he did naturally inherit of his father, he hath, like lean, sterile and bare land, manur'd, husbanded, till'd with excellent endeavour of drinking good and good store of fertile sherris, that he is become very hot and

valiant. If I had a thousand sons, the first humane principle
I would teach them should be, to forswear thin potations
and to addict themselves to sack.

HENRY IV, PT. II, IV. iii. 93–136

## 2 *Strange Crocodile*

LEPIDUS: What manner o' thing is your crocodile?

ANTONY: It is shaped, sir, like itself; and it is as broad as it hath
breadth: it is just so high as it is, and moves with it own
organs: it lives by that which nourisheth it; and the
elements once out of it, it transmigrates.

LEPIDUS: What colour is it of?

ANTONY: Of it own colour too.

LEPIDUS: 'Tis a strange serpent.

ANTONY: 'Tis so. And the tears of it are wet.

ANTONY AND CLEOPATRA, II. vii. 47–56

## 3 *A Curse*

THERSITES: Now the rotten diseases of the south, the guts-
griping, ruptures, catarrhs, loads o' gravel i' the back,
lethargies, cold palsies, raw eyes, dirt-rotten livers,
wheezing lungs, bladders full of imposthume, sciaticas,
lime-kilns i' the palm, incurable bone-ache, and the rivelled
fee-simple of the tetter, take and take again such prepos-
terous discoveries!

PATROCLUS: Why, thou damnable box of envy, thou, what
meanest thou to curse thus?

THERSITES: Do I curse thee?

PATROCLUS: Why, no, you ruinous butt, you whoreson in-
distinguishable cur, no.

THERSITES: No! why art thou then exasperate, thou idle im-
material skein of sleave silk, thou green sarcenet flap for a
sore eye, thou tassel of a prodigal's purse, thou? Ah! how

the poor world is pestered with such water-flies, diminutives of nature.

PATROCLUS: Out, gall!

THERSITES: Finch-egg!

TROILUS AND CRESSIDA, V. i. 20–41

## 4 *A Farewell*

CRESSIDA: And is it true, that I must go from Troy?

TROILUS: A hateful truth.

CRESSIDA:                              What! and from Troilus too?

TROILUS: From Troy and Troilus.

CRESSIDA:                              Is it possible?

TROILUS: And suddenly; where injury of chance
 Puts back leave-taking, justles roughly by
 All time of pause, rudely beguiles our lips
 Of all rejoindure, forcibly prevents
 Our lock'd embrasures, strangles our dear vows
 Even in the birth of our own labouring breath.
 We too, that with so many thousand sighs
 Did buy each other, must poorly sell ourselves
 With the rude brevity and discharge of one.
 Injurious time now with a robber's haste
 Crams his rich thievery up, he knows not how:
 As many farewells as be stars in heaven,
 With distinct breath and consign'd kisses to them,
 He fumbles up into a loose adieu,
 And scants us with a single famish'd kiss,
 Distasted with the salt of broken tears.

TROILUS AND CRESSIDA, IV. iv. 30–48

# List of 'Characters' in Shakespeare's Plays

Note (1) The plays are in the order assigned to them in Chambers' *William Shakespeare*.

(2) Line-numbering as in Craig's one-volume Oxford Shakespeare.

258

9) Act III, Sc. VII, ll. 70–79     *A Pious Prince*
10) Act IV, Sc. IV, ll. 47–58     *A Carnal Cur*
11) Act IV, Sc. IV, ll. 166–175     *The Several Ages of Villainy*

COMEDY OF ERRORS

1) Act II, Sc. I, ll. 7–29     *The Principle of Subordination*
2) Act III, Sc. II, ll. 1–28     *A Fair Disloyal Husband*
3) Act IV, Sc. II, ll. 31–45     *A Sergeant*
4) Act IV, Sc. III, ll. 12–33     *Sergeant Again*
5) Act IV, Sc. IV, ll. 26–41     *The Universal Principle of Trouncing*
6) Act V, Sc. I, ll. 55–86     *A Jealous Railing Wife*
7) Act V, Sc. I, ll. 235–249     *Schoolmaster Exorcist*

TITUS ANDRONICUS

1) Act I, Sc. I, ll. 150–156     *The Nature of Death*
2) Act II, Sc. I, ll. 81–89     *A Cut Loaf*
3) Act V, Sc. I, ll. 124–144     *A Notorious Active Villain*

THE TAMING OF THE SHREW

1) Act I, Sc. II, ll. 65–76     *A Gold-Gilt Wife*
2) Act I, Sc. II, ll. 193–214     *A Wild-Cat Tamer*
3) Act II, Sc. I, ll. 169–181     *A Contrary Wooer*
4) Act II, Sc. I, ll. 237–256     *A Gentle Lady Slandered*
5) Act II, Sc. I, ll. 284–292     *Virtues Misconstrued*
6) Act III, Sc. II, ll. 1–20     *Jesting Wooer*
7) Act III, Sc. II, ll. 44–74     *Uncouth Bridegroom, Horse, and Lackey*
8) Act IV, Sc. I, ll. 191–214     *A Tamer of Shrews*
9) Act IV, Sc. III, ll. 101–114     *A Tailor*
10) Act V, Sc. II, ll. 131–180     *The Character of Marriage*

THE TWO GENTLEMEN OF VERONA

1) Act I, Sc. I, ll. 28–35     *Bootless Love*
2) Act I, Sc. I, ll. 63–69     *Ill Effects of Love*
3) Act II, Sc. I, ll. 18–35     *Character of Love's Metamorphosis*
4) Act II, Sc. IV, ll. 63–75     *A Ripe Young Man*

5) Act II, Sc. IV, ll. 127–143 — *One Conquered by Love*
6) Act II, Sc. VII, ll. 72–79 — *True Lover Indeed*
7) Act III, Sc. I, ll. 81–105 — *The Contrary Character of Wooing*

8) Act III, Sc. I, ll. 174–187 — *Essential Love*

LOVE'S LABOUR'S LOST

1) Act I, Sc. I, ll. 161–172 — *The Refined Traveller*
2) Act II, Sc. I, ll. 39–54 — *A Courtly Mocker*
3) Act II, Sc. I, ll. 56–63 — *Wit, Beauty, and Simplicity*
4) Act II, Sc. I, ll. 64–76 — *An Eloquent Jesting Courtier*
5) Act II, Sc. I, ll. 226–247 — *A Lover Enchanted with Gazing*
6) Act III, Sc. I, ll. 8–27 — *Humoresque Love*
7) Act III, Sc. I, ll. 183–198 — *Love's Critic Caught*
8) Act IV, Sc. II, ll. 21–34 — *An Illiterate*
9) Act IV, Sc. II, ll. 67–74 — *Conceited Pedant*
10) Act IV, Sc. III, ll. 324–349 — *A Character of Love*
11) Act V, Sc. I, ll. 2–6 — *Good Talk Characterized*
12) Act V, Sc. I, ll. 10–29 — *Peregrinate Pedant*
13) Act V, Sc. II, ll. 60–70 — *Love's Scorner Scorned*
14) Act V, Sc. II, ll. 316–335 — *The Ape of Form*
15) Act V, Sc. II, ll. 460–470 — *A Courtly Tell-Tale*

ROMEO AND JULIET

1) Act I, Sc. I, ll. 152–158 — *A 'Clam'*
2) Act I, Sc. I, ll. 180–187 — *Paradox of Love and Hate*
3) Act I, Sc. I, ll. 196–200 — *The Character of Love*
4) Act I, Sc. I, ll. 210–222 — *Fair She that Will not Love*
5) Act I, Sc. IV, ll. 53–95 — *Queen Mab*
6) Act II, Sc. III, ll. 1–30 — *The Order and Balance of Nature*
7) Act II, Sc. IV, ll. 13–18 — *Love-Hit*
8) Act II, Sc. IV, ll. 19–38 — *A Fashionable Duellist*
9) Act III, Sc. I, ll. 5–33 — *Character of a Quarreller*
10) Act III, Sc. II, ll. 71–85 — *Paradox of Appearance and Reality*

11) Act IV, Sc. I, ll. 89–106 — *A Drugged Person*
12) Act V, Sc. I, ll. 37–54 — *An Apothecary*
13) Act V, Sc. I, ll. 66–74 — *The Needy Outcast*

RICHARD THE SECOND

| | |
|---|---|
| 1) Act I, Sc. III, ll. 156–173 | *The Exile* |
| 2) Act I, Sc. III, ll. 233–246 | *Just Judge Cruel Father* |
| 3) Act I, Sc. IV, ll. 23–36 | *Seeker of Popular Favour* |
| 4) Act II, Sc. I, ll. 33–39 | *The Character of Excess* |
| 5) Act II, Sc. I, ll. 172–184 | *A Patriotic Prince* |
| 6) Act IV, Sc. I, ll. 281–289 | *Majesty Outfaced* |
| 7) Act V, Sc. II, ll. 7–21 | *Popular Usurper* |
| 8) Act V, Sc. II, ll. 23–36 | *A King Outcast* |
| 9) Act V, Sc. III, ll. 1–12 | *A Riotous Prince* |

A MIDSUMMER NIGHT'S DREAM

| | |
|---|---|
| 1) Act I, Sc. I, ll. 26–38 | *The Ardent Wooer* |
| 2) Act I, Sc. I, ll. 67–78 | *The Nun* |
| 3) Act I, Sc. I, ll. 128–149 | *Love Subject to Time and Crosses* |
| 4) Act I, Sc. I, ll. 232–241 | *The Nature of Love* |
| 5) Act II, Sc. I, ll. 32–57 | *Rogue Goodfellow* |
| 6) Act II, Sc. I, ll. 122–134 | *Fairy Companion* |
| 7) Act II, Sc. I, ll. 202–210 | *Spaniel Love* |
| 8) Act III, Sc. II, ll. 198–219 | *Girlhood Love* |
| 9) Act III, Sc. II, ll. 378–393 | *Ghosts and Fairies* |
| 10) Act V, Sc. I, ll. 1–22 | *The Character of Poetry* |

KING JOHN

| | |
|---|---|
| 1) Act I, Sc. I, ll. 184–216 | *Worshipful Society—The New-Hatched Knight and the Traveller* |
| 2) Act II, Sc. I, ll. 423–445 | *Princes Well-Matched* |
| 3) Act II, Sc. I, ll. 455–467 | *Gargantuan Thunderer* |
| 4) Act II, Sc. I, ll. 495–509 | *Conceited Love* |
| 5) Act II, Sc. I, ll. 561–586 | *Character of Commodity* |
| 6) Act III, Sc. I, ll. 6–18 | *A Woman Fearful* |
| 7) Act III, Sc. I, ll. 113–129 | *Lion into Calf* |
| 8) Act III, Sc. IV, ll. 22–36 | *Despair unto Death* |
| 9) Act III, Sc. IV, ll. 90–98 | *Grief a Companion* |
| 10) Act IV, Sc. II, ll. 219–229 | *One Marked for Villainy* |

THE MERCHANT OF VENICE

| | |
|---|---|
| 1) Act I, Sc. I, ll 1–7 | *Strange Melancholy* |
| 2) Act I, Sc. I, ll. 15–40 | *Troubled Trader* |

3) Act I, Sc. I, ll. 50–56            Nature's Opposites
4) Act I, Sc. I, ll. 77–99            The Affectation of Gravity
5) Act I, Sc. II, ll. 48–57           Solemn Teuton
6) Act I, Sc. II, ll. 58–69           Chameleon Frenchman
7) Act I, Sc. II, ll. 70–81           Illiterate Englishman
8) Act I, Sc. II, ll. 90–96           Drunken German
9) Act I, Sc. II, ll. 24–38           Futile Valour
10) Act II, Sc. II, ll. 204–212       A Sober-Seeming Man
11) Act II, Sc. IX, ll. 86–100        A Likely Ambassador of Love
12) Act III, Sc. I, ll. 55–78         A Character of Common
                                              Humanity

13) Act III, Sc. II, ll. 149–175      A Rich and Biddable Bride
14) Act III, Sc. II, ll. 272–291      An Inveterate Foe
15) Act III, Sc. II, ll. 293–297      A Choice Friend
16) Act III, Sc. V, ll. 62–78         A Bragging Jack
17) Act IV, Sc. I, ll. 40–62          The Humour of Hate
18) Act IV, Sc. I, ll. 70–83          The Stubborn Jew
19) Act V, Sc. I, ll. 83–88           Man Without Music


HENRY THE FOURTH, PART I

1) Act I, Sc. II, ll. 26–43           Gentlemen of the Shade
2) Act I, Sc. II, ll. 217–239         A Politic Offender
3) Act I, Sc. III, ll. 29–64          Brisk Courtier out of his
                                              Element

4) Act II, Sc. I, ll. 73–99           Exalted Thuggery
5) Act II, Sc. III, ll. 42–69         Troubled Soldier
6) Act II, Sc. III, ll. 107–117       Trusty Wife!
7) Act II, Sc. IV, ll. 3–20           A Good Mixer
8) Act II, Sc. IV, ll. 109–115        A Drawer at an Inn
9) Act II, Sc. IV, ll. 116–126        Stout Warrior!
10) Act II, Sc. IV, ll. 271–281       The Fat and the Lean
11) Act II, Sc. IV, ll. 497–536       Twin Characters of Falstaff
12) Act III, Sc. I, ll. 36–51         Birth of a Wizard
13) Act III, Sc. I, ll. 121–134       Friend and Foe of Poetry
14) Act III, Sc. I, ll. 146–168       A Tedious Necromancer
15) Act III, Sc. I, ll. 176–190       A Rough Warrior Schooled
16) Act III, Sc. II, ll. 29–91        Politic Prudence and Imprudence
17) Act III, Sc. II, ll. 93–117       Model for a Prince
18) Act III, Sc. III, ll. 16–23       One not Unnecessarily Virtuous

19) Act III, Sc. III, ll. 27–59     *Knight of the Burning Lamp*
20) Act IV, Sc. I, ll. 94–110     *Golden Youth in Arms*
21) Act IV, Sc II, ll. 12–53     *A Recruiting Officer*
22) Act V, Sc I, ll. 85–92     *An Active-Valiant Gentleman*
23) Act V, Sc. II, ll. 47–68     *A Modest Young Warrior*

## HENRY THE FOURTH, PART II

1) Induction, ll. 1–20     *Rumour*
2) Act I, Sc. II, ll. 198–226     *Falstaff Young and Falstaff Old*
3) Act I, Sc. III, ll. 26–33     *One Misled by Hope*
4) Act II, Sc. III, ll. 16–32     *Model for Youth*
5) Act II, Sc. IV, ll. 129–141     *A Bottle-Ale Rascal*
6) Act II, Sc. IV, ll. 148–161     *A Captain—Forsooth!*
7) Act II, Sc. IV, ll. 260–277     *Character of a Good*
                              *Companion*
8) Act III, Sc. II, ll. 326–361     *A Cheese-Paring of a Man*
9) Act IV, Sc. II, ll. 4–30     *A Rebel Bishop*
10) Act IV, Sc. III, ll. 93–136     *The Nature of Sherris-Sack*
11) Act IV, Sc. IV, ll. 22–48     *Humouring a Humoursome Prince*
12) Act IV, Sc. V, ll. 63–78     *Fathers Over-Careful*
13) Act V, Sc. I, ll. 68–86     \* *Like Justice Like Man*

## MUCH ADO ABOUT NOTHING

1) Act I, Sc. I, ll. 9–17     *A Youth of Promise*
2) Act I, Sc. I, ll. 178–184     *Handsome Lady Unhandsomely*
                              *Praised*
3) Act I, Sc. III, ll. 10–19     *A Man in his Humours*
4) Act I, Sc. III, ll. 28–39     *A Cankered Villain*
5) Act II, Sc. I, ll. 76–84     *The Common Course of Love*
6) Act II, Sc. I, ll. 141–151     *Villainous Jester*
7) Act II, Sc. I, ll. 245–271     *An Infernal Ate of a Women*
8) Act II, Sc. I, ll. 358–364     *A Merry Lady*
9) Act II, Sc. III, ll. 7–23     *Soldier into Lover*
10) Act II, Sc. III, ll. 24–37     *A Man Hard to Please*
11) Act III, Sc. I, ll. 49–56     *A Proud, Self-Endeared Woman*
12) Act III, Sc. I, ll. 59–70     *A Humour of Perversity*
13) Act III, Sc. II, ll. 7–14     *A Merry Sound Man*
14) Act III, Sc. III, ll. 130–148     *Fashion*

15) Act IV, Sc. I, ll. 160–166    *An Innocent Lady*
16) Act V, Sc. I, ll. 92–99    *Antic Youth*
17) Act V, Sc. I, ll. 162–178    *Wit Discredited*

### HENRY THE FIFTH

1) Act I, Sc. I, ll. 22–69    *Sudden Scholar*
2) Act II, Sc. II, ll. 93–144    *A Mere Traitor*
3) Act II, Sc. IV, ll. 23–40    *Two Characters of One King*
4) Act III, Sc. I, ll. 3–17    *Men Set for War*
5) Act III, Sc. II, ll. 30–59    *Three Filching Swashers*
6) Act III, Sc. II, ll. 83–91    *The Knowledgeable Scot*
7) Act III, Sc. VI, ll. 26–40    *Fortune*
8) Act III, Sc. VI, ll. 64–92    *Counterfeit Soldier*
9) Act IV, Sc. I, ll. 28–47    *A King Commander*
10) Act IV, Sc. I, ll. 106–118    *The King but a Man*
11) Act IV, Sc. I. ll. 260–304    *Character of Ceremony*
12) Act IV, Sc. III, ll. 40–67    *Old Soldier*
13) Act V, Sc. II, ll. 136–176    *A Blunt Wooer*

### JULIUS CAESAR

1) Act I, Sc. II, ll. 71–78    *A Friend too Common*
2) Act I, Sc. II, ll. 134–140    *Oppressive Greatness*
3) Act I, Sc. II, ll. 191–209    *The Lean Thinker*
4) Act I, Sc. II, ll. 300–307    *A Shrewd Blunt Fellow*
5) Act I, Sc. III, ll. 157–160    *Popularity*
6) Act II, Sc. I, ll. 61–69    *A Man in Suspense*
7) Act II, Sc. I, ll. 141–153    *An Associate Fit and Unfit*
8) Act II, Sc. I, ll. 234–256    *A Man Perturbed*
9) Act II, Sc. I, ll. 292–303    *A Constant Noble Woman*
10) Act III, Sc. I, ll. 58–73    *A Fixed and Constant Man*
11) Act III, Sc. II, ll. 220–234    *A Plain Man, No Orator*
12) Act IV, Sc. I, ll. 12–40    *An Unmeritable Man*
13) Act IV, Sc. II, ll. 13–27    *A Hot Friend Cooling*
14) Act V, Sc. V, ll. 68–75    *A Complete Man*

### AS YOU LIKE IT

1) Act I, Sc. I, ll. 1–27    *A Gentleman Basely Bred*
2) Act I, Sc. I, ll. 147–182    *Two Characters in One*
3) Act I, Sc. II, ll. 200–208    *A Low-Spirited Youth*

4) Act I, Sc. III, ll. 75–79      *Inseparables*
5) Act I, Sc. III, ll. 117–125      *A Swashing Young Man*
6) Act II, Sc. III, ll. 46–62      *Old Faithful*
7) Act II, Sc. IV, ll. 30–56      *Love Fantastic*
8) Act II, Sc. VII, ll. 12–61      *The Fool*
9) Act II, Sc. VII, ll. 139–166      *A Character of Man's Ages*
10) Act III, Sc. II, ll. 78–82      *A True Labourer*
11) Act III, Sc. II, ll. 390–409      *The Marks of a Man in Love*
12) Act III, Sc. III, ll. 432–451      *One Who Could Cure Love*
13) Act III, Sc. V, ll. 109–136      *The Inventory of a Handsome*
     *Youth*

14) Act IV, Sc. I, ll. 11–21      *All the Melancholies—and then*
     *One*

15) Act IV, Sc. I, ll. 22–40      *The Traveller*
16) Act IV, Sc. I, ll. 149–165      *Capricious Love*
17) Act V, Sc. IV, ll. 40–54, 71–91      *Character of a Courtier and of*
     *his Quarrel*

TWELFTH NIGHT

1) Act I, Sc. III, ll. 15–48      *Two Characters in One—*
     *A Foolish Talented Knight*
2) Act I, Sc. V, ll. 78–105      *The Fool—and his Zanies*
3) Act I, Sc. V, ll. 147–175      *A Persistent Young Man*
4) Act I, Sc. V, ll. 278–284      *A Noble Suitor Answered*
5) Act I, Sc. V, ll. 288–297      *A Singing Suitor*
6) Act II, Sc. III, ll. 153–169      *An Affectioned Ass*
7) Act II, Sc. IV, ll. 73–80      *A Changeable Man*
8) Act II, Sc. IV, ll. 95–105      *An Incomparable Lover*
9) Act II, Sc. IV, ll. 109–123      *An Untold Love*
10) Act II, Sc. V, ll. 157–180      *An Aspirant to Greatness*
11) Act III, Sc. I, ll. 68–76      *The Wit of the Fool*
12) Act III, Sc. IV, ll. 196–203      *The Swaggering Swearer*
13) Act III, Sc. IV, ll. 254–266      *A Devil of a Fellow*
14) Act III, Sc. IV, ll. 304–313      *Another Devil*
15) Act V, Sc. I, ll. 55–63      *A Stout Fellow*

HAMLET

1) Act I, Sc. II, ll. 76–86      *The Pseudo-Mourner*
2) Act I, Sc. II, ll. 92–106      *Stubborn Sorrow*

3) Act I, Sc. III, ll. 58–80            *Prudence Personified*
4) Act I, Sc. V, ll. 13–22             *A Man Horrified*
5) Act I, Sc. V, ll. 74–80             *One Unprepared for Death*
6) Act I, Sc. V, ll. 169–180           *Pretenders to Inside Knowledge*
7) Act II, Sc. I, ll. 77–84            *Lover Distracted*
8) Act II, Sc. II, ll. 200–210         *Old Men*
9) Act II, Sc. II, ll. 584–596         *The Actor*
10) Act III, Sc. I, ll. 159–170        *Paragon of Princes—Blasted*
11) Act III, Sc. II, ll. 1–17, 33–40   *The 'Ham' Actor (a, b)*
12) Act III, Sc. II, ll. 59–79         *The Well-Balanced Man*
13) Act III, Sc. IV, ll. 53–63         *A Godlike Monarch*
14) Act III, Sc. IV, ll. 96–102        *A Vice of Kings*
15) Act IV, Sc. II, ll. 11–23          *Court Sponge*
16) Act IV, Sc. VII, ll. 81–92         *The Horseman*
17) Act V, Sc. I, ll. 201–215          *Dead Jester*
18) Act V, Sc. I, ll. 104–125          *Dead Lawyer*
19) Act V, Sc. II, ll. 111–128         *The Absolute Card of Gentility*

THE MERRY WIVES OF WINDSOR

1) Act I, Sc. IV, ll. 10–16            *An Honest Servant*
2) Act II, Sc. II, ll. 202–221         *Persevering Pursuer*
3) Act II, Sc. II, ll. 238–243         *Soldier, Courtier, Scholar*
4) Act III, Sc. II, ll. 70–74          *A Likely Young Wooer*
5) Act III, Sc. III, ll. 55–71         *An Absolute Court Lady*
6) Act IV, Sc. IV, ll. 29–39           *A Hunter's Ghost*

TROILUS AND CRESSIDA

1) Act I, Sc. II, ll. 12–31            *A Composite Brute*
2) Act I, Sc. II, ll. 202–206          *A Shrewd Sound Man*
3) Act I, Sc. II, ll. 271–276          *The Spice and Salt of a Man*
4) Act I, Sc. III, ll. 75–137          *The Nature of Degree*
5) Act I, Sc. III, ll. 142–184         *The Scurrilous Mimic*
6) Act I, Sc. III, ll. 188–196         *Insubordination Imitated*
7) Act I, Sc. III, ll. 264–283         *Provoking Challenger*
8) Act II, Sc. II, ll. 51–60           *The Nature of Value*
9) Act II, Sc. III, ll. 174–190        *The Plaguy Proud Man*
10) Act II, Sc. III, ll. 249–270       *A Monstrous Fine Fellow*
11) Act III, Sc. III, ll. 245–274      *A Stupid Vain Warrior*
12) Act IV, Sc. IV, ll. 30–48          *A Farewell*

13) Act IV, Sc. V, ll. 54–63        *A Wanton*
14) Act IV, Sc. V, ll. 95–112       *A True Knight*
15) Act V, Sc. I, ll. 20–41         *A Curse*
16) Act V, Sc. I, ll. 98–110        *A Promise-Breaker*

ALL'S WELL THAT ENDS WELL

1) Act I, Sc. I, ll. 45–53 ⁴        *A Lady of Birth and Breeding*
2) Act I, Sc. I, ll. 91–110         *Secret Ambitious Love (a)*
3) Act I, Sc. II, ll. 24–48         *Model Courtier*
4) Act I, Sc. III, ll. 39–56        *Contented Cuckold*
5) Act I, Sc. III, ll. 199–225      *Secret Ambitious Love (b)*
6) Act II, Sc. I, ll. 51–59         *The Courtier Coached*
7) Act II, Sc. III, ll. 1–8         *Philosophical Persons*
8) Act II, Sc. III, ll. 124–151     *Character of True Honour*
9) Act II, Sc. V, ll. 47–54         *A Light Nut*
10) Act III, Sc. II, ll. 3–10       *A Melancholy Man*
11) Act III, Sc. VI, ll. 5–12       *A Bubble*
12) Act IV, Sc. III, ll. 74–87      *Life a Mingled Yarn*
13) Act IV, Sc. III, ll. 277–328    *A False Character of a Captain*
14) Act IV, Sc. III, ll. 370–380    *The Conscious Worm*

MEASURE FOR MEASURE

1) Act I, Sc. I, ll. 66–72          *Retiring Greatness*
2) Act II, Sc. II, ll. 109–123      *Man in Authority*
3) Act III, Sc. I, ll. 4–41         *A Character of the Life of Man*
4) Act III, Sc. I, ll. 232–239      *A Hard Man*
5) Act III, Sc. II, ll. 113–121     *A Cold Man*
6) Act IV, Sc. I, ll. 61–66         *Great Place*
7) Act IV, Sc. II, ll. 81–88        *A Just Deputy*
8) Act IV, Sc. II, ll. 146–160      *One Insensible of Mortality*

OTHELLO

1) Act I, Sc. I, ll. 19–33          *Counter-Casting Soldier*
2) Act I, Sc. I, ll. 41–55          *Selfish Service*
3) Act I, Sc. III, ll. 76–94        *A Mere Soldier in Love*
4) Act II, Sc. I, ll. 60–65         *An Incomparable Bride*
5) Act II, Sc. I, ll. 109–112       *Variable Woman*
6) Act II, Sc. I, ll. 148–160       *A Virtuous Simple Woman*

7) Act II, Sc. I, ll. 240–255        *A Slipper and Subtle Young*
                                                        *Knave*
8) Act III, Sc. III, ll. 19–28       *A Vexatious Wife*
9) Act III, Sc. III, ll. 155–161     *The Nature of Reputation*
10) Act III, Sc. III, ll. 166–176    *Jealousy*
11) Act III, Sc. III, ll. 453–463    *One Set on Revenge*
12) Act IV, Sc. III, ll. 130–133     *A Cogging Villain*
13) Act IV, Sc. III, ll. 26–33       *Love Desolate*
14) Act V, Sc. II, ll. 337–355       *Love Awry*

KING LEAR

1) Act I, Sc. I, ll. 57–63, 71–78    *Two Unspeakable Loves (a, b)*
2) Act I, Sc. II, ll. 1–22           *The Bastard*
3) Act I, Sc. IV, ll. 299–313        *A Daughter Cursed*
4) Act II, Sc. I, ll. 39–58          *The Parricide*
5) Act II, Sc. II, ll. 11–26         *A Superserviceable Knave*
6) Act II, Sc. II, ll. 75–89         *Halcyon Rogues*
7) Act II, Sc. II, ll. 94–110        *An Affected Plain Knave*
8) Act II, Sc. III, ll. 1–21         *A Bedlamite (a)*
9) Act III, Sc. I, ll. 1–17          *Old Majesty Distraught*
10) Act III, Sc. IV, ll. 28–32       *Helpless Wretches*
11) Act III, Sc. IV, ll. 49–62       *A Bedlamite (b)*
12) Act III, Sc. IV, ll. 84–99       *A Courtly Serving Man*
13) Act III, Sc. IV, ll. 118–122     *The Fiend Flibbertigibbet*
14) Act III, Sc. IV, ll. 131–145     *A Bedlamite (c)*
15) Act IV, Sc. II, ll. 29–36        *Unnatural Child*
16) Act IV, Sc. IV, ll. 1–6          *Mad King*
17) Act V, Sc. III, ll. 131–140      *A Declared Traitor*

MACBETH

1) Act I, Sc. III, ll. 39–47         *Witches*
2) Act I, Sc. IV, ll. 1–14           *Penitent Traitor*
3) Act I, Sc. V, ll. 17–26           *Scrupulous Ambition*
4) Act I, Sc. V, ll. 39–55           *Woman into Fiend*
5) Act I, Sc. VII, ll. 39–45         *One Not Ruthless*
6) Act II, Sc. II, ll. 37–41         *Sleep*
7) Act II, Sc. III, ll. 98–103       *A Man Disillusioned*
8) Act III, Sc. I, ll. 49–57         *A Royal Nature*
9) Act IV, Sc. III, ll. 125–132      *A Prince Simply Virtuous*

10) Act V, Sc. III, ll. 22–28      *One without Love or Hope*
11) Act V, Sc. V, ll. 19–28      *The Nature of Life*

## ANTONY AND CLEOPATRA

1) Act I, Sc. I, ll. 1–13      *A Captain Transformed*
2) Act I, Sc. II, ll. 155–166      *A Woman Infinite (a)*
3) Act I, Sc. IV, ll. 55–71      *Tough Soldier*
4) Act II, Sc. II, ll. 241–248      *A Woman Infinite (b)*
5) Act II, Sc. III, ll. 15–38      *A Man Born Lucky*
6) Act II, Sc. VII, ll. 47–56      *Strange Crocodile*
7) Act III, Sc. XI, ll. 194–200      *Desperate Courage*
8) Act V, Sc. II, ll. 76–92      *An Incomparable Emperor*

## CORIOLANUS

1) Act I, Sc. I, ll. 172–190      *Character of the Mob*
2) Act I, Sc. I, ll. 234–242      *A Worthy Foe*
3) Act I, Sc. IV, ll. 48–61      *An Awe-Inspiring Soldier*
4) Act II, Sc. I, ll. 42–74      *An Humorous Blunt Politician*
5) Act II, Sc. I, ll. 76–104      *Character of the Tribunes of
the People*
6) Act II, Sc. I, ll. 224–240, 278–287   *A Popular Hero (a, b)*
7) Act II, Sc. III, ll. 15–26      *The Many-Headed Multitude*
8) Act III, Sc. I, ll. 253–260      *Fearless Bluntness*
9) Act III, Sc. I, ll. 318–322      *Rough and Ready Soldier*
10) Act III, Sc. II, ll. 7–13      *Underdogs*
11) Act III, Sc. II, ll. 110–123      *Hero into Suppliant*
12) Act III, Sc. III, ll. 24–30      *Rash Choler*
13) Act IV, Sc. II, ll. 50–53      *A Self-Feeder*
14) Act IV, Sc. V, ll. 234–252      *War and Peace*
15) Act IV, Sc. VI, ll. 91–96      *An Inspiring Leader*
16) Act IV, Sc. VII, ll. 35–57      *A Failure Analysed*

## TIMON OF ATHENS

1) Act I, Sc. II, ll. 39–54      *Parasites*
2) Act I, Sc. II, ll. 141–152      *Flatterers*
3) Act I, Sc. II, ll. 200–214      *Excessive Generosity*
4) Act II, Sc. II, ll. 113–121      *Whoremaster Man*
5) Act II, Sc. II, ll. 214–229      *Cold Ungrateful Men*
6) Act III, Sc. II, ll. 72–83      *Ungrateful Flatterer*

7) Act III, Sc. V, ll. 7–37   *The Nature of Homicide*
8) Act IV, Sc. III, ll. 24–43   *The Character of Gold (a)*
9) Act IV, Sc. III, ll. 133–167   *Whores*
10) Act IV, Sc. III, ll. 177–197   *Teeming Mother-Earth*
11) Act IV, Sc. III, ll. 221–232   *Indifferent Nature*
12) Act IV, Sc. III, ll. 251–277   *Two Kinds of Misanthrope*
13) Act IV, Sc. III, ll. 321–351   *Beastly Life*
14) Act IV, Sc. III, ll. 384–395   *The Character of Gold (b)*
15) Act IV, Sc. III, ll. 321–456   *Thievery*
16) Act V, Sc. I, ll. 25–33   *The Fashion of Promising*

### PERICLES

1) Act I, Sc. I, ll. 12–18   *A Gracious Queen*
2) Act II, Sc. I, ll. 31–38   *Voracious Miser*
3) Act IV, Sc. VI, ll. 178–184   *Door-Keeper in a Brothel*
4) Act V, Sc. I, ll. 107–114   *A Goodly Mother Matched*

### CYMBELINE

1) Act I, Sc. I, ll. 40–56   *A Rare Courtier*
2) Act III, Sc. III, ll. 11–55   *Court Life and Country Life*
3) Act III, Sc. IV, ll. 157–168   *Woman into Wag*
4) Act III, Sc. V, ll. 70–79   *A Woman Compounded of Excellences*

5) Act IV, Sc. I, ll. 7–17   *A Rival Measured*
6) Act IV, Sc. II, ll. 47–56   *A Competent Sad Youth*
7) Act IV, Sc. II, ll. 169–181   *The Nature of Princes*
8) Act V, Sc. IV, ll. 153–174   *Death the Debt-Payer*
9) Act V, Sc. V, ll. 83–88   *A Perfect Page*

### THE WINTER'S TALE

1) Act I, Sc. II, ll. 60–75   *Boys Eternal*
2) Act I, Sc. II, ll. 163–171   *Child in the House*
3) Act I, Sc. II, ll. 284–296   *Guilty Love*
4) Act II, Sc. III, ll. 9–17   *A Sensitive Lad*
5) Act II, Sc. III, ll. 95–107   *Father and Son Matched*
6) Act III, Sc. III, ll. 58–68   *Adolescence*
7) Act IV, Sc. II, ll. 23–32   *A Snapper-Up of Unconsidered Trifles*

271

8) Act IV, Sc. III, ll. 55–70    *A Country Hostess*
9) Act IV, Sc. III, ll. 135–146    *A Woman Perfect in All Things*
10) Act IV, Sc. IV, ll. 156–161    *A Queen of Curds and Cream*
11) Act IV, Sc. III, ll. 181–215    *A Pedlar of Ballads*
12) Act IV, Sc. IV, ll. 687–701    *A Thriving Cut-Purse*
13) Act IV, Sc. III, ll. 757–767    *Cut-Purse Courtier*

THE TEMPEST

1) Act II, Sc. I, ll. 120–129    *Bold Swimmer*
2) Act II, Sc. II, ll. 25–44    *A Man-Monster*
3) Act III, Sc. I, ll. 37–48    *The Sum of Excellences*
4) Act III, Sc. III, ll. 95–102    *Guilt*
5) Act IV, Sc. I, ll. 146–158    *The Nature of Art and of Life*
6) Act V, Sc. I, ll. 33–57    *The Magician*

KING HENRY THE EIGHTH

1) Act I, Sc. I, ll. 50–66    *A Self-Dependent Spider of a Man*
2) Act I, Sc. I, ll. 102–114    *A Man of Power and Malice*
3) Act I, Sc. II, ll. 111–124    *The Corruption of the Best*
4) Act II, Sc. III, ll. 23–33    *The Nature of Woman*
5) Act II, Sc. IV, ll. 11–42    *A True and Humble Wife*
6) Act II, Sc. IV, ll. 131–141    *A Queen of Earthly Queens*
7) Act III, Sc. I, ll. 124–136    *A Patient Constant Wife*
8) Act III, Sc. II, ll. 111–120    *A Man Distraught*
9) Act IV, Sc. II, ll. 31–75    *Two Characters of One Great Man*
10) Act V, Sc. V, ll. 18–39    *A Pattern for all Princes*